THE FUTURE OF
ISLAM
AND THE
WEST

Clash of Civilizations
or Peaceful Coexistence?

Shireen T. Hunter
Foreword by Marc Gopin

Published with the Center for Strategic
and International Studies, Washington, D.C.

PRAEGER

Westport, Connecticut
London

Library of Congress Cataloging-in-Publication Data

Hunter, Shireen.
  The future of Islam and the west : clash of civilizations or
peaceful coexistence? / Shireen T. Hunter.
      p.   cm.
  Includes bibliographical references and index.
  ISBN 0-275-96287-3 (alk. paper). — ISBN 0-275-96288-1 (pbk. :
alk. paper)
  1. Islam—Relations—Christianity.   2. Christianity and other
religions—Islam.   3. Middle East—Relations—Europe.   4. Europe—
Relations—Middle East.   5. Islam—Iran.   6. Islam—Saudi Arabia.
I. Title.
DS65.5.E8H861998
303.48'25604—dc21   97-52799

British Library Cataloging in Publication data is available.

Library of Congress Catalog Card Number: 97-52799
ISBN: 0-275-96287-3
      0-275-96288-1 (pbk.)

First published in 1998

Praeger Publishers, 88 Post Road West, Westport, CT 06881
An imprint of Greenwood Publishing Group, Inc.

Printed in the United States of America

∞™

The paper used in this book complies with the Permanent
Paper Standard issued by the National Information Standards
Organization (Z39.48-1984).

10 9 8 7 6 5 4 3 2 1

Contents

Foreword

The most important question facing the global community today is how to respond to the extremely rapid pace of transformation in international relationships that is accompanied by and in part caused by the unprecedented degree of social change occurring in many parts of the world. It is by now a truism that these developments have been unleashed, like pressured water from a corked bottle, by the unraveling of Cold War alignments and the remarkable shift into prominence of international democratic and capitalist institutions. The sinking into poverty of many and the fantastic and increasing prosperity of others have also created enormous tensions in many regions and cultures.

It has been tempting in such an environment to search intellectually for new alignments and, in a darker way, to search for new enemies. This is not a sinister desire by any means. But the Cold War did provide a sense of order to a very dangerous world. Even if that order had as its capstone the possibility of a global nuclear holocaust, it is remarkable how much more comforting it was for many of us to be familiar with that fateful danger, recognize the challenge, and respond to it with all our might technologically, than it is now not really to know from whence a mortal threat to our civilization could come next. Real dangers lie ahead, but it will be a while before we become accustomed psychologically to the amorphous quality of future threats, be they from despotic regimes with weapons of mass destruction; from the further unraveling of large concentrations of power, as in China;

from global economic depression in an astonishingly interconnected marketplace; from catastrophic industrial accidents; from
internally generated social turmoil and terrorism; or from some
combination of all of these.

One of the regions going through the most dramatic socioeconomic shifts is the Middle East—particularly the Arab lands.
The emerging generations are facing a chaotic world with enormous challenges to their economic well-being and the very fabric
of their culture. There are many complicated reasons for this upheaval, and several of those causes are brilliantly analyzed in
Shireen Hunter's study.

The danger to global stability, international relations, and the
West's relationship to this region will emerge, however, not from
the most crass expressions of violence that have emanated from
this region and not from the religious expression of that extreme
response, but from the misunderstandings that Westerners have
of the complex and multivalenced realities of Islam and its interaction with the political regimes of the Middle East. Another danger
to stability is the West's natural tendency to see the worst and
darkest set of possibilities for the future, without envisioning and
then enabling the best set of cultural and political possibilities to
emerge from this region.

It is an interesting question why the West has a rather arrogant confidence in exporting Western-style democracy and capitalism to Africa, for example, no matter how often this may lead
to disastrous results, whereas there is a dark set of fears associated with Arab and Islamic culture in the Middle East. I believe
the fears emerge from two sources. One is the tragic uses to
which Islam has been put by a minority of clerics who are deeply
angry at Western culture and the resulting terrorism in Islam's
name. The latter has struck a deep chord of fear in the average
Westerner because, at least in part, that is the devastating psychological impact that terrorism has. It is one of the most effective
ways to stimulate warfare between large groups, because it
strikes behind the walls of security that countries and civilizations
spend fantastic sums creating. Furthermore, it cannot be gainsaid
that there are old Western/Christian rivalries with and fears of
the "other" great missionizing and conquering religion of the
West—Islam.

That having been said, it is immensely dangerous to move from analyzing the sources of some intercultural anxiety to declaring what must be a clash of civilizations that will result in decades or centuries of antagonism, if not outright warfare. That grossly oversimplifies the reality of the present and shuts off the possibilities of the future.

Islam is, like all religions that I have analyzed, a complex amalgamation of centuries of sources and traditions, often pointing in very different directions, as far as the basic issues of tolerance, coexistence, peace making, and war making are concerned. Group psychology, economics, leadership styles, power distribution, external and internal issues of resource distribution have a direct effect on the religious hermeneutic activity of a particular generation at a particular point in time. This is also constantly evolving, despite the fact that traditionalists in most religions like to present themselves as adhering to an unchanging and unchangeable tradition. Islam is especially susceptible to this evolutionary quality because it is a far more decentralized religion than is commonly believed. It may be that various political leadership styles in the Middle East have been and continue to be authoritarian, and that this, in turn, has affected the leadership style of some clerics. But the religion itself is rather diffuse in terms of power concentration, and this is why Islam as it is expressed in India and South Africa, for example, has always had a remarkably different tone, than, say, the style of Saudi Arabian Islam.

All of this points to the need to understand deeply how external factors affect the growth and evolution of religious traditions and to address the perils and the possibilities of the Middle East's future, both culturally and geopolitically, as the author of this volume has done so well.

Despite legitimate Western fears of terrorism, it is also time to recognize that there is nothing unique about Islam when it comes to the choices of war or peace, pluralism, or authoritarianism. Judaism, Christianity, Confucianism, Buddhism, Taoism, and Shintoism have all had periods in which some in their midst utilized repressive religious laws or theological principles to commit unspeakable acts of brutality and terror. Indeed, this is one of the critical foundations of the Western drive to the secular, democratic state.

How Islam moves into the twenty-first century will depend on the internal dynamics of predominantly Islamic countries, but also on the political/cultural interaction of the West with these countries. If Islam is treated by the West as inherently destructive, then an adversarial religious hermeneutic will continue to emerge from this region, and the opportunity to generate a movement toward democracy and international stability will evaporate. If, on the other hand, there is a cooperative, respectful cultural interaction, an honest conversation may emerge in which Muslims will become partners with the West in making the challenging changes necessary to create more and more democratic institutions in their midst. The West, in turn, will come to recognize its role and responsibility, together with local regimes, for the continuing socioeconomic circumstances that are generating so much misery and so much dangerous upheaval in these cultures.

One of the more intractable barriers to future relationships has clearly been the Arab-Israeli conflict. However that conflict evolves or resolves, it should be noted that here as well as in the Middle East, choices are being made by key religious figures—quite conservative in their orientation—that this political conflict not devolve into conflict among religions but that, on the contrary, religion becomes a vehicle of peace making. I refer to key contacts, publicly acknowledged now, between Israel's chief rabbis and prominent Islamic leaders, even in Iran. Once again, the choice is in the hands of the generation as to whether a religious civilization becomes a vehicle of violence or a vehicle of coexistence. The West has a choice as to whether to nurture movement toward coexistence or make it more difficult.

One last word about a possible future toward which this volume paves the way. What the Western-style democracies have in common with Islam is the moral commitment to the individual. Throughout Islam's history that commitment has expressed itself theologically and legally with regard to the economic well-being and the dignity of members of the *Ummah*—the basic formula for social and economic justice. The West has committed itself particularly to the human rights of the individual, suggesting that human dignity resides primarily in the defense of those rights. If, instead of seeing the clash of civilizations, we begin to see all the multivalenced causes of conflict and violence and, alternatively, envision the ways in which civilizations can learn from each other and help each other to grow and evolve, we may witness an emerging multicultural commitment to truly dignify the life of the individual in the future of the Middle East. The future thus provides the opportunity to work jointly toward the dignity of the individual as it is expressed through his or her social, cultural, and economic welfare, and simultaneously, through the evolution and maturation of democratic institutions. The future also invites us to work toward the dignity of the individual as it is expressed by his or her human rights.

Shireen Hunter's enlightening scholarship helps us to see that a positive outcome of this meeting of civilizations is within reach.

Marc Gopin
January 1998

Marc Gopin teaches religion and conflict resolution at George Mason University in Fairfax, Virginia, and he is a senior associate in the CSIS Preventive Diplomacy Program. He received rabbinic ordination at Yeshiva University and his doctorate at Brandeis University.

Introduction

John Buchan, then a major in the British Army Intelligence Corps, based his 1916 novel *The Greenmantle* on a possible Muslim revolt that, had it happened, would have turned the fortunes of the World War I against the allied forces. Buchan wrote:

> Islam is a fighting creed, and the mullah still stands in the pulpit with the Koran in one hand and a drawn sword in the other. Supposing there is some Ark of the Covenant which will madden the remotest Muslim peasant with dreams of Paradise? What then, my friend? Then there will be hell let loose in those parts pretty soon. I have reports from agents everywhere, peddlers in South Russia, Afghanistan horse dealers, Turcoman merchants, Pilgrims on the road to Mecca, sheriffs in North Africa, sailors on the Black sea Coasters, sheep-skinned Mongols, Hindu fakirs, Greek traders in the Gulf as well as respectable consuls who use ciphers. They tell the same story. The East is waiting for a revelation.[1]

Nearly three-quarters of a century later, the American political columnist Charles Krauthammer expressed a similar fear when he wrote that the United States potentially faced two sustained geopolitical threats; the second of these threats emanated from the same region also mentioned in John Buchan's *Greenmantle*, in the form of "an Islamic World united under the banner of Iranian-style fundamentalism in existential struggle with the infidel West."[2]

Before Krauthammer wrote his article, other commentators

bridging several centuries had warned that "keeping Islam at bay was Europe's preoccupation from 1359, when Gallipoli fell to the Turks, until the last occasion on which the Ottoman soldiers stood at the gates of Vienna, in 1683. Islam is once more a preoccupation in the face of the Islamic Revolution."[3] Soon after Krauthammer's article and several years before Samuel Huntington in his article in *Foreign Affairs* popularized the notion of a coming clash of civilizations between Islam and the Western democracies, Bernard Lewis, in an article entitled "The Roots of the Muslim Rage," wrote that in the Muslim world the West faced

> a mood and a movement transcending the level of issues and politics and the governments that pursue them. This is no less than a clash of civilizations—the perhaps irrational but surely historic reaction of an ancient rival against our Judeo-Christian heritage, our secular present, and the worldwide expansion of both.[4]

Most of these ideas were introduced before the collapse of the Soviet Union and the emergence of a paradigm vacuum as a result of the discrediting of Communism. More than a decade before the demise of the USSR, the image of the Ayatullah Ruhollah Khomeini calling on Muslims to rise up against what he called the "global arrogance" resembled the mullah with the Koran in one hand and the sword in the other depicted by the colorful imagery of John Buchan's *Greenmantle*, except that now, instead of the sword, the mullah held a Kalashnikov rifle or Scud missile. The ayatullah also raised fears both in Western chancelleries and in the corridors of the Kremlin, fears similar to those expressed by Buchan's high official of the Foreign Office—of a Muslim World awakened and united, threatening the interests of an essentially secular although at least nominally Christian Western world and the atheist Soviet Union.

Yet Sir Walter Bullivant in *The Greenmantle* was not concerned about Islam's ideological—its civilizational—threat to the Western Christian world. As he reminded the young agent that "beyond Persia you remember, lies India," his concern was with the threat that a Muslim uprising could pose to Britain's control of India, to its mastery over the Indian Ocean and the Persian Gulf, and hence to its overall naval supremacy, which was the basis of Britain's global power.

The Greenmantle was written, however, before the time of universalist ideologies, unless one considers religion an ideology, which in fact it is. In 1916 the Russian czar was still in power and the world had not heard of Hitler and his National Socialism although Lenin was soon to return to Russia. Even earlier, Napoleonic France had combined imperial ambitions with ideological aspirations rooted in the French Revolution, providing a foretaste of the ideological era in international relations that was to come about a century later.

But after the experience of World War II during which the liberal democracies of Europe and America fought not only Germany but also its ideology, Nazism, and after more than four decades of Cold War during which the liberal democracies were locked in an existential struggle against Communist totalitarianism and were engaged in a fierce competition with it for the hearts and minds of the rest of humanity, international politics and relations had become thoroughly ideologized.

This is not to suggest that during the Cold War ideological motives and goals had replaced or superseded other more traditional state interests and objectives—the quest for security, economic advantage, military power, and political influence and prestige—as the basic determinants of their external behavior. On the contrary, even during the Cold War, more often than not ideological interests and objectives had to be abandoned or relegated to second place because their pursuit endangered more tangible interests; but the pursuit of the tangible interests had to be rationalized and justified as in perfect harmony with the ideology and the other values of the state concerned as well as in the service of some higher, unselfish objective.

Unlike in previous centuries when dynastic and state interests (raison d'être) were sufficient justification for state action, since the World War II the behavior of states, although inspired and motivated largely by similar impulses, has had to be cloaked in a higher ideal: making the world safe for democracy; creating a classless, socialist Utopia; or establishing an Islamic order. However, the role of ideology—and of any other value system—should not be reduced to a mere instrument of legitimization of actions undertaken under the impulse of other motives. Rather, by shaping states' visions of the good and the desirable, ideology moves them in particular directions. Ideology became one of the factors—and, at times, a determining one—in shaping state behavior. Also affected by this ideologization of international politics has been the methodology of studying state behavior and determining the dynamics behind it.

Most important in this new methodology has been the analysis of the external behavior of states and the nature of interstate relations in the context of one or two overarching paradigms such as the East-West conflict or the North-South dichotomy, coupled with explanations of international developments in light of these paradigms.

The End of History and the Clash of Civilizations

The ideologization of international politics and the paradigmatic methodology of studying it bear most responsibility for advancing two paradigmatic theories—the end of history and the clash of civilizations—to replace the East-West conflict as the principal determinant of the character of international relations in the post-Soviet era.

Francis Fukuyama has explained that because the history of mankind has been shaped by the clash of ideas, each idea struggling to establish itself as the universal creed and to organize society and polity according to its specific blueprint, the victory of Western liberal democracies in the Cold War, which established the superiority of Western ideas over socialism and the triumph of good over evil, brought history as defined in the above sense, to an end.[5]

Yet the idea of a cosmic battle between good and evil, light and darkness, that ends in the victory of good over evil and light over darkness and ushers in a blissful eternity is nothing new. Zoroaster originated it three thousand years ago.[6] Because of this Hegel said that the history of the world began with the Persians because they were the first to conceive of the world with a beginning, a cosmic battle between two opposite forces, and a denouement that brings history and the world to an end.[7] In Zoroastrianism, which deeply influenced Judaism, Christianity, and ultimately Islam, this denouement comes about as a result of divine intervention. Fukuyama maintains that this denouement already has happened as a result of the West's victory over Communism. Although he does not say it outright, Fukuyama implies that he believes the liberal Utopia has been achieved and those who live by its edicts have reached nirvana, and others also can reach this level provided they live by the rules of Western liberalism. He also contends that no future ideology for a fundamental social restructuring and reorganization could likely become a rival or the antithesis of Western liberal ideology. His end-of-history theory clearly reflected the afterglow of the first flush of victory over Communism. Fukuyama, however, left unanswered the questions of what would determine the character of interstate relations in the posthistorical era and what would be the main dynamics of conflict and cooperation among states.

Bernard Lewis introduced the concept of the clash of civilizations before the final collapse of the Soviet Union, but it did not immediately capture people's imaginations. Samuel Huntington popularized it in 1993 because, by then, many observers in the West were bewildered by the fact that the rest of humanity did not rush to embrace the triumphant Western creed, by the persistence of a wide range of interstate disputes, and even by the reemergence of conflicts long dormant. Although it had been assumed during the Cold War that interstate conflict was mainly— albeit not solely—caused by ideological differences and rivalries, the essence of the theory of the clash-of-civilizations is that if large parts of humanity still refuse to see the obvious superiority of Western liberal ideas and do not accept them, it is because of differences and deeply rooted incompatibilities in the collective makeup and value systems of states and countries—in other words, because of their cultures and civilizations.

The theory of the clash of civilizations goes even further, however, and posits certain fundamental assumptions about what constitutes the core of individual and collective identities and value systems, about what motivates the behaviors of different states, and about the basic incompatibility of some civilizations with that of the West. In terms of the evolving nature of the international relations, the following are the most consequential premises of Huntington's thesis:

• Religion, including its sectarian variations, appears to constitute the core and the defining element of a civilization. Yet there are exceptions. For example, Huntington refers to the Latin American civilization rather than the Catholic civilization, despite the fact that the overwhelming majority of Latin Americans are Catholic, whereas he talks about the Slavic-Orthodox civilization.

It is not clear whether he considers what he calls Western civilization as Christian and, if so, which creed defines it, or whether he considers it based on an undivine religion, secular humanism. His emphasis on Western liberal views and his assertion that some civilizations are inherently incompatible with its values indicate that for him the distinguishing feature of Western civilization is its secular nature. Despite these ambiguities, religion occupies a central place in Huntington's definition of civilizations.[8]

• Civilizations—religions, in other words—will become the defining element of collective identity, surpassing ethnicity, language, sectarian affiliation, and class. Huntington therefore greatly underestimates the significance of ethnic, linguistic, and other distinctions within a particular civilization zone. According to some of his detractors, Huntington "conflates ethnicity with civilization, assuming that all Muslims, for example, are part of a vast ethnic group whose primordial values lead them inevitably to persecute heretics, veil women and establish theocratic regimes."[9]

• Civilizational factors will be the main motivator of state actions. Civilizational affinity or hostility similarly will determine the pattern of interstate alliances and enmities. Huntington's emphasis on civilizations as the core of collective identity challenges the nation-state as the principal unit of the international system; for example, Huntington maintains that at times two different civilizations could, and most probably would, coalesce against a third one. Huntington believes that the Islamic and the Confucian civilizations could coalesce against the West.

• Islam and Confucianism, because of their fundamentally different belief and value systems, are particularly at odds with Western civilization and its democratic, secular, and liberal social and political ethos. Huntington writes that "Western ideas of individualism, liberalism, constitutionalism, human rights, equality, liberty, the rule of law, free markets, the separation of church and state, often have little resonance in Islamic, Confucian, Japanese, Hindu, Buddhist, or Orthodox cultures."[10]

• A clash between Western civilization and some or all of these cultures is inevitable although, Huntington notes, this clash need not be violent. The inevitability of a clash derives from the universalist vocation of Western civilization as well as from its global appeal and hence its existential challenge to other civilizations.

Huntington elevates the role of civilization as a factor shaping the behavior of states far above that accorded to earlier universalist determinants of state behavior such as political ideologies. In the past, tensions between ideology and other determinants such as security or economic advantage were recognized and played an important role in most analyses and theories of state behavior, but Huntington's thesis presents civilizational factors as overwhelmingly superior. Huntington therefore does not address the interaction between civilizational and other factors and the role of other determinants in mitigating or enhancing the impact of civilization. Although Huntington distinguishes sharply between ideology and civilization, he tends to weigh civilizational factors as determinants of state behavior more heavily than was done in the case of ideology in the past. Because Huntington believes that civilizational factors will supersede and submerge other dichotomies, such as between rich and poor and North and South, his theory of the clash of civilizations has important implications for the evolution of relations between the Western world and other nations, which in Huntington's scheme are clustered around a civilizational concept.

Implicit in Huntington's theory of a clash of civilizations also are a near-total homogeneity of value and belief systems within each civilization, the sui generis and immutable character of civilizations and their values, the absence of conflict among countries that belong to the same civilization, and the supremacy of belief systems among all the possible determinants of state behavior.

Ideology, Civilization, and Culture: How Different Are They?

Because of the central role that Huntington and his followers ascribe to civilizational factors as determinants of states' external behavior, it is important first to establish what is meant by civilization. In particular, it is necessary to determine to what extent civilizational factors are different from ideologies and other belief systems, a distinction critical to the methodology of assessing the relative role of civilizational factors in the shaping of the external behavior of states and in determining patterns of international conflict and cooperation.

Ideology and Civilization: Problems of Definition

Clifford Geertz points out that an irony of the ideological age has been that the term ideology itself has become thoroughly ideologized; a concept that at one time meant only a collection of impractical and idealistic political proposals has become what *Webster's Dictionary* defines as "the integrated assertions, theories and aims constituting a politico-social program, often with an implication of factitious propagandizing; as Fascism was altered to fit the Nazi ideology."[11] Whether this ideologization of ideology is a positive or a negative development and whether it is a valid interpretation of reality, the fact is that *Webster's* definition or a variant has become the accepted meaning.

The definition of civilization (or culture, which subsumes civilization as the outward manifestation of itself) also presents problems: In its broadest sense, culture means "the totality of socially transmitted behavior patterns, art, beliefs, institutions, and all other products of human work and thought characteristic of a community or population."[12] Clifford Geertz defines culture as "a historically transmitted pattern of meanings embodied in symbols, a system of inherited patterns of meanings embodied in symbols, a system of inherited conceptions expressed in symbolic forms by means of which men communicate, perpetuate, and develop their knowledge about and the attitudes towards life."[13]

Ideology—in the narrow sense of a system of social, economic, and political thought and guidelines for its implementation—thus becomes only one part of a specific culture and only one manifestation of its collective thought. This would also be true of a people's religion that, as a belief system, is only one element of a culture and a civilization. So defined, these concepts would produce no dichotomies between a people's ideology and its civilization because the ideology is subsumed in the civilization. Thus, when Huntington advances the thesis of the clash of civilizations, he in fact is saying that the battle of beliefs and values will continue and history, contrary to Francis Fukuyama, will not end.

Yet the continuing battle of beliefs and values cannot be reduced to a clash among civilizations because the battle has always been and will continue to be as much *within* civilizations as *be-*

tween them. This intra-civilizational conflict can be seen in what Henry Louis Gates, surveying the past two centuries, describes as "the perennial *Kulturkampf* between faith and secularism."[14] Within a single civilization, such a dichotomy, or battle, explains the current Islamist-secular divide within Muslim societies better than does the more widely accepted concept of specificity deriving from the assumed fusion of religion and politics within Islam. This is certainly not a clash between two civilizations but a clash within a single one.

Nor are clashes limited to Islam. Similar battles of beliefs and values divide Hindu and Jewish societies. The assassination of the Israeli prime minister, Yitzak Rabin, in November 1995 revealed the extent and the depth of the religious-secular divide within the Jewish state. The extent of the divide was demonstrated during the Israeli parliamentary elections of May 1996 when the religious parties made a strong showing. Given the depth of divergences between the two groups, some commentators worry about a potential cultural war between Israel's secular and Orthodox Jews.[15]

Western societies are not free of such dichotomies. The age-old and ongoing battle between faith and secularism was apparent recently in France during the controversy about whether the fifteen hundredth anniversary of the baptism of Clovis, also considered the birth of France as a country and nation, should be celebrated and whether the Pope should visit France on that occasion. France ultimately decided to celebrate the simultaneous coming of Christianity and the birth of the French nation in the lands of contemporary France, amid cries that "France is no longer secular."[16] The pope's trip to France in September 1996, which included a visit to Reims cathedral, led to counterdemonstrations by the secularists.[17]

In the United States, a similar debate about the proper place of faith and secularism has been going on for years; it is perhaps best symbolized by the ongoing argument whether prayer should be permitted in public schools. Advocates of the religious over the secular are certainly not limited to the so-called Christian fundamentalists or to the religious right. For example, during a speech at the Mississippi College School of Law, Justice Antonin Scalia of the U.S. Supreme Court criticized what he considers the excesses of secularism and defended the right of believers to assert their beliefs and values, even at the risk of being thought simpleminded by those he called "worldly wise."[18]

This discussion also implies that cultures are neither static nor the products of single factors. Instead they possess an incremental, cumulative, and composite character and result from the fusion of many intrinsic and extrinsic factors. They are living organisms in a constant state of evolution, and they change in response to internal and external stimuli in the context of the dynamics of challenge and response. The following observation by anthropologist Kevin Avrush captures the dynamic and changing character of cultures and civilizations:

> Traditions and states are recent and modern because they are continually caught up in processes of social and cultural construction. They are invented and reinvented, produced and reproduced, according to complex, interactive, and temporally shifting contingencies of material conditions and historical practice. They are products of struggle and conflict, of material interests and of competing conceptions of authenticity and identity.[19]

Judgments about a culture and the evaluation of its impact on the behavior of a collectivity therefore should take place within a particular rather than an unlimited time frame. This is also necessary because at different times various components of a culture, including its more narrowly defined sociopolitical ideology, acquire a greater or lesser salience and exert a greater or lesser influence in defining a collectivity's self-identity and in shaping its external behavior.

Judeo-Christian principles and traditions, for example, form an important part of Western civilization. But their salience within Western culture has been in decline, and their role in shaping the collective self-identity of Westerners or in determining the internal and external behavior of Western societies and states has been eroding, albeit to different degrees in different societies. A secular social and political belief system based on the centrality of the individual and with its particular dogma and claims to universality and superiority over other belief systems and at times a degree of intolerance toward them has principally shaped the character of Western societies and to some degree influenced their external behavior.

Because cultures and civilizations are composites or, as Nigel Harris has noted, "multiple suits of clothes,"[20] at times different segments within a single society make use of different aspects of its cultural heritage as the foundation of their sociopolitical philosophy and as instruments to legitimize power or to challenge it. In prerevolution Iran, for example, a mix of pre-Islamic Persian traditions and Western theories of modernization constituted the ruling elite's sociopolitical philosophy and the basis of its legitimacy. The opposition used Islam and several leftist ideologies to present an alternative and to challenge the regime's legitimacy.

Hence the dichotomy between culture and ideology is false. The ideological battles of the twentieth century have been, indeed, civilizational clashes, but they have been within civilizations as much as or more than between them. If we assume that such civilizational clashes will be the order of the day in the twenty-first century, they will be ideological disputes as well, and they will perform the sociopolitical functions of ideologies and will have a similar impact on states' external behavior. Therefore the methodological tools for the analysis of civilizational factors in defining the collectivities' self-identities, their values, and their world views, as well as in shaping their external behavior, should be the same techniques used in assessing the impact of ideology.

Islam's Salience

On the broader plane of relations between civilizations, many in the West see Islam as the most likely candidate for a civilizational clash with the West. A number of characteristics of Islam, especially in an abstract and ahistorical context, make it an ideal contestant.

Islam is a communal religion and, as such, in structure if not always in practice it presents an all encompassing and internally cohesive set of rules—both legal and ethical—for the organization of collective and individual life and the mechanisms for implementation. Islam aspires to be the principal component of a Muslim's self-identity and the main focus of allegiance. Islam also wants to create a new sociopolitical community based on a common faith, the *Ummat-ul Islam*, distinct and different from other communities. Moreover, during the past three decades, Islam—or rather new interpretations of it—has been undergoing a revival as a social and political ideology. Islam cuts across continents, nationalities, and ethnic groups and thus besides Christianity is the only other global religion.

None of the other candidates—such as Confucianism—for the role of the West's antagonist seems to match Islam as a system of beliefs, values, and guides for sociopolitical organization; they are too nebulous and unstructured. Confucianism is relevant only to China although it is influential in other parts of East Asia.

Two additional factors enhance Islam's position as the West's preferred antagonist. First, Islam is a proselytizing creed with a belief in its own ultimate victory and universal prevalence, no matter how serious the tribulations of the journey. If truly carried to its logical conclusion, this tendency, by the nature of Islam's very existence, would make Islam a serious challenge to the West's sense of its own civilizational superiority and belief in its ultimate victory even if Islam were dormant and devoid of political activism. If Islam is viewed in this abstract way, without analysis of historical practice, the theory of a clash of civilizations between Islam and the West gains plausibility.

Second, for more than one thousand years, Islam was the main enemy, the hostile "other," of the West. This well-established cultural memory makes it no surprise that any challenge from the Muslim world conjures up barely forgotten images of enemies at the gate and reawakens fears of a repetition. With its burden of history, Islam is the ideal candidate for the new enemy figure that will fill the gap created by the fall of Communism. This predilection for seeing Islam as the enemy is strengthened by the assumption that Islam's specificity and uniqueness, especially the assumed fusion of the spiritual and the temporal, are necessarily carried into practice, render Islam impervious to change, and make it by definition the antithesis of Western secular humanism.

The burden of history is not, however, all on one side. Not only does the West feel threatened by Islam, but also many Muslims—though by no means all—feel threatened by the West. Muslim memories of Western domination are more recent and hence far more fresh than Western recollections of the fall of Gallipoli or the siege of Vienna. These Muslims are also concerned about the dilution and possibly the disappearance of their civilization under the influence of what Bernard Lewis has characterized as "the seductive allure" of Western civilization. Thus the thinkers and theoreticians of the recent Islamist movements have also talked of a civilizational conflict between Islam and the West. Rashid Ghannushi, the exiled leader of the Islamist movement in Tunisia, sees that the inexorable expansion of Western civilization from Europe to the Americas and to Eastern Europe is now trying to penetrate the East—through, he believes, the intermediary of Israel. In Ghannushi's words: "The West as a concept of civilization has seen its center of gravity move from Western Europe to America to Eastern Europe. Israel represents the projection of this center into the East to wipe out its specific character, its spiritual wealth, and humankind's hope for a new renaissance."[21]

The Impact of Oil

From the West's point of view, more important than atavistic fears of an Islam resurgent is the fact that, by ironies of geography, geology, and history, Islam is also the creed of a part of the world that holds high strategic importance for the West. From the Caspian Sea to the Persian Gulf, from the peaks of the Caucasus to the sands of Arabia and the steppes of Central Asia, the oil and gas on which the awesome industrial and military might of the West depends is buried under lands populated by the Muslims. This same oil has for some time been the only hope of the Muslim world for overcoming its poverty and underdevelopment. No analysis of the theory of a potential clash of civilizations between Islam and the West, nor any answer to the question of whether the clash could be replaced by peaceful coexistence, can be found without accounting for the explosive marriage of Islam and oil. This also explains why the rise of Hindu fundamentalism, equally at odds with the West's liberalism, does not generate the same concern and anxiety. Similarly, awareness of civilizational incompatibility between the West and the Confucian world became more acute after the emergence of China and other Asian countries as potential economic competitors to the West and, in the case of China, even military and strategic rivals.

Thus it is the combination of the strategic significance of Muslim lands and Islam's perceived potency as a belief system and frame of reference for both spiritual and temporal life that makes Islam an important challenge. However, because of the ideologization of international politics, even recognition and acceptance of this would be unlikely to change fundamentally the discourse on relations between Islam and the West because every act of state must be justified on the basis of some higher value or goal. Western leaders justified the Persian Gulf War of 1990–1991 on the basis of punishing aggression and restoring democracy to Kuwait rather than securing Arabian oil fields. They also explain competition for power with Islamic states in terms of preserving and spreading Western liberal values rather than securing oil supplies at a favorable price.

Unlike secular ideologies such as Communism or fascism, which do not respond to people's deepest emotional and psychological needs or provide answers to the "why" of human existence, Islam as a divinely inspired creed is not easily susceptible to the instruments used to combat other ideologies that in the past have challenged the Western liberal creed. Like other religions, Islam can lose a war and not lose itself. Therefore all-out Western opposition to Islam and an ideological war against it could cause more damage to specific Western interests than whatever challenge Islam could pose to the West's civilizational and ideological supremacy.

Good versus Bad Islam

Since 1979 when the Iranian revolution demonstrated Islam's potential political potency, Western academics and policymakers have tried to resolve the dilemma of countering Islam's challenge without waging an all-out struggle against Islam itself by distinguishing between Islam as a religion and the new militant ideology that claims to represent Islam's true spirit. Islam limited to its religious dimension causes no clash with the West, in terms of civilization or of political reality. This dimension of Islam is unconcerned about politics and does not resist the penetration of Western economic, political, and cultural influences and—tacitly, if not explicitly—the supremacy of the West in the international economic and political systems. Islam limited this way is often proclaimed to be compatible with Western democratic ideas and hence capable of undergoing a process of reformation and enlightenment that would eventually bring it even closer to the Western value system and would transform it into a factor relevant only to private life, similar to the position that religion, at least the nonorthodox variety, occupies in the West.

Militant and revolutionary Islam, however, appears to recognize no boundaries between the private and the public domains and attempts to regulate the totality of individual and collective life. It is viewed as a totalitarian—an antidemocratic and anti-Western—creed. It is backward looking and xenophobic, which makes it fear Western ideas and presence. It opposes Western presence in the Muslim lands and challenges the West's global supremacy. The Islam that preaches this is the nemesis of Western civilization.

During the years immediately following the Iranian revolution, the division of Islam into good and bad versions took on a distinct ethnic and sectarian coloring. Shi'a Islam and the Persian traditions of Iran were said to be responsible for the excesses of its new Islamist ideology and its behavior. Sunni Islam was said to be more democratic and egalitarian and, because Sunnism lacked an established clergy independent of government control, less vulnerable to schemes that advocate the establishment of Islamic governments and a re-Islamization of society and polity in countries that, according to the Islamists, are now only nominally Muslim.

Even Islamist-movement leaders such as Hassan al-Turabi of Sudan, trying to soothe the anxieties of Westerners, have resorted to such arguments. That the history of the development of Islamist movements, as well as the essence of Shi'a doctrine of political power and the nature of government, did not support this theory was barely considered. Even after Islamist movements became active and visible in the exclusively Sunni countries, their militancy was often explained as the result of exogenous, especially Shi'a, influences and hence incompatible with Sunni traditions.

The division into good and bad Muslims according to sect has reasserted itself. Commenting on the tepid reaction of Palestinians and Sunni Arab governments to Israeli attacks on Lebanon in the spring of 1996, Jim Hoagland concluded that the Shi'as—or those inspired by the Shi'a revolution in Iran—represented the radical Islam, hence the bad Islam. To Hoagland, the reaction of Sunni Arab governments to the Israeli raids was evidence that these attacks had driven "a huge wedge between the two dominant branches of Islam" and that Israel may have "fashioned an alliance with major forces in the Sunni world against the radicals which either belong to or revere the Shi'ite revolution that started in Iran."[22]

Whether that was a correct assessment of Israel's relations with Sunni Islam, the implications of these distinctions for the future of relations between Islam and the West are considerable. If extremist Islam is viewed as essentially an aberration caused by myriad factors exogenous to the essence of mainstream Sunni Islam, it can be eliminated by attacking its root causes, presuming they can be identified and isolated. And because this theory assumes that the other, good, Islam is both capable of evolution and reform and not inherently either totally incompatible with Western values or necessarily anti-Western, the risk of conflict between Islam and the West is reduced.

Not all Western scholars and observers distinguish between good and bad Islam. They do agree that one type of Islam—the militant version—is the more dangerous and imminent threat to the West, civilizationally and otherwise, and hence must be contained and eliminated. But they disagree with the view that Islam is capable of evolution and reformation and hence of convergence with Western values. They conclude that until the total secularization of Muslim societies and the relegation of Islam to only the domain of private conscience, a degree of civilizational clash is inevitable. Proponents of this view also believe that any effort to involve even the least extremist Islamist groups in the political process would be dangerous because it would recognize Islam's role as a political and hence public force. Moreover, the Islamists would try to subvert the entire process.[23]

Limits of the Dualist Theory of Islam

The problem with most theories of the nature of Islam, its compatibility with Western ideas, and its ability to evolve and reform—as well as the debate about the inevitability of a clash of civilizations, the possibility of peaceful coexistence, or even some degree of convergence—is that discussions deal mostly in an abstract, static, and ahistorical way with the role and place of Islam as an organizer of Muslim societies and polities and as a determinant of Muslim external behavior.

Yet it is impossible to determine in the abstract the impact of Islam. For example, it is futile to try to establish in the abstract whether Islam is compatible with democracy: powerful arguments can be made for both sides. The fact is that the development and consolidation of democratic systems require the existence of many social and economic conditions and not only mere adherence to a secular creed; this is illustrated by the large number of modern governments that can be described as secular and either totalitarian or authoritarian. Moreover, in reality, Islam is not merely a static body of ethical and legal rules and regulations that, once revealed, have remained unaltered through the centuries; Islam is also the sum of the lives and experiences of Muslims, as lived in different territorial contexts and historic eras, with each other and with non-Muslims.

Like other traditions and cultures described earlier, Islam has, in the words of Kevin Avrush, been "caught up in processes of social and cultural construction" and has been "invented, reinvented, produced and reproduced, according to complex, interactive and temporally shifting contingencies of material conditions and historic practice."[24]

The evolution of Islam's relations with other societies has followed a similar path. From the beginning of its expansion beyond Arabia, Islam not only affected and shaped the cultures and societies of conquered peoples, but it was itself affected and shaped by the preexisting civilizations. Islam has also been affected by the new creeds and cultures that have made inroads into Muslim societies during the past two centuries.

Thus understanding Islam and analyzing its relationship to other ideas and civilizations can be accomplished correctly only within specific frames of time and space. Any other approach leads to incomplete and hence inaccurate generalities that would represent only one aspect of Islam, not its totality.

The same principle applies to other great ideas and civilizations, including the Western liberal tradition. For example, the current understanding of democracy—the balance between individual and collective rights and responsibilities and the relationship between the majority and ethnic and religious minorities in Western societies—is different from what it was in the nineteenth century. In the first half of the twentieth century, cultural relativism or multiculturism were not even heard of. Also in the last century, despite the Enlightenment and the separation of church and state, ethical values that are deeply rooted in religion to a great extent determined the acceptable parameters of secular legislative action. Until very recently, for example, homosexual relations in England were legally prohibited by laws that derive from the religious prohibition of the homosexual act; indeed in England the practical separation of church and state is still a matter of custom rather than of law and principle because the British monarch is both the head of state and the head of the Church of England and defender of the faith. The separation of church and state has evolved there only in the past 100 years.

In discussions of whether Islam and democracy are compatible, the questions "What kind of democracy?" and "What kind of Islam?" must, therefore, be answered first. This applies also to the broader context of Islamic versus Western values.

Evolution of Religion and Secularism

A democratic system of government that operates on ethical rules rooted in religious beliefs is clearly more compatible with Islam—and with any other divinely inspired religion—than is the present Western system in which ethical issues in the main are considered to be in the private domain. The modern Western liberal state in matters of religion is (borrowing a phrase from Leonard Binder) agnostic if not atheist.

All segments of Western societies do not accept this. Debates over birth control, abortion, and euthanasia show that the *Kulturkampf* between faith and secularism and their respective domains is still continuing in the West. Many Westerners still believe in the eternal value of certain religiously rooted ethical norms, and a significant segment of the Western population seems to hold religiously based ethical values higher than existing laws and social norms, even being willing to challenge secular laws and norms to uphold religious edicts. Antiabortion groups believe that maintaining the right to life of an unborn child, on the basis of the belief that life can be given and taken only by God, is a higher value and justifies and legitimizes the illegal and antisocial act of setting fire to abortion clinics. In addition, if one believes opinion in the West that Western civilization lacks a spiritual or ethical purpose and that societal ills result from this supposed spiritual vacuum, it is conceivable that in the future the balance between faith and secularism may be altered in favor of faith. The French government's decision to commemorate the fifteen-hundredth anniversary of the baptism of Clovis despite opposition by the pure "laicists" led some to point out that "an approach between absolute secularism and state religion is in the process of developing in Europe in regard to religion."[25]

A reverse process is quite likely to take place in many parts of the Muslim world. In countries such as Iran, the existence of governments based on Islam (or that claimed to be) has led to a deterioration of material aspects of life and a perpetuation or a worsening of political repression. This deterioration has led to a turning away of the population from religion and gravitation toward a more secular system of politics and governance.

The coalescence of these trends—a greater acceptance of a role for religion in the West and a greater secularization in the Islamic world—could in time create a common ground where the two civilizations could meet. Conclusions based on the current relative weighting of secularism and faith in Western and Islamic countries—and on whether civilizational relations are conflictual or cooperative—may not be valid in the next decade. Unlikely also is that a convergence at the level of civilization would end conflict between the West and all or part of the Muslim world unless at the same time fundamental change took place in other aspects of their relations, notably in the tremendous gap in their relative political power and economic well-being.

Real Cause of the Clash

A civilizational rapprochement—or at a least narrowing of differences—between Islam and the West would not eliminate conflict because, contrary to Huntington's suggestion, the real cause of conflict between Islam and the West is not civilizational incompatibility. If this were the case, relations between the Western countries and all Muslim states would be hostile. Yet clearly this is not the case; even the West and Shi'a Islam had good relations under the Iranian Pahlavis. The West has had closer and more cooperative relations with Muslim countries such as Saudi Arabia and Pakistan where Islam is the core of the people's collective identity and the main organizer of society and, more important, the official state ideology to a far greater degree than is the case in some other countries with which the West has more difficult relations, most notably Iran.

This situation results from the fact that the underlying but largely unspoken and unacknowledged cause of the dichotomy between Islam and the West is the question of power and the consequences of its exercise—that is, influence at the regional and global levels. This balance of power, which is heavily weighted in the West's favor, gives the West a tremendous influence over the fate of the Muslim states and peoples. The Western countries exercise through a variety of financial and military means a good deal of influence on the internal politics of Muslim countries, including support for regimes and governments that are less than reasonably supported by the majority of their own people. This Western support, in turn, often perpetuates narrowly based elites and excludes the chance for large segments of the population to share power and the advantages that flow from it.

In the international arena also, it is the West that exercises a hegemonic influence in that it sets the rules of the game in both economics and politics; this is often prejudicial to Muslim countries and, indeed, to all other less developed states. Western officials and experts have admitted, for example, that the only group to have lost out in the Uruguay Round negotiations on the international trading system was the Third World. Voting or veto power in international institutions—the UN, World Bank, IMF— also reflects this bias, as does even the allocation of the world's airwaves. Prevailing opinion in the Muslim world has been that the West has been able to maintain such an unequal balance of power because of the subservience of Muslim governments to the Western powers; to change this unequal correlation of forces, the internal power structures of Muslim states should be changed.

Over the years, groups that represent a range of—mostly secular—political ideas such as liberal nationalism and varieties of socialism have challenged the existing governments and their legitimacy. The Islamists are only the latest in a long line; earlier secular groups also resented and challenged with varying degrees of intensity and vehemence Western supremacy and its controlling influence in international life. The anti-Western views and sentiments of certain segments of Muslim populations are more the consequence of these internal and external disequilibria and structural inequalities than of civilizational incompatibilities. Similarly, the main reason for the West's dislike of the Islamists is their temerity to challenge the West's global superiority and their unwillingness to live by the rules set by the Western powers.

Centrality of Power and the Role of Ideology

Any analysis of the role of Islam in Muslim societies as well as of the question of the future state of Islam-West relations, including the debate about the inevitability of a clash of civilizations or the possibility of a modus vivendi, must recognize the central role played by interest- and power-related issues and goals. Some Western analysts have recognized this; Graham Fuller wrote in 1995 that "a civilizational clash is not so much over Jesus Christ, Confucius, or the Prophet Muhammad as it is over the unequal distribution of world power, wealth, and influence."[26] Indeed, the clash is between the "civilization of the poor and the powerless and that of the rich and the mighty. It is a conflict between those who have power and those who do not, those who control the world's destiny and those who are subjects of control."[27] Therefore an essential part of any analysis of relations between Islam and the West needs to be the linkage between belief systems, including ideology, power, and their use for the maintenance, acquisition, legitimation, and delegitimation of power, both within states and among them. The same also applies to the function of belief systems, as well as their role as instruments for explaining existing conditions and for transforming them, so as to improve one's own situation.

Sociopolitical Functions of Ideology and Its Role in Foreign Policy

In addition to their role as instruments of legitimation and delegitimation of power and its uses, ideologies and belief systems perform several other functions. Ideologies make sense in a systematic and at least superficially coherent manner of complex and at times seemingly unintelligible conditions and, in doing so, also provide psychological comfort. Ideologies perform these functions by providing

• scapegoats and making them responsible for the ills of particular groups, societies, and countries;
• identifiable objects of hostility such as a corrupt elite, big powers, global imperialism, or Islamic extremism. Ideologies ease the pain of individuals and states and to some degree reconcile them to their conditions; and
• higher values that facilitate the acceptance of existing hardships and inequalities.

Ideologies thus contribute to the functioning of societies because, as Clifford Geertz has remarked, they bridge "the emotional gap between things as they are and as one would have them to be, thus insuring the performance of roles that might otherwise be abandoned in despair or apathy."[28] At any given time in the history of a nation, any belief system that best performs these functions gains the largest number of adherents.

In the field of foreign policy and the external relations of states, ideologies and belief systems exert a good deal of influence principally by affecting states' perceptions of external realities and their impact on their own interests and, to some degree, defining these interests; garnering popular support for policies undertaken for other reasons, notably the quest for power; and legitimizing questionable acts by justifying them on the basis of higher values to obtain popular support for policy. Thus ideologies and belief systems provide a blueprint or, as Zbigniew Brzezinski has put it, an action program for the acquisition and uses of power.

Despite these important functions that ideology performs in the field of foreign policy, its exact impact on states' external behavior is not easily determined because, important as it is, ideology is only one determinant and not even the most important one. Theoreticians such as Hans J. Morgenthau of the so-called realist school have maintained that all politics, including international politics, are about power and that ideologies serve as disguises.[29] Others, the idealists, have argued that in most cases states more often act from ideological motives, and they point out that, even if one accepts that the search for power is the principal impulse behind state behavior, the method by which a state acquires and uses power is also very important. At this level it is ideology that has a determining impact because it is essentially an action program.[30]

Whichever interpretation is considered valid, both illustrate that ideology is only one of the determinants of state behavior. The impact ideology makes is often enhanced or mitigated by factors such as geopolitical conditions, economic needs, elite interests, the process of decision-making, the character of regimes, and influences emanating from regional and international systems and balances of power. At the times that significant incompatibilities and even outright conflicts emerge between a state's ideological goals and its other interests, more often than not ideology is relegated to a level of lower priority although, in a skillful use of ideology, leaders often justify nonideological activities as being in perfect harmony with state ideology. In particular, when the pursuit of ideological goals has conflicted with the security or even the actual survival of a state, ideological objectives either have been abandoned or their achievement has been pushed so far into the future that it strips them of any immediate operational value. In explanation, F. S. Northedge remarked that a "state must survive and somehow prosper . . . [and] in the final resort the nation's will to survive is irresistible."[31]

The subordination of ideology to other interests and realities occurs more frequently at later stages of the adoption of a belief system as the guiding principles of a governing elite. This is so because most ideologies initially are change oriented and aim to alter existing structures and balances of power that they view as unfair and to create new ones according to their own blueprints. Their efforts to alter the existing system inevitably generate resistance from the status quo and those who benefit from it, thus setting in motion the dynamics of challenge and response that ultimately result in the emergence of a new equilibrium.

In today's Muslim world we can observe all these functions of ideology and their interplay with other elements. In particular, the question of power and its relationship to ideology is relevant to the debate about Islam's role within Muslim societies; this debate is clearly and directly related to the question of power and who yields it. Islam as an ideology is used to delegitimize and challenge the existing power structure within many Muslim societies, but it is also used by existing power elites to legitimize and perpetuate their own status. To achieve their purposes, both sides have recourse to scriptural texts and their interpretations.

In the history of the Muslim world this practice is not new. On the contrary, since Islam's early days, theoretical debates in the Islamic communities have been directly related to the question of power and who should wield it and to what ends.

The external behavior of Western states also bears witness that power and interest rather than ideology have been the critical factors in driving their foreign policies. Both before and since the age of ideology, Western behavior has been determined primarily by security concerns, political and economic interests, and the drive for power and prestige, not by some value- and belief-related factors such as ideology and civilization. Western powers, like all countries, have used value-based arguments to justify, rationalize, and legitimize decisions and actions undertaken for other reasons, and the Western governments have used value-related arguments to garner popular support for more worldly objectives. This has been especially true when achievement of worldly goals has required considerable material and personal sacrifices on the part of Western people.

During World War I, the American public might not have been willing to make the sacrifices it did to restore the balance of power in Europe, but it was prepared to make these sacrifices "to make the world safe for democracy." More recently, just before the decision to go to war with Iraq in 1991, many Americans opposed military action on the grounds that it was prompted by a desire to protect the Arabian oil fields; they chanted, "No blood for oil." It was only after U.S. leaders convinced them that Operation Desert Storm was necessary to stop Saddam Hussain (a totalitarian dictator in the mold of Hitler), to uphold principles of international law, and to provide a chance for democracy to flourish that they wholeheartedly supported retaliation against Iraq.

This is not to suggest that Western countries have not been interested in spreading their values or that the failure of other countries to observe certain values and norms that the West considers essential has not affected Western attitudes toward them. It is clear that the Western countries have favored the dissemination of their own value system, partly out of belief in its superiority and universality and partly out of a belief that ideological affinity leads other countries to be more responsive to Western interests and priorities. This has occurred, however, only where the pursuit of such goals has been judged not to endanger other Western interests. Whenever there has been such a conflict, the ideological and value-oriented goals have been subordinated to more important security, political, and economic interests: if, for example, parliamentary elections in countries important to the West could lead to the unseating of a pro-Western government or to the coming to power of a less malleable leadership, Western countries have not favored it.

By contrast, in the case of governments with which the West has not been on good terms and where parliamentary elections could bring to power a government receptive to Western interests and priorities, the West has insisted that the democratic norms be upheld. For example, Western countries have not been especially interested in open and fair elections in most of the Muslim world because the West has calculated correctly that such elections would lead either to the replacement or to the serious weakening of existing pro-Western governments. Western states not only have not flinched when their favored governments have denied the fruits of free elections to their opponents but also have helped them eliminate their opponents, for example, in Algeria since 1992. This rule has applied also to other pro-Western Muslim countries such as Egypt, Saudi Arabia, Morocco, Tunisia, and several Gulf and Arab states.

The West has also used the human rights issue, which constitutes such an important component of Western values and diplomacy, to pressure those countries that, in one form or another, either threaten Western interests, pose some kind of actual or potential security or economic challenge to those interests, or simply refuse to follow the West's lead on important issues. Thus the West often uses the human rights argument to justify hostile policies—including covert efforts to destabilize governments when security, economic, and other interests seem to require it—toward governments with which it differs on other grounds. Likewise, a country's dismal human rights record has rarely been much of a hindrance to the establishment of close relations. During the Iran-Iraq war, for example, the West overlooked Iraq's use of poison gas against the Iraqi Kurds in Halabja; the West did not end military, economic, and political support to Iraq. Nor has Turkey's denial to its Kurdish citizens of their most basic human rights—including the right to proclaim their separate identity—plus the practice of torture in Turkish prisons and Turkey's other lapses in observing human rights reduced Western support for Ankara.³⁷

Even more significant is that the West appears to have little or no problem with a Muslim country organizing its internal life according to the principles and requirements of Islam, provided that this in no way threatens or challenges Western interests. Thus the West seemed to have little problem with the government of Ja'afar Numeiry in Sudan when it began to impose Islamic rule upon Sudanese society and government because Numeiry did not challenge the West or its regional allies. By contrast, the West has put Sudan's current military-Islamist government on its list of pariah states, partly because of its Islamization policy but mainly because of the Sudanese government's opposition to Western policies in the Middle East and its alleged aid to Islamist groups, including extremist factions that engage in terrorism.

Saudi Arabia is another example of a country where civilizational incompatibility—the clash of values—is no hindrance to close relations with the West provided that the external behavior of the country does not threaten Western interests or have the potential to become a competitor on a regional or an international level.

This pattern of the relationship between ideology on the one hand and the requirements of power and interest on the other has also prevailed in the West's relations with countries other than Islamic states with which it has had ideological incompatibility. The main reason for animosity toward the Soviet Union, for example, was not the incompatibility between the Western and the socialist ethos as much as it was the fact of growing Soviet power and the threat it posed to Western interests. This was noted before the Cold War was fully under way, following the Soviet Union's extension of its sphere of influence in Eastern Europe, in the Balkans (the Greek-Turkish crisis), and in the Middle East (the Azerbaijan crisis with Iran). Thus before the occurrence of the above-noted events, President Harry Truman did not feel the United States had any particular reason to be concerned about the nature of the Soviet system, and he did not see the Soviet system as a barrier to an understanding with the USSR. Truman wrote that the Russians "evidently like their government or they wouldn't die for it. I like ours, *so let's get along* [emphasis in original]."[33] Truman's views changed "only when he grew to fear the prospective growth of Soviet power. Truman disliked tyrants and believed in self-government, but not enough to do anything about them unless he saw U.S. interests engaged."[34] The presidents who followed him also faced similar dilemmas and responded in the same way. For example, from the mid-1970s through the 1980s, the undemocratic nature of Communist China did not prevent the United States from forging a strategic alliance with China against their common enemy, the Soviet Union.

Throughout the 1960s, 1970s, and 1980s, the West similarly helped Romania in economic and other ways because of the relatively independent posture that Romania's leadership adopted in foreign policy, thus distancing itself from Moscow. Domestically, however, the Romanian regime remained one of the most repressive and rigidly socialist of all East European governments. The tolerance and complicity of the Western countries was also extended to authoritarian and undemocratic regimes of rightist tendencies. The long list of authoritarian figures who benefited from Western support includes Marcos of the Philippines; Pinochet of Chile; a coterie of other Latin American dictators; Mobutu of Zaire; military rulers of South Korea, Pakistan, and at times Turkey; the shah of Iran; and last but by no means least during the 1980s, Saddam Hussain of Iraq.

This line of argument is not intended to ascribe to Western governments a tendency to practice conscious hypocrisy. On the contrary, decisions of how to approach governments whose character and behavior have been incompatible with Western values have been made after, at times, agonizing debate and desperate efforts to reconcile the conflicting demands of ideals and interests. The choice to sacrifice ideals often comes from the conviction that the alternative would do more harm, not only to Western interests but also to the general good. (Of course, the tendency to view what is in one's own interest as compatible with the general good is a common failing of humans and societies.) The result, nevertheless, is that Western governments and publics have often overlooked "the extent to which they have tolerated and even aligned themselves with evil regimes when their own interests were not endangered or when it served their interests to do so."[35]

This inconsistency is often the consequence of the ideologization of international relations and the popularization of foreign policy, especially if its implementation requires popular sacrifice. The role of ideology in creating an image of an enemy that can rally people around their government and lead them to accept burdens must not be underestimated. At times, fighting a clearly identified enemy becomes the most potent force that unifies a people. The emergence of the theory of civilizational clash during the last several years should be understood, at least partly, in this context.

With the end of the Cold War and the collapse of the Soviet Union and with the absence of another country that could credibly challenge Western supremacy, the West is lacking a believable enemy figure, making it more difficult to reach consensus on foreign policy issues within individual countries as well as among allies. Thus, at least for commentators with the requisite psychological and analytical bent, there is utility in finding an ideological enemy against which to unite. Speaking within the American context, Irving Kristol noted: "With the end of the Cold War, what America really needs is an obvious ideological and threatening enemy, one worthy of its mettle, one that can unite all Ameri-

cans in opposition. . . . Where are invading aliens when America
most needs them?"[36]

Which Islam, Which West?

The popularity of the theory of a clash of civilizations has led to
some generalization and to sweeping statements on the nature of
relations between Islam and the West, as well as to ambiguity in
the definitions of Islam and the West, which are both civilizational and geopolitical concepts.

Because in the real world it is not civilizations but countries
or groups of countries that clash, it is important to determine first
what is meant by the Islamic world and what is meant by the
West. Does Islam mean all countries where most people profess
Islam or only those that have a particular type of Islamic government? If it means all Muslim countries, a clash between Islam and
the West appears unrealistic and highly improbable because most
Muslim states have good relations with most key Western countries—the United States and the West European states.

The definition of the West is clearer, but not completely so. It
does include Western Europe and the United States, and, according to Huntington, Japan is also part of the West. But Huntington
considers other countries to be on the borderline of either opting
for or opting out of the West. Australia may be opting out of the
West, whereas Mexico and Turkey want in but are not yet accepted. Huntington's analysis is flawed here, however, because
he equates the leanings of existing elites with the views of the
majority although, in reality, the situation is not clear-cut. Not all
Turks or all Japanese want to be part of the West; and not all
people in countries with anti-Western governments are antago-
nistic toward the West or toward its culture. Indeed, the clash of
civilizations within Muslim countries, and to a lesser degree in
the West, is more intense than it is between Islam and the West.

On the basis of both historical experience and current conditions, relations between Islam and the West cannot and should
not be discussed in overly general terms. Instead they should be
analyzed at a more specific and parochial level and within the
specifics of time and space. Only this way can a realistic and
relatively more accurate assessment be made of both the relative
role of civilizational factors in determining the state and the prospects for Muslim-Western relations—whether they will be conflic-

tual or cooperative. Only a pragmatic and specific approach, not a general and abstract one, can answer whether an accommodation between Islam and the West can take place in a gradual and evolutionary manner or whether it can happen only after conflict and confrontation.

Goals and Methodology

The goals of this study are to subject to historical analysis certain basic and commonly held views of the nature of collective identity and community, the place and role of ethnicity, the nature of government and politics, and the vision of interstate relations in Islam. This task is necessary to demonstrate the practical application of these concepts in individual Muslim societies over the centuries and their continuing evolution. Such an approach provides

• an assessment of likely trends in the internal evolution of individual Muslim societies and in intra-Muslim relations, notably the potential for the formation of a more closely knit Islamic community of states that could present a united front to the West;
• an analysis of the factors behind both the revival of Islam as a potent political force during the past few decades and its new militancy and anti-Western dimensions, as well as the different manifestations of this revival. Special attention is paid to the role of Islam as an ideology used by both the state and various social and political groups for legitimizing and delegitimizing power and for maintaining or gaining power;
• an analysis of the causes of the anti-Westernism of the Islamists for establishing the relative weight of civilizational and noncivilizational factors;
• an assessment of the relative role of Islam in determining the character and pattern of external relations of Muslim states, especially Islam's impact on the nature of relations with the West;
• an assessment of the likelihood of a civilizational clash between Islam and the West, as well as the likelihood of peaceful coexistence; and
• suggestions that could help minimize the risk of conflict between the West and the Islamic world and maximize the chances of their reconciliation.

The methodology is both historical and empirical. A historical approach helps illustrate the unfolding of the Islamic experience over the centuries as experienced by various Muslim peoples in different parts of the Islamic world. It illustrates the specific shape of abstract Islamic concepts when they are applied to different sociopolitical, historical, and cultural contexts, thus making Islamic civilization a diverse phenomenon. It further illustrates that over the centuries Islam has been affected by and, in turn, has affected the dialectics of power and ideology in various Muslim lands. Special treatment is given to the question of Islam's long contact with the West and the consequences for Muslim societies and for Islamic political thought, which includes the more recent Islamist theories.

A complementary empirical approach helps to draw the pattern of Islam's interaction with other cultural, political, and economic forces within Muslim societies and the pattern of relations between the Islamic countries and the West. Thus it helps identify the more tangible causes of rift between the Islamic world and the West. Evidence produced by these historical and empirical analyses helps to identify the directions in which the dynamics of Muslim societies and the relations between Islam and the West are most likely to evolve. Thus it suggests ways to prevent a prolonged dichotomy in Muslim societies between the Islamic and the secular and a conflict of civilizations between the Islamic world and the West.

1

Unfolding of the Islamic Experience

The principal arguments of those who foresee an inevitable clash between the Islamic world and the West are based on the specificity of Islam, in particular its supposed fusion of the spiritual and temporal domains, and on its alleged inherent incompatibility with secular, liberal Western political ideology. It is interesting that both the Islamists and the Western adherents of the theory of the clash of civilizations share this belief. Islamists also believe that Islam is unique and all encompassing. They have built their vision of an ideal Islamic society upon an Islamic Utopia that they claim existed during the brief period of the prophet Muhammad's rule in Medina.

Yet neither the Islamist view nor the Western view is supported by historical evidence; on the contrary, an objective and impartial reading of the history of the Islamic experience in its different temporal and territorial contexts shows that Islam has not been as different from other religions as is often proclaimed, nor has there ever been an Islamic Utopia as some Islamists believe. It is therefore critical to start with an understanding of the historic Islam—as opposed to abstract Islam—to discern the likely trends in relations between Islam and the West and especially to assess the risks of conflict between the two worlds.

The Early Islamic Community: Myth and Reality

Between A.D. 622 when Muhammad, the Prophet of Islam, arrived in Medina and A.D. 632 when he died, he exercised both spiritual and political leadership over his followers in the new

Muslim community, first in Medina and later in other parts of Arabia that he conquered for Islam. Although brief, this period influenced deeply the later development of Islam's political and social theory and has held tremendous fascination for successive generations of Muslims as the perfect model of what an ideal Islamic society and state—an Islamic Utopia—was, could be, and should be. The intensity of Muslims' fascination and preoccupation with this ideal period of Muslim life and, hence, their urge to re-create this Utopia has ebbed and flowed throughout their history.

During the past few decades, as Islam has experienced a renewed social and political vibrancy, the vision of this ideal Muslim community has acquired a central place in the theories of various Islamist thinkers and movements. Indeed, the re-creation of such an ideal society, or at least its approximation, is declared to be the main goal and aspiration of followers of the Islamist movements.

The period of the Prophet's spiritual and temporal rule has also produced several widely held views among Muslims—certainly among the Islamists—as well as among a good many Western scholars of Islam regarding Islam's conception of the basis of collective identity; the nature of society and politics, notably the relationship between private and public, sacred and profane; the state; the nation; sovereignty, including who possesses it and who should wield it; and the source of legitimacy in an Islamic polity.

This period and, to a lesser degree, the period of the rule of the four early caliphs—the *Rashidun*, or rightly guided—have acquired great importance as the principal sources of guidance regarding these central issues[1] for successive generations of Muslims. This has been true partly because there are relatively few specific and clear *Qur'anic* injunctions on these issues and partly because those that do exist are often ambiguous; at times they are even contradictory. This paucity of clear and precise Islamic injunctions also largely explains the disagreements, controversies, and schisms that have developed over the centuries, beginning as early as the immediate aftermath of the Prophet's death, among both Muslim political theorists and Muslim communities. Indeed, disagreements about the correct interpretation of these injunctions—as well as divergences in the interpretation of the body of information related to the Prophet's sayings, his views on various matters, and his actual behavior concerning political and social issues faced by the Muslim community—are at the heart of the current debate in the Muslim world about what constitutes true Islam and the true Muslim society and polity.

Islamic Theory of Society and Polity

The *Qur'an* and the Prophet's *Sunna* (his behavior and conduct) do not provide adequate and unambiguous guidance on the necessary qualifications for an Islamic polity and its governing rules beyond those principles of the general conduct of the individual and collective lives of Muslim people and the source of authority and legitimacy within that polity. Nevertheless the following concepts have generally been accepted by both Muslims and non-Muslim students of the faith as forming the fundamentals of Islam's political theory.

The Sovereignty of God and the Fusion of the Spiritual and the Temporal

The view most widely held, both within the Islamic community and also by non-Muslim students of Islam, is that in Islam sovereignty belongs not to the community, that is, not to the people, and not to a single individual such as a king, a prince, or an emperor; sovereignty belongs to God. From this basic principle two others follow: in the Muslim community the ruling authority—the form of which was specified neither in the *Qur'an* nor by the Prophet's *Sunna*—can rule only as God's regent; and in Islam there is no clear distinction between what is religious and belongs to God and what is temporal and belongs to man—because both belong to God. Bernard Lewis has argued that the Muslims have not had to choose between God and Caesar because, in Islam, "there was no Caesar, there was only God."[2]

The issue of the fusion of the spiritual and the temporal in Islam is important because it is at the heart of the arguments that maintain that, because of this fusion, Muslim societies, unlike those that profess Judaism or Christianity, are incapable of political modernization and of creating the requisite separation of religion from politics and statecraft.

Yet viewed in a historical context, it is clear that the Muslim faith and Muslim societies have not been much different from those of Christianity or Judaism. The reality is that for centuries the separation between Caesar and God in Christianity was less clear-cut than is often believed while the separation between the two in Islam has been more pronounced than is usually assumed. The empire of Charlemagne and the Holy Roman Empire, for example, combined spiritual and temporal power. Until the past two centuries, popes combined political rule with spiritual leadership. Throughout modern European history, the political conflicts between the papacy and the kings and princes of Europe testify to the considerable fusion of the spiritual and the temporal in Christendom, in fact if not in theory. As late as the middle of the nineteenth century, European political thinkers such as Joseph Demaistre argued that both temporal and spiritual power rested with the pope, who then bestowed temporal power upon the king. Even today, Queen Elizabeth II of Great Britain, who is both head of state and head of the Church of England and defender of the faith, combines spiritual and temporal power.

In Orthodox Judaism, with its elaborate legal and social systems and tradition of prophet-kings such as David and Solomon, this fusion of the spiritual and the temporal is even greater. As Norman L. Zucker pointed out: "Orthodox Judaism provides for total regulation of society. All temporal acts have spiritual relevance and must, accordingly, conform to a strict religious code of law that is subject to rabbinic interpretation."[3] These "traditional Judaic conceptions of law and society have survived and coexist uneasily and in frequent conflict with the secular Jewish nationalism of late nineteen century origin."[4] Since the creation of the state of Israel, this situation has led to what has been characterized as "secularization conflicts" because "religious issues are not 'private matters' affecting only the rabbinate and the observant; they are of primary public concern because they involve claims of legitimacy that are dependent on the state for action and enforcement."[5]

Islam, however, is a collective and communal religion, in the sense that it enjoins the members of the community to behave in prescribed ways not only individually and in relation to their God but also toward one another. In this sense a degree of overlap exists between the domains of public life and private life. Religion in Islam is not only a matter of private conscience but also of social duty. The Muslim has a religious duty to enjoin the good and to warn against evil. There is nothing in Islam, however, that orders the Muslim to force others to accept his faith. On the contrary, the principle of "enjoining the good and warning against evil" (*Amr Bil-Ma'ruf va Nahy Men al Munkar*) is balanced by the injunction that there is no coercion or compulsion in faith (*La Ikrah fid Din*). Believers in other religions such as Christianity also have a code of conduct that they try to propagate among nonbelievers. And the Islamic community's social conscience is not much different from that of the Christian community's, which also has a set of rules of behavior with emphasis on charity, compassion, modesty, and solidarity among Christians and encourages Christians to urge the observance of the faith on their coreligionists.

It is true, however, that even though the fusion of religion and politics, temporal and spiritual, in Islam has not been much greater than in other religions—and hence cannot be held responsible for a lesser degree of secularization in the Muslim world—the question of who could or should act as God's regent within the Islamic community has occupied Muslims since the Prophet's death and still remains at the heart of the Islamist-versus-secular debate in the Muslim world.

From the concept of the sovereignty of God, in Islam it follows that the principal goal and, indeed, the raison d'être of the community is to create conditions in which Muslims can worship and serve God and prepare for the afterlife. This has not meant, however, that Muslims should disregard the worldly aspects of life. On the contrary, in its concept of human nature Islam encompasses both its physical and its spiritual needs, and the achievement of balance between these two aspects of life is the essence of Islam. The balance that Muslims should strive to achieve is illustrated by a saying attributed to the prophet Muhammad to the effect that Muslims should live their lives as though they were going to die the next minute or as though they were going to live forever; they should attend equally to demands of spiritual salvation and of worldly well being.

Divine Source of Law and the Supremacy of the Shari'a

Because sovereignty belongs to God, it follows that the divine will is the source of law in the Islamic community. This law was revealed to the Muslims through the Prophet and is embodied in the *Qur'an* and in the Prophet's *Sunna*. The *Qur'an* and the *Sunna* together constitute the *Shari'a*, the Islamic law. Added to the *Shari'a* over the years is the *Fiqh*, or jurisprudence, based on the interpretation of these primary sources.

Because the source of the *Shari'a* is the divine will as expressed through the *Qur'an* and the Prophet, it cannot be altered or tampered with by mere mortals, even if they are doctors of law; therefore the *Shari'a* is everlasting and not subject to change. It can be interpreted only according to well-established and fairly inflexible rules and methods, methods that are manmade and thus can be changed, a process that can open new possibilities for interpreting the *Shari'a* to make its rules adaptable to circumstances.[6]

Universal and Transethnic Character of Islam

Another widely accepted view is that Islam is a universalist creed that does not recognize racial, ethnic, or other differences among Muslims; adherence to Islam is the only criterion for membership in the Muslim community and all Muslims therefore form a single community. Some commentators conclude from this premise that Islamic political theory is inherently incompatible with the notion of ethnically based political and territorial entities and, hence, with the modern nation-state and the international system based on it. Adherents of this view believe that, once in power, the Islamists will try to eliminate the existing interstate boundaries and create a united Islamic community. Because of the implications of these ideas for relations between Islam and the West, it is important to assess their validity. It is true that the Muslim community, in the *Qur'an* and in the prophetic tradition, is referred to as the *Ummah*, in the sense of the Muslims forming a community apart. The problem, however, has been to determine whether this concept of *Ummah* excluded all the non-Muslims living in the midst of the Muslims and whether the *Ummah* delegitimized ethnically based entities even though they professed Islam.

There is some evidence that the notion of the *Ummah* initially embraced all believers—as opposed to idolaters—and included non-Muslims. For example, in the main political document remaining from the Prophet's time in Medina, often called the Constitution of Medina, the concept of the *Ummah* also included the Jews of Medina, or at least some of them.[7] Moreover, the *Ummah* of this document consisted of various tribes that were responsible for regulating the conduct of their own members. It also emphasized, however, that the *Ummah* should act collectively to enforce order and, in particular, to confront the Muslims' enemies. Thus, as Nazih Ayubi has pointed out, the concept of the *Ummah* is an attempt to create a religion-based community that to some degree transcended tribal distinctions, but it "does not negate sub-units completely."[8] In other words, the existence of clan, tribal, and ethnic differences is recognized within the *Ummah*.

For two obvious reasons the *Ummah* does not refer to anything comparable with modern notions of the nation-state: First, Islam was revealed within a system that was tribal. Therefore the particular characteristics of the *Ummah* owed more to the tribal nature of Arab society and less to any conscious delegitimization of ethnically based units. Second, at the time of the revelation of Islam, the concept of nation-state in its current use was unknown to all communities, Muslim and non-Muslim alike. The real meaning of the unity of the Islamic *Ummah* is that Muslims, regardless of their ethnic origin, should maintain their solidarity.

In this sense, solidarity within a religious community as expressed here by the term *Ummah* is not limited to Islam. In the Christian world, the empire of Charlemagne and the Holy Roman Empire were based on the concept of the unity of the Christian community, and the Holy Roman Empire could be interpreted as a Christian *Ummah* community. That Islam does not address the issue of the nation-state does not mean that Islam opposes it as fundamentally incompatible with the realization of the Islamic mission. Nor does this seeming neglect imply that the present territorial nation-states are anti-Islamic and, hence, illegitimate and should therefore be abolished—by force if need be—to create a single Islamic community. Acceptance of this interpretation implies that nothing in the Islamic injunctions can be interpreted as delegitimizing the present international political system simply because it is based on nation-states. Indeed, both the early and the more recent history of Islam are steady reassertions of ethnic particularisms and the erosion of religious universalism and, hence, the gradual but inexorable fragmentation of the *Ummah*.

Post-Prophetic Islamic Community: Persistence of Ethnic and Class Distinctions and the Early Fissure of the Community

The lack of clear and unequivocal injunctions in the *Qur'an* and in the Prophet's *Sunna* about the character of the Islamic state, the form of its government, and the basis of its legitimacy caused an important political crisis within the Islamic community immediately after the Prophet's death. It also caused the earliest and the most significant schism in Islam, that between the Shi'as and the Sunnis.

Problem of Succession

Whether or not the Prophet had appointed a successor was the first major disagreement to develop within the Islamic community. Those Muslims who believed he had not done so and had left that decision to the community came to be known as the Sunnis. Today they constitute the overwhelming majority of the Muslims. Those who believed that the Prophet had appointed a successor by telling his followers just before his death that "whomever I am the leader, Ali is the leader" came to be known as partisans of Ali—*Shi'at-ul-Ali.* Today, they constitute the main minority within the Islamic community.[9]

Those who did not believe in the Shi'a theory of the Prophet's succession faced two additional questions—how a successor should be chosen and what qualities a successor should possess. The Prophet—if the Shi'a claim is ignored—and the *Qur'an* had been silent on the issue of succession. When they chose the Prophet's successor, the early Muslims—almost all were of Arab origin and of tribal culture—applied their tribal traditions. But these differed among tribes. Among the south Arabian tribes, for example, the tradition of a kingdom with a "semi-divine king" was strong. Diverse traditions contributed to the early schism among the Muslims.[10] Southern Arabian tribes felt more comfortable with what was essentially a hereditary system of successorship; by contrast, northern Arab tribes favored a form of elective process.

When Sunnism prevailed, so did the elective traditions of the northern tribes. Although devoid of any divine attributes, these traditions consequently became an important part of the Islamic political heritage. At their heart are three principles—*Shu'ra*, consultation; *Agd*, contract between the leader and the community; and *Bay'a*, oath of allegiance—that have also acquired significant contemporary relevance in the debate on the compatibility of Islam and democracy, an issue related to the more general question of Islam's ability to reform and reconcile itself with modernity. Hence, the principles also have a bearing on the debate about the inevitability of a clash between Islamic and Western civilizations or the potential for coexistence and even cooperation between the two. This is so in part because of the early emergence of two distinct systems of leadership: the Shi'a system based on lineage, the dynastic system; and the Sunni system based on the principle of election, the electoral system. This distinction has led contemporary Western scholars of Islam to maintain that Sunni Islam is inherently more democratic than the Shi'a version, reflecting one aspect of the practice of dividing Islam into good and bad variants referred to in the Introduction.

These Western scholars could be correct if the principles noted above were interpreted in a broad and liberal fashion. Historically, however, they have not been so interpreted, a fact that reduces greatly the supposed differences between Sunnism and Shi'ism concerning their ability to reform and their compatibility with democracy. Indeed, because the process of consultation was carried out only among notables of the tribe and did not include all tribal members or their representatives, the electoral methods of the Arabian tribes of Islam's early period were more akin to oligarchies or feudal systems than to modern popular democracies.

The consultative and electoral aspects of the process were diluted further after the death of the second caliph, Omar. Before his death he had assigned six people the task of choosing his successor. Although consultation in this narrow sense was far from modern notions of participatory politics, the existence of this process is important for the prospects for liberalization of Muslim societies, provided that other conditions in Islamic countries permit the establishment of political systems that are more democratic.

The early Muslim community also had to determine the qualifications of the Prophet's successor. This produced the first case of the inherent contradiction between Islam's universalist vocation and egalitarian principles and the parochialism of the Muslim community. Which vision—the universal or the parochial—would prevail? Would it be Arab tribal customs and hierarchies or Islam's new egalitarian creed symbolized in the *Qur'anic* verse, "The noblest of you in the eyes of God are the most pious." The dividing line was between those who maintained that the Prophet's successor should be a member of his tribe, the Quraysh, and those who based their argument on the *Qur'anic* verse and believed that any Muslim should be eligible to succeed the Prophet, provided that he had the required qualities of piety and justice. The first principle, tribalism, prevailed and produced another schism, between those who accepted that the Prophet's successor should be from his tribe and those who did not. The latter came to be known as the Kharijis, those who have left the community.[11]

The Kharijis and their interpretation of the conditions and qualities required for accession to the leadership of the Islamic community later would become popular with Arabs who belonged to the lesser tribes, as well as with increasing numbers of non-Arab converts. In short, from the earliest Islamic period, two phenomena of particular relevance to the current debate about Islam emerged: the early assertion that class and ethnic distinctions influence Muslims in matters related to interpretation of Islamic injunctions, and the appearance of the notion of an establishment Islam as separate from a more populist or revolutionary Islam.[12] In other words, the Qurayshites were the elitists, the establishment, of the early Islamic community while the Kharijits were its populists, the revolutionaries.

The emergence of schisms so early in the life of the Islamic community and the causes of the schisms reflect the impact of nontheological factors on the evolution of Muslim community. It also clearly illustrates that issues and disputes surrounding successorship to the Prophet and the qualifications of successors were in essence about the issue of power, about who should wield it, and about who should benefit from its fruits. This is not surprising because any system of thought and value, once implemented in a societal context, affects the character of relationships and the equation of power within society. Those who claim to hold the essence of the system exert the greatest influence within it because it is they who set the rules within which the society functions. Because of this direct relationship between ideas and power, struggles for power have often been reflected in diverging religious theses and ideological schisms. The current debate between Islamists and other political forces is also largely about power.

Expansion of Islam: Impact on the Development of Islamic Theory of State and Politics

The tribal traditions of Islam's birthplace may have been sufficient to provide the first blueprints for the organization of the Muslim community immediately after the Prophet's death, but the expansion of Islam to vast territories beyond Arabia created a far more complex and heterogeneous community. This vast community could no longer be governed and administered solely according to the tribal traditions of Arabia, especially since many of the peoples conquered by Arab Muslim armies had advanced civilizations and longer experience in governing and administering extensive empires than the Arabs.

To govern their new conquests, the Muslims thus had to build their states and develop their governments "through innovation, improvisation and borrowing".[13] A great deal of this had to be borrowed from civilizations that the Muslims considered as belonging to the era of darkness, ignorance, and corruption—the *Jahiliya*.

Jahiliya and Pre-Islamic Civilizations.   The pre-Islamic Arab conception of history was primitive: the rise and the decline of tribes. They had no sense of "linear development in history."[14] Perhaps for this reason they were not interested "in the distant past or the origins of the cosmos."[15] In this historical vacuum Islam emerged. It is no wonder that the Islamic theory of history is simplistic: human history is divided into two clearly delineated periods—before and after the advent of Islam. The earlier time is characterized by idolatry, corruption, injustice, oppression, despotism, and greed. It is the era of *Jahiliya*, and the Hellenic, Roman, and Persian civilizations all belong to *Jahiliya*.

The concept of *Jahiliya* is very significant for understanding the evolution of Islamic thought. In the later periods of Islam, especially since the encounter of Islam with the Western world, all shortcomings of Islam and the Islamic world have been attributed to the influence of *Jahili* cultures. *Jahiliya* has also a special place in the Islamists' discourse. They accuse all current Muslim governments of being of *Jahili* culture. This interpretation of the relationship between Islam and pre-Islamic cultures and civilizations is also laden with racial connotations because all pre-Islamic cultures were non-Arab, although the Muslim Arabs have admitted that pre-Islamic Arabia also was part of the world of *Jahiliya*. Nevertheless, the Arab *Jahiliya* possesses some redeeming features, especially for modern secular Arab intellectuals: the Arab tribal system is considered to have been democratic, and the emergence of despotic rulers in the Arab world is attributed to the impact of the Byzantine and, especially, Persian cultures.

It is important to note that, if these issues are approached not through the prism of faith but in light of historical evidence it becomes clear that the Islamic concept of *Jahiliya* distorts the realities of life in pre-Islamic societies, including the assumption of a total lack of ethical and moral values.

An example of *Jahili* influences on the despotic nature of later Islamic rulers illustrates this point. Many despotic tendencies of Islamic governments have been blamed on Persian notions of kingship and the divine source of imperial power in Sassanid Persia: because the basis of a king's authority in Persian theory is the Divine Light, *Far-e-yazdani*, that is bestowed on him directly by God, *Ahuramazda*, the king is therefore omnipotent and not accountable to the people or to judgment based on a body of law. This interpretation, however, ignores the important consideration that the Divine Light remains only as long as the monarch rules according to the principles of the Good Religion, *Behdin*— the Zoroastrian faith. If the king deviates, he loses the Divine Light and hence his legitimacy and his right to rule and, in so doing, he also brings misfortune on his people as punishment.

It is immaterial whether this principle was observed in practice in Sassanid Iran. The important point is that the king's authority was based on his upholding the faith and living by its rules. In the Sassanid tradition the fusion between the temporal and spiritual and between religion and politics was greater than in Islam. The Sassanid kingship was based on the Good Religion and was governed by its rules and was at its service. These rules were considered necessary for the welfare of the society, and the welfare of the society was viewed as necessary for the preservation of religion. One of the few surviving Sassanid documents about social and political issues, *Nameh-e-Tansar* (*Book of Tansar*), states: "Do not be surprised that I enthusiastically consider the welfare of the mundane world a prerequisite for the sustenance of the religious conjunctions. *Religion and state are born twins. They will never be separated* [emphasis added]."[16]

A case can even be made that the Sassanid state overidentified with the church and, along with the excessive influence of Zoroastrian priests in the latter days of the dynasty especially when the state failed to provide for the society's welfare, contributed to the erosion of its popular base and facilitated the Arab conquest. Despite these historic realities, these notions are popular with contemporary Islamists, including those of Iranian origin, who characterize their own pre-Islamic culture as *Jahili.*

Notwithstanding the above, the impact of other civilizations did shape Islam's political thought and led to the development of at least three traditions.

The first intellectual trend was expressed through what have been characterized as advice books, *Andarz Nameh* in Persian, on the politics and ethics of governance for kings and princes. These works, which in Western scholarship on Islam have been called the mirrors of princes, were inspired by Persian Sassanid traditions. Most were written in Persian, by Persians, and were modeled on the earliest known work of the type, *Karnamak-e-Ardeshir-e-Papakan*, written in Pahlavi for the founder of the Sassanid dynasty, Ardeshir Babekan. The most famous and elaborate was *Siyasat Nameh* (*Book of Politics*), by Khajeh-e-Nizam-ul-Mulk, the Persian vezir of the Saljuq kings Alparsalan and Malekshah. The mirrors were therefore a synthesis "between Sassanian ideals and Islamic theory."[17] The Sassanid influence was reflected in the theory that maintained that the king—the sultan—was directly chosen by God and is directly responsible to him. The Islamic influence was reflected in the view that maintained that the purpose of the sultan's government was the creation and maintenance of conditions that would ensure the establishment of Islam and the observance of its rules.[18] These mirrors were also partly political tracts and, by holding up the ideal of justice, their authors voiced an implicit protest against contemporary shortcomings.[19]

The second intellectual trend was influenced by Greek philosophy. Those Islamic thinkers and theorists who were influenced by Greek philosophy, including Ibn Sina (Avicenna), Ibn Rushd (Averroës), and Fakhr ed-Din-Razi, tried to prove the compatibility and harmony between Islam and classical political philosophy. The most prominent representative of this group of Islamic thinkers was Al-Farabi, who in his *al Madinat-al-Fadila* (*The*

Good City) tried to show that the ideal political system envisaged in Plato's *Utopia* and that created by the divine law of Islam were one and the same. For these Islamic philosophers, like the authors of the mirrors, the key concept behind the theories was justice, interpreted as meaning the "harmonious relationship of society in a divinely appointed system, the component parts of which were in perfect equilibrium."[20]

The main problem with these theories as well as with the approach taken in the mirrors was that they did not provide for a mechanism to deal with abuse of power by the ruler. The mirrors held up the ideal standard of justice and, in this way, might have moderated the autocratic tendencies of the monarch or the caliph. The Islamic political philosophers did not provide such a mechanism either.

The traditions of the mirrors and the appreciation of Greek philosophy were particularly strong in the eastern regions of the Islamic world, where Persian culture and Hellenic traditions were strongest; and most thinkers were not Arab but of either Iranian or Persianized Turkic origin.

The third trend was the juridical school. Although not all theoreticians of this school were Arab, the most important were. Thus this trend can to some degree be attributed to the reaction of the Arabs to what they saw as the pollution of Islam by the new converts who, the Arabs believed, were still under the influence of their pagan cultures. There was also an element of political power struggle involved in this Arab reaction as the non-Arabs, especially the Persians, came to acquire a good deal of influence in the bureaucratic structure of the Abbasid caliphate. The development of the juridical school was, in part, a response to the erosion of the centrality of the ethnic Arabs within the Islamic empire and the fear that Islam would be contaminated by non-Islamic—non-Arab—elements. These fears strengthened during the Abbasid period, when a "transformation of the administration and society under the influence of Sassanian traditions took place."[21]

The essence of the juridical school was that government and rulership must be based on the *Shari'a* and not be influenced by non-Islamic traditions. This sentiment was apparent in the *Kitab-ul-Kharaj* (*Book of the Land Tax*), which was addressed to the Abbasid caliph, Harun-al-Rashid; the author, Abu Yusuf, implicitly protested against the adaptation of Islamic principles to Sassanid and other influences.[22]

Despite the juridical school's insistence on the supremacy of the *Shari'a* and its more rigid interpretation of the primary sources of the Islamic law, it too adapted theory to external realities. It did this out of both political necessity and self-interest.

Theory as Justification of Reality. Does ideology—a system of thought and value—shape external reality or merely explain, justify, or refute reality? Although this will never be settled, in practice ideology does all these things, albeit to varying degrees during different periods and through the agency of different actors. At the beginning of its emergence, any ideology—and religion is an ideology defined in this sense—tends to shape external reality to a greater extent by determining the perceptions and the actions of the adepts who, under its influence, try to alter existing conditions. Later, however, ideology must adapt, partly to external developments generated by its own advent, partly in response to new external power equations, and partly because of the persistence of preexisting influences—influences that often begin to reassert themselves after the first burst of the new ideology's energy is spent.

Even the most elaborate ideologies—including religious systems that claim to be universal and timeless—cannot and do not provide guidance and answers for all future contingencies societies based on these ideologies are likely to face. Interpretation of existing ideological sources and even innovation—to adapt an ideology's precepts to new needs and conditions—are inevitable consequences and become part of the unfolding of any ideological experience within specific territorial and temporal spheres. In this context, two groups play the essential roles: those who wield power and use ideology to justify, legitimize, and explain the exercise of power; and those who contest the existing power structures, establish contending power centers, and seek justification for their positions and legitimacy for their own exercise of power.

This process has characterized the history of the development of Islamic political thought and its various schools, including those aspects concerning sources of political power and the elements of its legitimacy. In Islamic tradition, too, theoretical differences and innovations have occurred in response to specific political conditions. For example, Nazih Ayubi, quoting al-Jibiri, notes that the controversy that emerged among Islamic thinkers during the rule of the Umayyad caliphs on the issue of predetermination vs. free choice was, in reality, a political rather than a theological issue. It was related to the question of the legitimacy of the rule of the Umayyad caliphs. Because the Umayyads had based their rule on the absolute divine will and as part of a predetermined godly plan, they promoted the school of Predetermination. The dissenters, along with those who contested the Umayyads' rule and legitimacy, resorted to the theory of free will.[23]

Other Islamic theorists, too, developed new interpretations and put the weight of their intellectual power and reasoning behind a particular line to defend and legitimize the existing power situation and the requirements of the ruler. Thus the Islamic theorist, Al-Jahiz, who elaborated the concept of the Imamate—in its Sunni version—was essentially moved by a desire "to justify the assumption of power by the Abbasids."[24] As a result, Al-Jahiz simultaneously denounced the Umayyads, declared their rule to be illegitimate, and attacked the Shi'as. He also asserted the right of the community to rebel against what he characterized as "usurpers and tyrants" who in the context meant the Umayyad caliphs.[25]

In addition to situations in which the elaboration of a particular theory has followed a change in actual political conditions—most notably a passing of leadership from one dynasty to another—three other factors have provided impetus to the development of new theories and new interpretations of existing notions: the decline of the power of the central authority, in this case the caliphate; the strengthening of the disintegrative forces within the Islamic community and the emergence of princedoms and kingdoms independent of the authority of the caliphate; and growing external threats to the cohesion and stability of the Islamic realm. The military threat posed to the Islamic realm and the center of its power—the caliphate—was the greatest concern of Muslim theorists. For the thinkers of the juridical school, the impact of non-Islamic traditions and of politico-religious concepts on the theory and practice of the Islamic state was also a threat to the unity and survival of the community.

Principal Stages in the Development of the Juridical School. The juridical school of Islamic political thought, in any significant fashion, also began under the rule of the Abbasids. The important point worth noting is that religious orthodoxy initially was prompted by a desire to reassert the centrality of the Arabs within the Islamic realm. The Abbasids came to power through the assistance of non-Arab and newly converted Muslims, especially the Persians, who were unhappy about the discriminatory policies of the Umayyads. The Abbasids ruled at first in the name of an Islamic rather than an Arab state, and a number of non-Arabs—especially Persians such as Fazl Ibn Sahl (the name he assumed after conversion to Islam) and the Barmaki brothers—occupied high offices in the court of the Abbasid caliphs. The Abbasids, however, soon reverted to favoring the Arabs, which rekindled earlier sociocultural grievances of the underprivileged groups.

These grievances increasingly acquired "the form of a cultural conflict, striving to express its political content in certain intellectual styles." Because these socioethnic movements "indulged in glorifying their non-Arab heritage and belittling that of the Arabs, defense of the Arab past, especially its Jahili period acquired for the latter the dimension of a struggle for national identity and even survival. . . . "[26] This desire to reassert the centrality of the Arab element in Islam was thus the beginning of the recording—and the interpreting—of the history of the pre-Islamic and early Islamic periods from the perspective of the Abbasid caliphate. In other words, knowledge was recorded from a statist point of view, which made religion subject to politics.

Although this process started under Caliph Al Mansur in the eighth century, elaborating the rules of thinking to justify and legitimize the state was not completed before the ninth century, during the time of the jurist Al-Shafi'i (d. A.D. 820). The close connection between the beginnings of the juridical school and the interests of the existing power structure made it natural that the institution of the caliphate and its place within the Islamic community and polity (plus its evolution under the impact of changing external circumstances such as the gradual fragmentation of the Abbasid Empire and the emergence of independent kingdoms and even rival caliphates) should constitute the main concern of the juridical school.

Al-Mawardi and His Theory of Caliphate and Sultanate: The Triumph of Power over Principle. A major theoretical innovation of the middle of the Abbasid period was the development of a theory of Caliphate to explain and regulate the relationship between the caliph/imam and caliphate/imamate on the one hand and the growing number of princes and kings with de facto independence from the caliphate on the other. A principal theorist of the theory of the caliphate was Al-Mawardi, who expounded his view in his *Ahkama-Sultaniyya* (*Principles of Government*).

Because the early Abbasid theoreticians sought to justify the overthrow of the Umayyads, their main goal was to demonstrate that the Umayyads were illegitimate because they had usurped the caliphate from Ali. Mawardi, by contrast, wanted to justify the continuation of the office of the caliphate and the caliph's position toward the growing number of kings and princes who wielded real power in the extended Islamic realm. The essence of Mawardi's theory of the caliphate, which survived until the time of the Ottoman caliphs, was as follows:

• The caliphate/imamate is obligatory by revelation and not by reason.
• The principle of the election of the imam cannot be tampered with. Nor can an imam, who has been duly elected, be replaced or challenged in favor of a worthier candidate. Mawardi reflected the political realities of his time, however, when the Buyid Iranian dynasty held sway over the caliph in Baghdad and nominated him; Mawardi maintained that the principle of election was valid even if there was only one elector.
• There can be only one imam at any time. This principle, too, recognized the political realities, namely the existence of the rival Fatimid caliphate/imamate in Cairo.

Beyond these basic principles, other aspects of Mawardi's theory of the caliphate, including qualifications of the imam and his elector or electors plus the nature and form of the contract between the imam/caliph and his electors, were essentially those of the early traditions of Islam. For example, the process through which the exchange and establishment of duties between the caliph and the electors was ratified was still called *Bay'a*. And Mawardi characterized the principal duties of the imam, from which all others derived, as the defense and maintenance of religion and the protection of the territory of Islam, including through waging of *jihad*.

Mawardi's concept of the authority of the imam was that of a simple delegation of authority for the purpose of applying and defending the *Shari'a*. According to Mawardi, the caliph inherited the judicial and executive functions of the Prophet. He had no legislative function, and his power of interpreting the *Shari'a* was limited since this had become the domain of the jurists (*Ulema*). The caliph exercised his authority in the realm through his governors, whose relationships with him were regulated within the office of *Imara*. The caliph delegated to the emir, the ruler, his religious, legal, military, and administrative functions. The emir was expected to govern according to the *Shari'a*; if he failed to do so, the caliph could depose him.

Because independent princes and kings increasingly obtained their offices by the use of military power instead of by appointment by the caliph, Mawardi introduced the notion of *Imarat-ul-Istiglal* (emirate by seizure). He determined that the caliph must recognize the conqueror's right in order to prevent him from open rebellion. Mawardi recommended this approach because he believed this was necessary for the public good and interest—*Masalahat*. Mawardi maintained that avoiding injury to the public welfare justified the relaxation of rules.

The fragmentation of the caliphate and the increasing number of independent kings—trends that prompted Mawardi to develop his theory of subjecting religion to political control, in effect trying to maintain the fiction of the latter's supremacy—continued and strengthened in the coming decades. Succeeding theoreticians further accommodated even more political realities and necessities while all the time trying to safeguard the position of the *Shari'a* as the organizing principle of the Islamic community. In short, the growing power of independent kings and princes caused the domains of religion and politics to grow more separate in reality if not in theory.

Imam Al-Ghazali.   The most prominent representative of the trend to subject religion to political reality while trying to perpetuate the fiction of the latter's supremacy was Imam Muhammad-al-Ghazali. During Al-Ghazali's lifetime (he died in A.D. 1111), a view began to emerge that the imamate was dead because occupants of the office of the imam/caliph lacked required qualifications. Al-Ghazali rejected this view. He developed a new theory that attempted to reconcile existing political realities with the need to preserve the community's religious life. He based his theory on the twin principles of the inevitability of accepting the existing power structure—the alternative would have been anarchy and the disruption of social life—and the need to preserve the community's religious life. To preserve the community's religious life, even if in a less than ideal manner, he accepted some diminution in the qualities of the imam and in the imam's designation by the holder of political power. To maintain the integrity of the Muslim religious community, Al-Ghazali developed a new relationship between the caliph/imam and the sultan: the sultan should designate the caliph and thus have the constituent authority, but the validity of the sultan's own rule should depend on his oath of allegiance to the caliph and on the caliph's appointment of the sultan.

Al-Ghazali believed that by maintaining discipline and stability the sultan would ensure the application of the *Shari'a*, thus allowing Muslims to live their lives according to the divine will as revealed to them by the *Qur'an* and the Prophet. Despite its recognition of the fact of the sultan's power, Al-Ghazali's theory implicitly conditioned the legitimacy of the exercise of that power on its permitting the unhindered practice of Islam by the sultan's subjects. This implicit bargain between the realities of political power and the requirements of Islam would become the rule across the Islamic realm, until the bargain was broken by the secularizing policies of the modernizing elites.

In Al-Ghazali's theory, the caliphate still embraced the totality of the Islamic government and was composed of three elements: the caliph, the sultan, and the jurists (*Ulema*). The jurists were the depositories of the *Shari'a*'s functional authority, which they expressed by approving the sultan's choice of caliph through the *Bay'a* and the *fatwa* (legal opinion).

The End of the Caliphate and the Theory of Ibn Taymiyya.   In essence, these theories of Islamic government concerned two goals: the maintenance of at least the symbolic unity of the Islamic community by the preservation of the office of caliphate and the preservation of the integrity and authority of the *Shari'a* as the main organizing principle of the Islamic community. Subsequent developments—the emergence of new military powers, mostly of Turkic origin—further eroded the caliph's position and authority. As a consequence, theories regulating the relationship between the caliph and the rulers became irrelevant because the rulers increasingly arrogated to themselves their rulership as a divine right bestowed upon them directly by God, not by the caliph. The main principle that legitimized the ruler's power became the need to maintain public order and avoid anarchy, and not appointment by the caliph. Jurists increasingly argued that the ruler had to be obeyed even if he disregarded the canons of Islam because any government was better than anarchy.

The destruction of the caliphate by the Mongols in A.D. 1258 completed the secularization of rulership, relieving it of the necessity for any religious legitimizing imprimatur. Only after the emergence of the Ottoman Empire with the fall of Constantinople in 1453 did the caliphate and the sultanate unite once more. The impact of these developments impelled Islamic thinker Ibn Taymiyya to develop his theory. The elaboration of Ibn Taymiyya's theory was an important turning point in the history of Islamic political thought because Ibn Taymiyya reversed the trend toward accommodating Islamic principles to political realities, even if the ultimate goal was to maintain at least the symbolic unity of the Islamic community and the centrality of the *Shari'a* as its organizing principle.

The disappearance of the caliph's office, which eliminated the outward symbol of Muslim unity, made it even more necessary to seek other means to restore the unity of the *Ummah*. This instrument of unity for Ibn Taymiyya was the *Shari'a* and the observance of the *Shari'a* by the ruler. Ibn Taymiyya was moved in part by his belief that the Muslim world's new Turkic-Mongol rulers lacked true commitment to Islam. He believed their conversion was superficial and that they continued to live more according to their tribal traditions, including the Mongol legal system, the *Yasa*.[27] Thus, while he reversed the trend of subjecting religious principles to political necessity by reasserting the supremacy of the *Shari'a*, Ibn Taymiyya, too, was in fact reacting to external developments. His attitude also had a racial dimension that reflected a tendency common among most Arab jurists to believe that only the Arabs could understand Islam and sincerely commit to it.

Ibn Taymiyya's theory reached into the traditions of early Islam and its leaders—the *Salaf*. But he also introduced a number of innovations, and his ideas contained points that created a degree of affinity with modern theories of participatory government. In fact he can almost be viewed as avant garde. His theory is also important because it has exercised a tremendous influence on the development of recent Islamist theories.

Ibn Taymiyya believed that

• unity of the Islamic community does not depend on fictitious political unity symbolized by the person of the caliph/imam but instead is based on the confessional solidarity of each autonomous entity within an organic Islamic whole;
• there is reciprocity in the act of allegiance between the ruler and the subject in the context of what Ibn Taymiyya calls *Mubaya'a*, the simultaneous pledging of allegiance by the ruler and the ruled;
• cooperation and solidarity, *Ta'awun*, is the ideal basis of relationship between the ruler and subjects; this follows from the principle of *Mubaya'a*, according to which the people through this oath of allegiance guarantee effective power to the ruler, and he pledges to them to maintain social peace and provide for their welfare;
• consultation, *Shu'ra*, is central in the management of society. In contrast with the practice during the early period of Islam when consultation was limited to the circle of notables, Ibn Taymiyya extended it to all members of the community because he believed all should participate in the administration of the state; and
• Muslims have a right to rebel if the ruler deviates from the *Qur'an* and the *Shari'a*.

Although Ibn Taymiyya ostensibly based his theory on early Islamic notions of state, government, and legitimacy, his principles demonstrate that he was in fact an innovator because many of his views did not reflect actual conditions in early Muslim societies. Nonetheless, Ibn Taymiyya advised against the frequent and indiscriminate use of the right of rebellion; like his predecessors, he warned of the dangers of anarchy and implicitly cautioned against challenging the established order.

Ibn Taymiyya's strength was the internal cohesion of his ideas; his was a more integrated system than notions of earlier theorists. By recognizing the people's right to rebel if the ruler deviated from the *Shari'a*, he provided an enforcement mechanism lacking in other schools of thought. Because of its cohesiveness and reliance on the *Shari'a*, Ibn Taymiyya's theory has acquired a degree of timelessness although it was unrealistic for its period. He was the first Islamic thinker to develop what amounts to a populist and almost revolutionary Islamic ideology.

Ibn Taymiyya was the last of the major Sunni theorists. The fifteenth to the mid-nineteenth centuries were a time of relative intellectual stagnation in the Muslim world, especially if mystical and theosophical works, mostly produced in the Shi'a world, are excluded. The next burst of intellectual vitality occurred only in the middle of the nineteenth century under the impact of encounters with the West and—with periods of ebb and flow—this has continued until the present day.

Shi'a Experience and Political Theory.   Shi'a political theory and its evolution have been affected deeply by the fact that Shi'ism lost the battle for the hearts and minds of the majority of Muslims. In the earliest period of the Sunni-Shi'a split, Persians gravitated toward Shi'ism; thus a number of scholars interpret the emergence of Shi'ism and the ensuing Sunni-Shi'a split as the result of the encounter between the Iranian and the Arab cultures. James Dormstetter has viewed the Shi'a doctrine of Mahdism as an Islamic adaptation of the pre-Islamic Iranian belief in the Divine Light. Certainly the ideas and concepts of the Zoroastrian faith, including its belief in the ultimate unfolding of the human experience as part of the divine plan and the concept of *Sayoshant* (Messiah), have influenced all monotheistic religions. But no clear evidence points to these concepts having a strong impact on the early development of Shi'ism. In fact, similar traditions of semidivine kings also existed among tribes of southern Arabia.

Nevertheless, some Sunnis have characterized Shi'ism as a conspiracy by the Persians against Islam,[28] but in a historical and sociopolitical context, this Sunni charge has no basis in reality. In fact, like many other aspects of the post-Muhammad unfolding of Islam, the emergence of Shi'ism is rooted in tribal and clan rivalries of Arabia. Nevertheless, Persian nationalism and resentment of the Arab conquest had a clear impact on the Iranian gravitation toward Shi'ism. The Arabs' discriminatory practices intensified the Persian Muslims' alienation from the Sunni establishment and their adoption of Shi'ism to demonstrate their protest against the inegalitarian practices by Sunni caliphs who favored the Arabs. The House of Ali (*Alids*), in contrast, treated the Persians with kindness, perhaps seeing in them potential allies against their Sunni rivals.[29]

The Shi'a thinking on politics and government, like that of the Sunnis, has also been shaped by the historical experience of the community. This experience has formed the Shi'a ethos and pathos, world view, and self perception. Most important was the decision of the Muslim community to elect Abu Bakr as the Prophet's successor despite the Shi'a belief that Muhammad had unequivocally appointed Ali as his legitimate successor. The consequence has been a state of mind in the Shi'as that "refuses to admit that majority opinion is necessarily true or right . . . and a rationalized defense of the moral excellence of an embattled minority."[30] Because of their history, Shi'as have come to believe that the limited number of followers of a creed or an idea does not prove its falsity, just as the popularity of another idea is no proof of its truth.

The second most important event in Shi'a history was the revolt of the third imam, Hussain Ibn Ali, against the Umayyad caliph, Yazid Ibn Mu'awiya, and Hussain's martyrdom for the sake of truth and justice. This event has had a paradoxical impact on the Shi'as' collective psyche and on the evolution of Shi'a political thought. On one hand, the defeat at Karbala marked the beginning of the end of the Shi'a struggle to restore the rights of the House of Ali, leading during the following centuries to a quietist and isolationist attitude toward the established centers of political power and a belief in the establishment's illegitimacy. This belief carried the implication for the Shi'as that a just society and government could not exist until the return of the twelfth imam, the Mahdi. The inevitable conclusion was that Shi'as should keep their faith and wait (*Intizar*) for his return and, in the meantime, refuse to grant legitimacy to temporal powers. On the other hand, Hussain's epic resistance endowed the Shi'a spirit with a belief in the need to rise against falsehood and injustice even in the face of overwhelming odds.

The third important element in the Shi'a experience was the practice of the sixth Shi'a imam, Ja'afar as Sadiq, of a quietist approach toward power and politics and his recommendation to his followers to adopt a similar approach and a prudent dissimulation of faith (*Taqiya*). This experience has led on the ideological level to a Utopian idealism, a latent potential for activism and even extremism, and a disengagement and aloofness from politics. On the practical level it has meant that, unlike their Sunni counterparts, Shi'a jurists and scholars have felt no need to develop theories to either justify or challenge existing political conditions and power relationships although they have had to devise practical arrangements with the holders of political power to preserve the safety of Shi'a communities. Shi'a pragmatism, however, has been different from that of the Sunnis because whatever necessary compromises were made were often "in the nature of ad hoc dispensations which never abrogated or diluted the basic Shi'a doctrinal position that all temporal authority in the absence of the hidden Imam is illegitimate."[31]

Safavid Rule and the Dilemma of Shi'a Theory. As long as the Shi'as lived under Sunni rulers, this simple theory of illegitimacy coupled with inevitable but ad hoc compromises met Shi'a needs. But the situation became different, when, under the Safavids in the sixteenth century, Shi'ism became the official religion of Iran. Suddenly there was a government that professed Shi'ism, which raised the question whether it was still illegitimate and not owed any allegiance by the faithful or whether it should enjoy at least a limited and conditional legitimacy.

Despite these new conditions and the questions they posed, the Safavid period did not lead to a sudden flourishing of new Shi'a political theories. This paucity of new ideas and theories was perhaps due to the fact that Shi'ism's "long existence as a scholastic relic had made it insensitive to politics."[32] In reality, however, a compromise between the Safavid rulers and the Shi'a religious leaders emerged on the basis of which the government would have a limited legitimacy contingent upon its adherence to the rules of the *Shari'a*, in its Shi'a version, and its defense of the faith against internal and external enemies. While religious thinkers and leaders never relinquished their power to proclaim political leadership illegitimate, the political leadership and the Shi'a *Ulema* in Safavid Iran developed a large degree of mutual dependence that, in its essence, continued until the constitutional revolution of 1906.

The influences and changes in the Shi'a world as a result of its encounter with the West in the nineteenth century eroded both the basis of this compromise and the mutual dependence and led to a flourishing of Shi'a political thinking.

Concluding Remarks

This discussion has led to several conclusions that challenge the validity of some widely held views about Islamic conceptions of state, politics, and the relationship between religion and politics. This challenge undermines assumptions about the inherent incompatibility of Islam with Western values and political systems that, if correct, would make a clash between the two inevitable.

Most important is the conclusion that the specificity of Islam is not as strong and as pronounced as some observers maintain. Islam is not the only religion in which there is a good deal of fusion between the public and the private and between the religious and the political. Nor are Muslim societies unique because of tension between absolute secularism and religion-based value systems. All religious belief systems that believe in the divine source of law and the supremacy of God-given law over man-made law are incompatible with a value system that makes the individual and the will of the majority the source of law and legitimacy. The incompatibility therefore is between religion and irreligion in general and not only between irreligion and a particular religion, namely Islam. In that sense, Christianity and Judaism—especially in their orthodox traditions—are as incompatible with absolute secularism as is Islam. The difference lies in the fact that, in the Western world, religion has lost the battle with secularism, whereas in the Muslim world and in Israel the contest continues.

Second, there is little in the *Qur'an* that deals specifically with questions of politics and governance beyond exhortations to uphold Islamic principles and justice. Moreover, many *Qur'anic* injunctions on these and other issues are contradictory and still others have meanings not intelligible to common mortals.[33] There is, however, enough in the *Qur'an* and in the sayings of the Prophet to indicate what kind of government and rulership is unacceptable to Islam. For example, Islam does not approve of despotic rule. The Prophet said that the *Qur'anic* injunction to the Muslims to obey God and those among them who have authority—their temporal rulers—does not apply if the ruler(s) do not follow the principles of Islam. Similarly, the injunction that there is no obedience in sin is further proof of Islam's objection to despotic and arbitrary rule. Therefore, contrary to Huntington's assertion that in Islam there is no concept of the rule of law, the foregoing shows that the Islamic sociopolitical system is indeed based on law—the divine law—although that law often has not been observed.

Beyond these general principles, nothing in Islam's earliest sources indicates the fusion of religion and politics or the specific shape and form that the government of a Muslim state should take. It has been partly because of this lack of clear *Qur'anic* or Prophetic injunction that several schools of political thought developed in Islam, and the process is continuing.

Islam does place in God the source of authority and law in Muslim society. It clearly elevates God-given law above man-made law. But this is not peculiar to Islam for all religions place God's commands above rules made by ordinary mortals. But historically, in real life the commands of God are often disregarded in favor of those made by men, or they are so loosely interpreted that they sanction and ratify man-made rules. Muslim communities have experienced this, but subordination of divine law to man-made rules and the dilution of God's commands have also been the experience in non-Muslim societies. In fact, a tension between the two systems of law has existed even in the thoroughly secularized West. For example, as recently as the autumn of 1995 during a referendum in Ireland about the right to divorce and remarry, the Pope reminded the Irish faithful that their first duty was to God's commands and, therefore, they should vote against the proposed divorce law.

Moreover, in Islam religion is not merely a matter of private conscience but also of collective conscience. Thus while Islam clearly states that there is no compulsion in faith, it nevertheless imposes on Muslims the duty of enjoining the good and warning against evil. The exercise of this duty toward followers of other faiths can be seen as both subversive and coercive. Islam does not consider belief and disbelief as morally equal. The result is that, rather than a complete fusing of religion and politics in Islam, their domains at times overlap; hence the widespread assumptions about their fusion. The relationship between the two nevertheless remains ambiguous, which makes it possible to argue in support of their fusion and also allow for interpretations that support the thesis of their separation.

Which trend ultimately prevails in a given Muslim society is determined by the interplay of a wide set of internal social, economic, and political factors and external influences. For the foreseeable future the two tendencies are likely to compete and clash and their influences to ebb and flow as various segments within Muslim societies compete for power and economic advantage and use Islam and secular ideologies as their instruments in this struggle.

The third conclusion is that throughout Islam's history, the domains of religion and politics have been separate in fact, if not in theory. Religion, even in the scheme of the theoreticians of the juridical school, never exerted more than moral authority over the political establishment; there were no means to ensure observance of Islamic rules by political leaders. The only alternatives for believers seem to have been open rebellion—with all that that implied in terms of damage to the peace, unity, and prosperity of the community and not to be contemplated hastily or condoned lightheartedly by the jurists—or total withdrawal from politics as with the Shi'as.

The fourth conclusion is that in practice religion has historically been subordinated to politics and to the requirements of external reality. Islamic political theories evolved in response to external challenges and, with few exceptions, attempted to accommodate them. A key concept in this context is that of *Masalahat*, the common good, a concept that encompasses security, order, and the overall well-being of the community and, at times, justifies the overlooking of religious laxities. *Masalahat* often stands in juxtaposition to religious rigidity and, in most instances, prevails. The concept of *Masalahat* affects not only the internal development of Muslim societies but also the conduct of their external relations.

The fifth conclusion is that the historical Islamic experience continues to unfold. As in the past, Islamic theory will evolve in the context of a dialectical interaction between religious principles and external developments, within Muslim countries and around them.

The sixth and final conclusion is that, despite the current ascendancy of secularism in the West, the battle between faith and disbelief and their respective domains has not been settled once and for all. In some Western countries—notably in the United States—a tendency is growing on the part of at least some of the population to accept a political role for religious institutions, recognizing that they have a right to take part in society's major debates and to express their views on a particular side.

Islamic Conception of International Relations:
Theory and Practice

Many Western scholars of Islam as well as Muslim theoreticians and political thinkers have held a polarized and simplistic view of what constitutes Islam's conception of interstate and international relations and the Islamic community's position in relation to others. The main flaw of this view is that it is not based on a historical analysis of the development of basic Islamic notions of the nature of relations between Islamic and non-Islamic peoples and countries and their application during Islam's historical unfolding within different spatial and temporal contexts.

On the contrary, the adherents of this polarized vision have taken a few basic Islamic concepts and have developed sweeping theories about Islam's views of international and interstate relations. And they have endowed these purported Islamic views with everlasting and immutable validity. Although different thinkers emphasize some elements more than others, the following are the principal components of this polarized view of Islam's concept of international and interstate relations:

• The idea of nation, which is inherently parochial, is alien to Islam, which is a universalist idea.
• Nationalism, a creed built upon the glorification of one's own distinct community and allegiance to it, is anathema to Islam, which demands the full and undivided loyalty of the believers.
• The nation-state as the political and institutional embodiment and expression of nationalism has no basis in Islam because the overall community of Muslims (*Ummah*) is the political as well as the spiritual and social expression of Islam.
• The Islamic world view and concept of the nature of interstate relations is polarized and, according to Western scholars, expansionist. The expansionist dimension derives from Islam's view of the world as divided into *Dar-ul-Islam* (the abode of Islam), a realm of peace and enlightenment, and *Dar-ul-Harb*. The latter is often translated as the realm of war but, more accurately, it means the realm of disbelief and corruption—namely, that of the *Jahili* societies that existed before Islam's advent and those societies that still refuse to embrace Islam. The second category constitutes the enemies of Islam and of the Muslims.

- As a result, Muslims have not had an elaborate and sophisticated concept of foreign policy beyond the mere management of conflict between *Dar-ul-Islam* and *Dar-ul-Harb*.

Western scholars of Islam who subscribe to this polarized vision believe that Muslims are required to wage *Jihad* until the *Dar-ul-Harb* is transformed into *Dar-ul-Islam*. They also believe that it is this proselytizing zeal and quest for the achievement of Islam's universalist vocation that endows it with an intrinsic expansionism.[34]

Several important consequences for the state of Islam-West relations derive from these assumptions, especially whether conflict or coexistence will carry the day in deciding the character of these relations. Those who believe that this is Islam's world view see the nature of Muslim relations with non-Muslims as inherently inimical and confrontational.

Western proponents of this view believe that to the Muslims the West collectively represents the *Dar-ul-Harb* that they must fight.[35] Their Muslim counterparts see the West as the archrepresentative of the *Jahiliya* and hence the enemy of Islam. If this view prevails, conflict—active or latent—will define the character of Islam-West relations. Yet neither historically nor currently has this been the case and it is unlikely to be the case in the future. The questions arise, therefore, why this idea persists and why such a wide gap exists between theory and practice.

The answers to these questions must be sought in the inherent ambiguities of the earliest Islamic sources and in the encounter of Islamic theory with external realities in different spatial and temporal contexts.

Islam's World View

If this polarized view has survived and remained influential among both Western and Islamic scholars it is partly because it does have some foundation in the earliest Islamic sources, namely the *Qur'an* and the *Sunna*. Passages in the *Qur'an* as well as certain of the Prophet's sayings indicate that Islam viewed the community made up of Muslims as an integrated social and political unit separate from all others. Moreover, within this community of believers no differences of race, ethnic origin, or color were to be recognized: The small group of the Prophet's companions included Salman the Persian, whom the Prophet called a member of his household, and Bilal the Abyssinian, who was the *Mu'azin* calling the faithful to prayer.

The composition of the Prophet's entourage came to represent the externalization of the deep egalitarian principle of Islam, encapsulated in the *Qur'anic* verse: "The noblest of you in the eyes of God are the most pious." It is ironic, therefore, that Huntington should maintain that Muslim societies have no sense of, or appreciation for, the egalitarian principles that form part of Western liberal traditions. This egalitarian principle does not mean, however, that Islam does not recognize the existence of ethnic and racial differences. Indeed, passages in the *Qur'an* acknowledge such differences within the Islamic community and even sanction them by characterizing them as signs of God. For example, the *Qur'an* says that God has divided you (people) into different ethnic groups so that you can get to know one another. In short, as is often the case with other *Qur'anic* injunctions, pronouncements on questions of identity are ambiguous and contradictory.

It cannot be denied that the *Qur'an* makes it a duty for Muslims to fight the nonbelievers, and the prophetic traditions also appear to put great value on *jihad*. According to one *hadith* (the method of relating Muhammad's sayings and behavior), the Prophet said that whoever fights to make Allah's word superior fights in God's cause and that even a single journey for this purpose is better than the world and everything in it.[36]

Yet other principles of Islam seem to reduce the importance of *jihad* and undermine its central position. The *Qur'anic* injunction that there is no coercion (compulsion) in faith clearly contradicts the duty to fight all of humanity until all have accepted Islam or have submitted to Islam's suzerainty. And *jihad* is not one of the prerequisites of salvation and accession to heaven as is, for example, regular prayer, fasting, or the paying of alms. It ranks even lower than the pilgrimage to Mecca, the *hajj*, which is obligatory only if a Muslim's financial resources permit its performance without prejudicing his other duties such as meeting the needs of his family and extending charity to his neighbors. Moreover, *jihad* does not always imply waging war against others but can mean battling one's own baser instincts and impulses; thus it comes to mean, more often than not, striving to become a better Muslim oneself rather than trying to convert someone else.

Jihad is compulsory only for the defense of the Islamic realm and not for the expansion of its dominions. In the Shi'a tradition, in fact, *jihad* cannot be fought for expansionist reasons because only imams can wage such a *jihad*. Because there has been no living imam among the Shi'as for more than a millennium, they must wait until the return of the Mahdi, which means that Shi'as cannot fight wars to spread Islam.

The foregoing implies that support can be found in Islamic sources for virtually any interpretation of Islamic theory of international relations, its implications for other peoples, and the prospects of conflict between Muslims and others. Thus any analysis and discussion of Islam's view of international relations in the abstract is futile, especially when these rather ambiguous and contradictory Islamic injunctions are compared with early twentieth century Western concepts of international relations. Indeed, if these ambiguous Islamic principles and specific actions flowing from them are compared with their contemporaries in the West, the differences do not appear to be as great as is often assumed.

For example, the concept of nation-state as both a political entity and a pole of identity and loyalty is also a recent one in the Western world, dating from the 1648 Treaty of Westphalia that ended the Thirty Years War between Catholics and Protestants. It then took nearly three centuries for the nation-state to supplant other sources of collective identity, loyalty, and frameworks of political organization. Before the consolidation of the nation-state in Europe, linguistic and regional identities as well as religious and personal loyalties—to kings, emperors, and princes—predominated.

A similar comparison can be made in regard to the purported inherent expansionism of Islam because of its belief in *jihad*. It is useful to remember that wars to expand the territory of one's faith have not been limited to Muslims. More or less at the time Sultan Mehmet the Conqueror was taking Constantinople—assuming that he did it to spread Islam rather than to gain glory, expand his dominions, and augment his wealth—Isabella of Aragon was not only re-Christianizing Spain and expelling Muslims and Jews but also financing Christopher Columbus's journey to discover India and spread the message of Christ. The Crusades are a better example of the spirit of *jihad* in Christianity. The Thirty Years War, too, was a form of *jihad* on the part of the Christian belligerents because each Christian faction thought it was fighting for God's sake to defend or establish the correct religion.

The only constructive way to develop a view of an Islamic theory of international relations, therefore, is through the study of the history of Islamic states' relations with other Muslim and non-Muslim states as well as their application of certain basic, albeit ambiguous, Islamic concepts bearing on international relations, especially regarding the interpretation of these principles to fit the external realities of the times and the internal needs of the states.

Note first, however, that, whether religious or secular, every ideology with a universalist vocation, that is, it believes in its own ultimate truth and triumph, is inherently incompatible with ideologies that do not share this conviction. Such ideologies are also proselytizing, a fact that brings them into inevitable conflict with adherents of other religious faiths or secular value systems with similar aspirations. Such ideologies are also change oriented and hence subversive in that they challenge existing value systems, bases of individual and collective identities and allegiances, social and political structures and hierarchies based upon these identities and allegiances, and the equilibrium of forces within and among communities.

In response, the challenge posed by a new and proselytizing creed generates resistance from collectivities and structures that feel threatened by it. Within this dialectic of challenge and response, concrete relationships take shape as the emerging ideology affects external realities and, in turn, is affected by them and is forced to adapt itself to them. Important to the adaptation of the ideology to external realities, including the resistance of existing sociopolitical structures, is the gradual delay of the realization of the ideology's universalist vocation, postponed so far into the future that it becomes transformed from a historical goal, achievable within historic time, into a messianic goal to be achieved at some distant and unknown time. The process of adaptation does not mean that the proselytizing zeal disappears completely and it cannot periodically resurface. It simply means that the manner in which it is pursued and the effects it produces are conditioned by a wide range of other variables.

During the early period of its manifestation, an ideology may overshadow other aspects and components of individual and collective identity; for a time, it can become the most important determinant of the behavior toward others of a given collectivity. Ideology, however, seldom obliterates other components of identity, nor does it eliminate the influence of other determinants of collective behavior. These remain dormant but tenacious and ready to reassert themselves when the ideological fervor wanes, which is often fairly soon. This process then leads to either the subordination of ideology to the demands of these preexisting forces or to creative interpretations of ideology that make the influence of nonideological forces appear compatible with the prescription of ideology.

Islam as an ideology has not been immune to the effects and consequences of the dialectics of challenge and resistance, which unleash a process of mutual transformation and accommodation. Even at its dawn, Islam was not capable of subduing ethnic and linguistic differences and loyalties among the Muslims; in Arabia, it was not even capable of submerging clan and tribal affiliations and allegiances, an important factor in shaping the Islamic experience. Some Muslim scholars blamed the strengthening of parochial and ethnocentric tendencies and loyalties within the young Muslim community on the Umayyads, but this explanation confuses the symptom with the cause. The Umayyad rule was a symptom of the tenacity of parochial affiliations and allegiances in the face of the challenge of Islam's egalitarian and universalist message.[37] Even today, in many parts of the Arab world, local loyalties not only supersede those owed to Islam but also those owed to recently formed nation-states. This process of challenge and response has shaped Islam's theory of international and interstate relations within the context of interaction over the centuries between Islamic notions and principles and external realities, along with the interaction between these principles and internal developments within Muslim communities.

Evolution of Islamic Theory of International Relations

The predominant perception in the West of the character of Islam's world view and theory of international relations is rather simplistic. It is also absolutist and dualistic. The dualism is represented by the West's insistence that Islam divides the world into *Dar-ul-Islam* and *Dar-ul-Harb* and its nonrecognition of divisions and distinctions within the two realms. Absolutism is reflected in two basic assumptions—namely, that the main impetus behind

Muslims' behavior toward other collectivities is the desire to spread the message of Islam or, failing that, to become martyrs; and Muslims, unless Islam's influence is diluted to a point where it has no hold on the collective psyche, will not rest until Islam has become the universal creed.

This view also implies that the Muslims tend to act as a single political bloc. Three important conclusions flow from this argument: it is not possible to reach compromise with Muslims on the basis of worldly quid pro quo; long-term coexistence with Muslims is inconceivable and the best one can expect is temporary truce or a cold war; and in dealing with the Muslims the West should also act as a single bloc. However, the history of Muslim interactions within the community and with non-Muslim peoples presents a different and more complicated picture, a pattern of behavior and accommodation to external realities that during various historical epochs has more in common with non-Muslim states than this simplistic description warrants.

The Pragmatic and Strategic Streak

Contrary to the assumption that Islam has no concept of international relations and foreign policy, the behavior of Muslim political and military leaders, beginning with the Prophet himself, demonstrates both a knowledge and an understanding of what we today call foreign policy and strategy and a keen sense of pragmatism and flexibility when circumstances have required it. In fact, the motives and behavior toward others of Muslim leaders and communities have not been much different from those of other leaders during various historical epochs. For example, instead of fighting until the total defeat or conversion of one side or the other, Muslims historically have often entered into treaty relations. For example, when the Prophet of Islam "was unable to prevail over the Jews of Medina and the Christians of Aqaba and Najran he concluded formal treaties with them. Moreover, he concluded the Hudaybiyya treaty, which brought a truce in 628 between the believers in Medina and the polytheists of Mecca when the former needed more time to gain strength against the latter."[38]

Since the foreign policy of all states at the time of the Prophet consisted largely of the conduct of wars and the negotiation of truces, the Prophet showed he was as capable as his contemporary kings, princes, and emperors of conducting foreign policy. His behavior also attests to Islam's capacity for compromise and accommodation to external realities and, if need be, to the bending of ideological precepts for the sake of the common good— *Masalahat*. Muslim leaders certainly did not embark on *jihad* against their non-Muslim neighbors unless they "had a good prospect for success."[39] Therefore, the charge that the only alternative for Muslims was total victory over the nonbelievers or martyrdom is simply not supported by historical evidence. Successive Muslim leaders signed treaties with non-Muslims for a variety of strategic and political reasons, and by the mid-seventeenth century, the Muslim governments were establishing more sustained diplomatic relations with the rest of the world.

Mixed Motives of Behavior

It is further argued that Muslims have been motivated historically by a zeal to spread the word of Allah. This certainly was a major motivation, especially during the early centuries of Islam; but it would be a mistake to underestimate conquest, glory, and treasure as other important motivators. The early Islamic conquests by the Arabs, followed by those of the Turks, can also be interpreted as the imperial cycle of the Arab and Turkic peoples, much like the cycle of the Assyrians, the Persians, and the Romans before them. With Muslims, too, ideals and baser motives were significant impulses for behavior. But just as the Crusades were fought not only for the sake of Jerusalem and Christianity— although these were important motives—the Islamic conquests were motivated in part by reasons other than the desire to spread Islam. The lure of riches (*Ghanimah*), for example, was a major impetus for Muslims to go to war.[40]

A More Complex World View

Historically, Islam's world view and concept of international relations has been much less simplistic and polarized than that represented by its supposed division of the world into *Dar-ul-Islam* and *Dar-ul-Harb*. The division of the world into *Dar-ul-Islam* and *Dar-ul-Harb* developed fairly late, during the Abbasid period, and like many other ideas was probably inspired by Persian Sassanid traditions. The Sassanids divided the world into two parts:

Eranshahr (home of the Aryans) and the non-*Eran*. *Eran* was also the land of *Behdin*, the good religion, namely, Zoroastrianism with its dualistic theory of good and evil, light and darkness, and the cosmic battle between them. The Muslims adopted this view, substituting Islam and non-Islam, *Dar-ul-Islam* and *Dar-ul-Harb*, for *Eran* and non-*Eran*.

This dualistic theory of the cosmos and of history never prevented the Sassanids from having relations with other governments and states, including their archenemies the Roman Empire and, later, Byzantium; nor did it condemn them to perpetual battle. By the same token, the dualistic theory of Islam has never meant a permanent state of war, with temporary truces interrupting periods of warfare, between the Muslims and others. On the contrary, the dualism and bipolarity of the Islamic world view was mitigated by the development of the concept of *Dar-ul-Ahd* or *Mo'ahada*, the domain of treaty.[41]

More important is the fact of the territorial and political plurality of the *Dar-ul-Islam* and its practical recognition by Muslims throughout their history. The gradual disintegration of the Islamic realm affected the evolution of Islamic political thought about the internal organization of the Muslim world. This process of fragmentation also affected the evolution of theories regarding Muslim interstate relations. The result was that Islamic thinkers eventually came to view the *Dar-ul-Islam* as more of a spiritual than a territorial or a political concept and argued that territorial and political pluralism were not incompatible with the unity of the Muslim community.[42]

By the time the modern law of nations began to emerge parallel with the birth of the nation-state, the decline of the Islamic world and the ascendancy of the West was under way. Thus the nature of modern international political systems and law was determined by the dynamics of the European state system and extended to the rest of the world. Muslim states that wanted to operate within this system were forced to accept these norms. The consolidation of the nation-state system within the Muslim world in the twentieth century, along with the rise of nationalism, accelerated the assimilation of the Muslim world into the international community.

Yet many questioned the value of this process and called for reintegration of the Islamic world; they were prompted by the growing domination of Muslim lands by foreign powers and by the need for the Muslims to regroup to reverse this process. These calls went unheeded, however, and nationalization of the Islamic world has continued unabated. The Muslim world has been plagued by internecine conflicts and by alliances between Muslims and outsiders against other Muslims. Despite much talk about pan-Islamism and Islamic union, the Islamic world has failed to achieve any real measure of unity and to act as a single bloc or political union. All Muslim states, as well as most Muslim intellectuals, have similarly accepted both the international political system based on the nation-state and the rules governing it.[43] Because of their belief that this system is discriminatory and is dominated by the great powers that disregard international rules whenever it suits their interests, they call for its reform. But in this the Muslims have not been alone; throughout the Third World a similar belief has given rise to various efforts to redress the balance of power within the international system, from the formation of the Non-Aligned Movement (NAM) to the demands in the 1970s to reform the international economic order.

In one field of international law—human rights—there are significant divergences of view between most Muslim states and Western countries. Here, too, however, the lines are much less clear-cut than would at first appear. For example, in the Muslim world a large percentage of the human rights violations such as the practice of torture, the denial of due process of law, and the disregard of freedoms and rights—including the freedom of expression—have very little to do with Islam and much to do with the nature of the Islamic world's political systems. Some of the most severe violations of human rights occur in those Muslim countries that have secular political systems.

Conflict also exists on certain other issues between Islamic principles and Western values that are based on the concept of natural law. This dichotomy is not limited to Islam, however, but exists also in certain values of Christianity and Judaism. It derives from the natures of the two legal and ethical systems, one inspired by God and one by man.

2

The Islamist Movement and Its Anti-Western Dimensions: Islamic Particularism or Sociopolitical Mutation?

The predicted clash of civilizations between Islam and the West relates in particular to the militant Islamist movement, which has strong anti-Western dimensions. The root causes of this phenomenon must therefore be established. Many experts explain the spreading wave of an Islamic revival in the past three decades, including its strongly political and militant version, in terms of the inherent characteristics of Islam: its supposed fusion of religion and politics, and the unity and integrity of the Islamic *Ummah* as a transethnic and transnational entity.

Yet the previous chapter demonstrated that both characteristics—particularly the existence of a unified Islamic *Ummah*—have been more myth than reality. To be sure, Muslims have always held as a goal the ideal of one day having a united Islamic community. At times this ideal has also justified the expansionist impulses of Muslim kings and potentates. As long as Islam maintains its hold, this will be a distant goal and will provide cover for more mundane aspirations of Muslim states and rulers, but in fact the united *Ummah* has not existed since the death of the Prophet.

The answer to the question of the fusion of religion and politics in Islam has been more ambiguous. In the Islamic world such a fusion has seldom existed in practice, but Muslims have always discussed whether this was the case and, if not, how to bring it about.

In reality these two inherent aspects of the Islamic experience contributed both to the resurgence of Islam as a potent social and political force and to its radicalization. Yet the Islamist phenomenon of the past three decades cannot be explained wholly or even largely in light of these factors.

This chapter will not provide a detailed analysis of the roots of the Islamic revivalist phenomenon; nor will it present a typology of its manifestations. During the past two decades, extensive and excellent work has been done in these areas by both Muslim and Western scholars.[1] Instead, this chapter will demonstrate the extent to which three factors have been central to the appearance of the Islamist phenomenon: the polarization of Muslim societies along cultural lines; the marginalization of the traditional and culturally Muslim elements of society; and efforts of traditional Muslims to change the power equation within their societies, which have been discriminating against them. This chapter, therefore, aims to show that interest and power-related issues have been central to the recent unfolding of the Islamic experience, without underestimating the impact of value and identity-related factors in this process, and to determine the reasons behind the anti-Western dimension of the Islamist movement. In particular, this chapter will attempt to assess the extent to which the Islamists' anti-Western feelings are rooted in civilizational factors—the specificity of Islam—and to what degree they stem from other causes—the struggle for global power and influence coupled with Western policies toward the Muslim world in the past two centuries. Answers to these questions will tell much about the inevitability of a civilizational clash or the possibility of peaceful coexistence between the West and the Muslim world.

If the Islamist phenomenon were due to intrinsic and immutable characteristics of Islam irrevocably at odds with the ideology and values—the civilization—of the West and Westernized Muslims, conflict between the two would be inevitable. If not, compromise, accommodation, and perhaps even convergence might be possible. It is thus essential to identify correctly the causes of the Islamist phenomenon, including the impact of non-Islamic factors, and its manifestations, as well as the main reasons for its anti-Western dimension.

This chapter, therefore, will also discuss the extent to which both the Islamist phenomenon and its radical discourse have been affected by the influence of secular radical ideologies exogenous to Islam and the Islamic world, especially as a factor in raising the political consciousness of the disadvantaged classes. The chapter further attempts to show that the rise of the Islamist phenomenon is another stage of a long history in which Islam as a living phenomenon interacts with other social, economic, and political forces and, in the process, affects and is affected by them.

This aspect of analyzing the Islamist phenomenon is critically important to the debate about whether a civilizational conflict between Islam and the West is inevitable or whether a modus vivendi between the two can be achieved.

Origins of the Islamist Phenomenon

At the risk of simplification but with the merit of providing clarity, it is possible to divide expert opinion on the principal causes of the rise of the Islamist movement into two schools: the Neo-Orientalist and the Neo-Third Worldist.

Neo-Orientalist Interpretation

The first school can best be characterized as Neo-Orientalist because its followers attribute the emergence of the Islamist phenomenon mainly to Islam's specificity rather than to the social, economic, political, and cultural dynamics of Muslim societies and the mutations caused by economic development and growing interaction with the outside world.

Followers of this school believe the Islamist phenomenon is the consequence of Islam's inherent characteristics and its incompatibility with modernism and, by extension, Westernism. They do not believe that Islam is capable of change and reform, and they therefore believe the convergence of Islam and Western ideas or their peaceful coexistence is nearly impossible. Thus the Neo-Orientalists are cultural determinists, believing that Muslims think and behave in certain ways because they are Muslims. The consequences and implications for the evolution of Muslim societies and for relations between the Muslim and Western worlds are considerable and largely pessimistic.

The adherents of this school believe that the only way the West can deal with the Islamist phenomenon is by resistance, suppression, and containment. They advise that the West help those Muslim governments that resist their Islamists until they are eliminated or subdued completely.

Neo-Orientalists speak harshly of scholars and analysts who do not share their views and who profess more optimism about Islam's capacity to evolve and the potential for peaceful coexistence between Islam and the West. Martin Kramer, for example, characterizes these scholars as "apologists." After warning that a century earlier other Westerners had entertained similar feelings, only to be disappointed, Kramer argues that the current phase of Islamic resurgence, like previous ones, could spend itself by the end of the century provided "it is not abetted by a misguided reprise of the Carter administration's policy toward Iran—a policy which in the name of human rights first inaugurated the era of the Ayatullahs."[2] Likewise, Amos Perlmutter has stated that optimists are naive and prone to wishful thinking. On the question of whether Islam can be compatible with democracy, he argues, "There is an amazing amount of ignorance and wishful thinking at work here. The issue is not democracy but the *true nature of Islam* [emphasis added]. Is Islam, fundamental or otherwise, compatible with liberal, human rights-oriented Western style representative democracy? The answer is an emphatic 'No.'"[3] He, too, seems to foreclose the possibility that a more liberal version of Islam will ever emerge.

Neo-Third Worldist Interpretation

By contrast, Neo-Third Worldist scholars are fully cognizant that certain inherent characteristics of Islam have contributed greatly to its relevance and vitality as a social and political idea throughout its history despite periods of dormancy. But they do not attribute its current resurgence, in its various manifestations, solely to these characteristics. Nor do they consider Islam to be incapable of change and adaptation; and they do not see it to be incompatible with certain concepts of Western liberal ideology. As a consequence they do not see an inevitable clash between Islam and the Western world.

They point instead to several of Islam's primary sources and to the history of Islamic experience to demonstrate Islam's capacity for change and adaptation, and they identify areas of compatibility between it and aspects of Western liberal ideology. Unlike Neo-Orientalists, these scholars do not see either an absolute or an inevitable incompatibility between Islam and democracy. On the contrary, they maintain that, properly interpreted (and provided other conditions are present), certain Islamic concepts provide an adequate basis for a version of democracy. These concepts include that of *Shu'ra, Bay'a*, or—even better—Ibn Taymiyya's concept of *Mubaya'a* (the simultaneous and mutual pledging of allegiance between the ruler and the ruled).[4]

The Neo-Third Worldists also see the latest wave of the Islamic resurgence not as the consequence of Islam's peculiarities but rather as a combination of economic deprivation, social alienation, and political disfranchisement. Francois Burgat, one of Europe's most distinguished scholars of the Islamist phenomenon, sees it as part of the broader North-South divide and considers its radical tone the consequence of a long period of the prosperous North's neglect of the South's problems and aspirations.[5] Burgat also sees a cultural dimension to this movement, not in the sense of aspiration to a pure and mythical Islam but rather as an effort at cultural emancipation and a quest for cultural autonomy. According to Burgat, in the Islamist phenomenon, "We are witnessing the third phase of the process of decolonization. The first phase was political—the independence movements. The second [was] economic—the nationalization of the Suez Canal in Egypt, or oil in Algeria. The last phase is cultural. . . . "[6]

The strategy that this group of scholars proposes for dealing with the Islamist phenomenon is opposite that suggested by the Neo-Orientalists. The Neo-Third Worldists do not believe that a policy of exclusion and repression alone will resolve the Islamist problem or prevent the emergence of conflict between the West and the Muslim world. Of the southern Mediterranean region, where he sees a dangerous misunderstanding developing between the northern and southern littorals, Burgat says that this misunderstanding is being aggravated "by the blindness of those in the West who think that the prevention of the materialization of this conflictual potential is only possible through exclusion and repression. . . . "[7]

Assessing the Merits of Each School

Both the Neo-Orientalist and the Neo-Third Worldist schools of thought contain elements of truth although the Neo-Third Worldist view more accurately reflects the Muslim world's historical and current realities. Any system of values, belief, and thought based on a divine source of inspiration is incompatible with a system that is based on only individual humans and their natural rights viewed in this light. Islam as a divinely based system of belief and values is indeed incompatible with the absolute secularism of Western liberal ideology, which itself has become a fairly dogmatic religion, claiming to be the only depository of truth and to have universal validity. To the extent that the Neo-Orientalists see an incompatibility between Islam as a system of value divinely inspired and Western secularism as a system based on individuals' inalienable natural human rights, the systems are indeed incompatible. But so are all other divinely based systems of belief and values such as Judaism and Christianity. Therefore, the Neo-Orientalist singling out of Islam is not justified. It is also clear that this aspect of Islam explains neither the Islamist phenomenon nor its anti-Western dimensions.

However this particular point is resolved, the ascendance in the West of one of these interpretations of Islam would make a great impact on the Western approach toward the Islamist movement and the Muslim world. The nature of relations between Islam and the West in the coming years will be affected greatly by the Western approach toward the Islamist phenomenon.

It is important, therefore, that the underlying causes of the Islamist phenomenon, and its anti-Western dimensions, be identified and assessed correctly and appropriate policies to deal with them be adopted. Like all other aspects of the Islamic experience, however, the identification and the assessment of the causes of the Islamist phenomenon cannot be carried out in the abstract; they need to be done in the proper historical and territorial context.

Process of Modernization: Rending of the Traditional
Societal Fabric

The Islamist phenomenon can be analyzed and understood only within the context of the socioeconomic development of Muslim societies and the cultural and political consequences of that development. These consequences include the cultural polarization of the Muslim societies and the disruption of their traditional sociopolitical fabric that also altered the equilibrium of power among various sectors of society.

Before the process of modernization in the Muslim world, which began timidly by the late eighteenth and early nineteenth centuries—at different times and at varying speeds in various countries—Muslim countries enjoyed cohesive and integrated societies. Economies were based on agriculture, artisanal manufacturing, and trade. Political systems were either monarchical—of the absolutist nature but tempered by Islamic law and notions of justice and the monarch's benevolence toward his subjects—or based on more primitive tribal structures. Family, clan, other small collectivities, and Islamic charitable organizations such as the pious endowments (*Awqaf*) were the only providers of what is now called social security.

The societies were characterized by strong class distinctions: the princes and the aristocracy, the notables and the landed gentry, the *Ulema*, the merchants, artisans organized within guilds, and peasants and other laborers. Despite these economic and class distinctions and notwithstanding sectarian differences, societies were culturally homogeneous and all members shared and adhered to the basic values of their particular version of Islam plus their own pre-Islamic traditions. Differences that existed among Muslim populations related to the level of personal piety of individuals, not to the overall validity and legitimacy of the primary value system that was based on Islam.

For several centuries before the late eighteenth century, the level of the collective self-confidence of the Muslims and their governments was high, and their belief in the superiority of their own value system was strong. This was so largely because they had not suffered any major defeats at the hands of the non-Muslim powers for several centuries. Their relations with non-Muslims, while fairly limited, had been essentially on an equal footing. Indeed, because of these factors, a degree of psychological and intellectual complacency—if not apathy—had taken over the Muslim world. This condition triggered a process of decline that coincided with a period of renewal and rebirth in the West, thus causing a gradual yet inexorable widening of the gap between the economic, military, and hence political strengths of the Muslim and Western states.

By the mid-nineteenth century, the simultaneous Muslim decline and Western regeneration had led to either the outright occupation and colonization of Muslim states or extensive political and economic penetration by non-Muslim powers through the establishment of regimes of capitulation and the obtaining of sweeping economic and political concessions thus severely undermining the sovereignty and independence of Muslim states. In short, the character of Muslim-Western relations had turned from that between two equals to that between the dominating and the dominated.

Muslim Reaction to Decline

The most important consequence of this process of decline and the ensuing economic and political domination of Muslim states by Western powers was psychological shock and the shattering of Muslim confidence in the strength and validity of their culture and value system, as well as in the social and political structures that these values had produced. This decline and its consequences generated soul-searching among Muslims about the causes of their predicament—a process that continues. The result of this inquiry has been the development of two schools of thought about the causes of and remedies for the Muslim decline.

Islam the Culprit, Westernization the Solution.   One school of thought maintained that Islam was the source of its own problems and that Westernization was the only way of overcoming them. The followers of this school, many of whom had studied in Europe, believed that Islam, at least the dogmatic and stagnant version prevalent in the nineteenth century Muslim world, was the main cause of the Muslims' decline. According to the members of this school, this rigid and atrophied Islam and its custodians, the *Ulema*, shared in the responsibility for Islam's decline because they had cooperated closely with the inefficient and corrupt Muslim political establishments and their absolute monarchies. It was the arbitrary and corrupt rule of these monarchies and their clerical allies that had opened the Muslim world to foreign economic and political penetration and domination.

Non-Arab Muslims in countries such as Iran and Ottoman Turkey considered Arab influences also to be sources of decline. The Arabs, for their part, viewed the impact of Persian and Byzantine cultural and political traditions as the cause of Islam's corruption and decadence and Turkish rule as responsible for their own decline.

The proponents of this school of thought believed that the scientific progress that caused the enhanced economic and political power of the West was due to the erosion of religious dogmatism and the triumph of rationalist thinking and method of analysis. This group suggested a twofold remedy to reverse the decline, improve the Muslims' conditions, and establish a more favorable balance of power between the Islamic and the Western worlds. First, pre-Islamic culture and traditions needed to be revived. This belief was especially strong in the non-Arab states although in Egypt interest was renewed in its pharaonic past. In the rest of the Arab world, this trend led to the romanticization of Arab tribal virtues and qualities of early Islam before they were contaminated by foreign cultures. Second, Muslims needed to emulate the West, most notably its secularization, constitutional governments and rule of law, and rationalist mode of thinking and scientific method of inquiry.

Islam Not the Culprit, Return to Islam the Solution.   Other Muslim thinkers formed a second school of thought, which promoted the thesis that alienation from Islamic principles was the cause of Muslim decline. Fereydoun Adamiyat, an Iranian historian, quotes an anonymous nineteenth-century Iranian author who lamented that the Muslims had reached such a sorry state that they had to adopt Christian laws and constitutions and forgot that the *Qur'an* is the best constitution.[8] This school of thought attributed Western penetration of the Islamic world to its fragmentation as a result of alienation from Islam. The remedy was to be more strict application of Islamic rules and principles. Members of this school, however, differed among themselves on the interpretation of Islamic rules. One group interpreted Islamic rules rigidly and did not admit to any dilution in these principles or any admixing with alien concepts; these were the traditionalists.

The other group interpreted Islam more liberally to make it compatible with rationalist thinking, science, and Western political concepts such as democracy. Allameh Muhammad Iqbal, one of the founders of the Pakistan movement in British India, maintained that the principle of *Ijma*—interpreted as the consensus of the entire community of Muslims, not merely the *Ulema*—amounted to an Islamic form of democracy.[9] The Tatar Muslim reformist from Kazan, Shihabeddin Marjani, struggled to show that Islam, once rid of "the narrow dogmatism and obscurantism of traditional theology . . . was perfectly compatible with modern science."[10]

These Muslim reformers were not averse to borrowing certain aspects of Western culture, especially its scientific and technological achievements. The reformers differed, however, on the degree of their liberalism in interpreting Islamic rules and the extent of their emulation of Western ways. Allameh Iqbal, for example, advocated a reinterpretation of Islamic dogma in light of history and the needs and requirements of individual Muslim societies at a particular time, but he did not approve of Muslims blindly following the ideas of the West: "This new wine [Western values] will weaken our minds, this light will only intensify the darkness."[11]

Another reformist from the Indian subcontinent, Sir Sayyid Ahmad Khan, believed by contrast that intercourse among cultures is the main engine of the march of civilization, and as a result, he was convinced that Muslims needed "to adopt such Western traits as would further their own national development."[12] He was also one of the more liberal interpreters of Islam and maintained that "if the principles yielded by the Qur'an were adopted, there remained no opposition between modern sciences and Islam."[13]

The Islamic reformists failed to generate a true reformation in Islam or to erode the influence and the hold on the Muslim populations of traditional Islamic leaders. One reason was that, by the late nineteenth century secularist and nationalist discourse was becoming more popular with the slowly expanding intelligentsia while the uneducated masses by and large remained faithful to Islam and to its traditional representatives. In addition, leftist ideas began to make inroads among the dissatisfied segments of society who saw the traditional clergy as part of the socioeconomic hierarchy that discriminated against them. This certainly was true in Iran and, to some degree, in Turkey, Iraq, and other Arab states.

The rather complicated notions of the Muslim reformists, aimed at demonstrating the compatibility of Islamic and Western secular liberal concepts, therefore would not attract either group. The newly emerging secularists saw the reformists as hindrances to total modernization of their societies. And the traditional Muslims were suspicious of the reformists' somewhat ambiguous Islamic credentials and believed that their appeal to Islam was merely for political and tactical reasons. The reformists appealed to Islam because they sensed its influence within society and its potential as a unifying element that could harness the energies of

Muslim states, thus enabling them to resist foreign encroachment. These suspicions about the depth and the sincerity of the
reformists' commitment to Islam were partially justified. The following examples illustrate this point.

*Afghani and Abduh: Muslim Reformers or Cynical Opportun-
ists?* Sayyad Jamal-ed-Din Asadabadi, known as Al-Afghani,
along with his disciple, the Egyptian reformist Shaikh Muhammad
Abduh, are two of the most important and influential pioneers of
Islamic reformism, men who were committed to Islam and
wanted to strengthen it by reforming it. This does not reflect
the whole of their complex intellectual makeup and their goals,
however, especially in Afghani's case. Aspects of Afghani's life
and work indicate that he was interested more in forging an alliance of Muslim states to enable them to resist the pressures of the
great powers, notably Britain, than in generating a true reformation of Islam. His use of Islam as an instrument of political mobilization seems to have been determined largely by his appreciation
of its hold on the populace and, hence, its usefulness as an instrument for arousing them against their governments, which
Afghani viewed as corrupt and responsible for the Muslim
world's domination by the great powers.

The interaction between Afghani's dissimulation of his Persian and Shi'a roots when
this suited his plans, along with his emphasis on his descent
from the Prophet and his claim to Afghan origin when this was
advantageous, betrays a degree of flexibility that cannot be easily
reconciled with a deep commitment to Islam.[14] Other evidence
suggests that Afghani was lax in observing religious rules; for
example, in a biography of Afghani, his nephew, Lutfullah
Asadabadi, related that while studying in the holy city of Najaf
Afghani got into trouble with his teachers, largely because of
"laxity in carrying out his religious duties."[15]

The interaction between Afghani and the French philosopher
Ernest Renan provides a further interesting and important insight
into both Afghani's flexibility and his thoughts about the sociopolitical role of Islam and religion in general and their relation to
scientific thinking. This exchange is important for understanding
the complexity of Afghani's personality and views and the political nature of his vocation.

On March 29, 1883, at the Sorbonne Ernest Renan delivered
a lecture on Islam and science, in which he eulogized Hellenism

as the source of science and progress in Europe and attacked Islam as an engine of "despotism, terror and persecution." He accused Islam of having destroyed the high civilizations of the Sassanids and the Byzantines and ultimately having shut off those countries that it conquered "from the rational culture of the spirit."[16] Yet Renan said that it was his conversations with Afghani, whom he characterized as an *asiatique éclaire* (an enlightened Asian), that prompted him to deliver his talk on Islam. Renan said:

> Shaikh Jamal-al-Din is an Afghan entirely liberated from the prejudices of Islam; he belongs to those active races of upper Iran, on the confines of India, where the Aryan spirit still survives under the superficial veneer of official Islam. . . . The freedom of his thought, his noble and loyal character gave me the impression while talking to him, that I had in front of me one of my ancient acquaintances, such as Avicenna or Averroës, or some other one of those *great unbelievers* who, for five centuries, upheld the tradition of the human spirit [emphasis added].[17]

Afghani's response to Renan's attack on Islam was not a rebuke or a condemnation of his characterization of Islam. Instead it was almost an endorsement of Renan's views. Afghani's only defense of Islam was that it was not much worse than other religions. In response to Renan, he admitted, "Islam did seek to stifle science and to arrest intellectual freedom but so did Christianity." The closing of Afghani's response to Renan is important because it shows both his true views on religion and the reason for his appeal to and use of Islam in his political struggle against Muslim potentates and European imperial powers. Afghani wrote:

> Every time that religion has the upper hand, it will eliminate philosophy; and the contrary takes place when it is philosophy which rules as a sovereign mistress. So long as humanity exists, the struggle will not cease between dogma and free inquiry, between religion and philosophy, a bitter struggle, from which fear, free thought will not emerge victorious, *because reason does not please the masses* and its teachings are understood only by a few choice spirits, and also because science, however beautiful it is, cannot completely satisfy hu-

manity which is athirst for an ideal which it likes to place in obscure and distant regions which philosophers and men of science can neither glimpse nor explore [emphasis added].[18]

A correspondence between Afghani and Abduh indicates that Abduh, too, shared his mentor's belief. After reassuring Afghani that he had managed to prevent the translation and dissemination of his answer to Renan's lecture in Egypt, thus averting the risk of protest and uproar, Abduh wrote:

We regulate our conduct according to your sound rule: We do not rut the head of religion except with the sword of religion. Therefore if you were to see us now, you would see ascetics and worshipers [of God] kneeling and genuflecting, never disobeying what God commands and doing all that they are ordered to do.[19]

This dissimulation of one's true beliefs, *Taqiya*, is particular to Shi'ism and, as Nikki Keddie pointed out, was practiced by Afghani and, as Abduh's communiqué illustrates, his disciples.[20] Evidence permits Kedourie to conclude, "One of Afghani's aims—of which his disciple Abduh knew and approved—was the subversion of the Islamic religion, and that the method used to this end was the practice of a false but showy devotion."[21] Other scholars also seem to have reached similar conclusions about Afghani's and Abduh's utilitarian approach toward Islam and Islam's role in the sociopolitical structure of Muslim societies. Keddie noted that Afghani had both an exoteric and an esoteric doctrine, and that he used Islam for political purposes.[22] Sylvia G. Haim, who shares this view, wrote that Afghani's bent was "utilitarian, skeptical and activist" and Afghani was "the very type of revolutionary conspirator activist so well known in Europe in modern times."[23] Haim also doubts Abduh's commitment to Islam, stating that if Islam is interpreted according to Abduh's vision, it "ceases to be properly a religion and is transformed into a system of ethics or rules for successful conduct in this life."[24]

These interpretations of Afghani's and Abduh's views and personalities cannot, of course, be taken at face value. They must be checked against other interpretations that produce a different image of these men.[25] It is clear, however, that Afghani was a political activist who wanted both to change the nature of the Muslim states—especially Iran's government—and to end their domination by imperial powers, especially Britain. Indeed, as Keddie has pointed out, Afghani considered the "strengthening of the Muslim World against Western, and especially British, encroachments as the most important task of his age and the necessary condition of meaningful reform."[26] As a pragmatist, Afghani also understood the important role Islam can play in mobilizing the masses against their governments and in uniting the Muslim states against the imperial powers. None of these characteristics, however, necessarily implies a lack of religious commitment by Afghani.

Of more contemporary relevance is that the debate about Afghani's and Abduh's real views helps explain the suspicion of the more orthodox Muslims and of the new breed of strict revolutionary Islamists of the whole phenomenon of reformist Islam. The revolutionaries believe that the reformists' use of Islam is merely a cynical tactic and they lack true commitment. In Iranian politics of today, for example, the hard-liners label as liberals the Muslim reformists and accuse them of wanting to subvert Islam from within, a charge that Kedourie makes against Afghani.

Early Reforms in the Muslim World

By the middle of the nineteenth century, the school of thought that attributed the Muslim states' decline largely to the specific characteristics of Islam and that saw the cure in secularization and the emulation of Western models became popular with the emerging Muslim intellectual elites. Most Muslim states began reform of their educational, administrative, and military systems along the lines of Western institutions.

The process of reform in the Ottoman Empire (*Tanzimat*); reform undertaken by Mirza Taqi Khan (Amir Kabir) and Mirza Hussain Mushir ul-Dauleh, prime ministers of the Qajar kings in Iran; and reform by Muhammad Ali and Khadiv Ismail in Egypt were the first responses aimed at arresting the process of decline.[27] Efforts at educational and social reforms were also undertaken by Muslims of British India, especially by Sir Sayyid Ahmad Khan. For example, on December 26, 1870, he organized the Committee for the Better Diffusion and Advancement of

Learning among Muhammadans of India,[28] and he also recommended the establishment of the Muhammadan Anglo-Oriental College of Aligarh.[29] In Central Asia, the leaders, such as Mahmud Khoja Behbudy, of the reformist *jadid* movement worked for educational reform.[30] Beginning in the early nineteenth century, the Muslim states also started sending students to European countries and availing themselves of the services of European experts.

The result of these two developments was the emergence of a new elite characterized by its familiarity with and appreciation of the West's culture and sociopolitical institutions. This new elite was distinguished from other groups within the society by its ideology instead of by its position within the social and economic structure of the country although initially, at least, the majority of the new elite belonged to society's upper echelon.

The ideology of this elite was based on the rationalist and positivist philosophy of nineteenth-century Europe and was imbued with concepts of constitutionalism and the rule of law. It also betrayed, to varying degrees, its anticlerical sentiment. As a result, members of this elite were extremely subversive toward the interests of the clerical and the political establishments in the various countries. This elite contributed greatly to the development of constitutionalist movements and, perhaps even more important, to the popularization throughout the Muslim world of the concepts of modern nationalism. Even the emerging socialist movement in nineteenth-century Europe did not leave these groups and countries unaffected.

The 1905–1906 constitutional revolution in Iran, the Young Turks revolt in 1908 in Turkey, and the nationalist movement in Egypt were partly the result of the emergence of this ideological elite. Yet the impact of this elite and the reforms this intelligentsia initiated in the respective countries were too small to challenge seriously the traditional power equilibrium of society, and their numbers were too limited to alter its cultural homogeneity based on the principles and practices of local Islam. Nor did members of this elite openly and defiantly challenge Islam and champion a militant secularism similar to the French Revolution's notion of *laïcité*. Nevertheless, by the turn of the twentieth century, a cultural split along the lines of modernists versus traditionalists was emerging within Muslim societies, a split that would continue and deepen in the coming decades.

This brief history of the Muslim reaction to decline and efforts to cope with it also demonstrates the difficulty the Muslim reformists have had in prevailing, challenged as they have been by both the unadulterated secularists and the orthodox and extremist Muslims. The secularists have considered the reformists to be too influenced by Islam, and the orthodox Muslims have doubted the reformists' Islamic credentials. Afghani and Abduh were not the only Muslim reformists whose commitment to Islam has been questioned. During Iran's constitutional revolution, similar charges were made against some of the progressive clergy who cooperated with the constitutionalists; for example, the Iranian Shi'a cleric, Sayyid Muhammad Tabatabai, who was the most ardent supporter of reformist ideology among the *Ulema*, was considered to have been influenced by the ideas of freemasonry. According to some sources, his father, Sayyid Sadiq, was a member of *Faramushhane*, which was set up in 1859 by an Armenian-Iranian reformist, Mirza Malcolm Khan, on the model of European Freemason organizations.[31]

Despite the historic difficulties that the Muslim reformists have encountered in gaining broad support for their views and in establishing their credibility as both Muslims and reformers, their example is nevertheless extremely important and encouraging in regard to the prospects of an eventual Islamic-modernist synthesis in the Muslim world. It also shows that Islam is not as impervious to reform as the Neo-Orientalists claim.

Ephemeral Triumph of Secularism, 1920–1970, and the Deepening Islamic-Secular Divide

It is difficult to imagine what would have been the fate of the Islamic reformist movement had there not been a World War I and the dramatic changes it produced in the international political system. Of equal importance for the destiny of Islam, reformist and otherwise, as an important sociopolitical agent was the Russian Revolution of 1917 and the creation of the Soviet Union, which for decades made Communist ideology the principal medium of radical discourse. In terms of Islam's evolution as a political and ideological force, the impact of the creation of the Soviet Union and Communism was stronger and longer lasting than the impact of World War I. What, for example, would have happened to Iran's experience with what can best be described as Islamic constitutionalism as embedded in the 1906 constitution if there had not been a combined Soviet-Communist threat? Would the *Ulema*, which had been granted the right to oversee the compliance of all legislation with Islamic principles and law, have prevented any kind of innovation? Or would the participation of reformist *Ulema* in the parliamentary experience have led to the development of a progressive jurisprudence and an incremental process of Islamic reformation? Similar questions can be asked about Turkey in the absence of a Mustafa Kemal and his policy of forced secularization and Europeanization. What is clear is that the triumph of secularism and ethnocentric nationalism in the Muslim world, which began during the 1920s and continued throughout the 1970s, set in motion forces that created deep fissures in the fabric of nearly all Muslim societies. This outcome, in turn, led by the late 1960s to a renewal of Islam's potency as a social and political force, a phenomenon that is still very much a part of the sociopolitical landscape of the Muslim world.

Secularization from Above: A Limited Success. During the period from the early 1920s until well into the 1970s, most Muslim societies underwent a process of state-directed secularization and cultural and political nationalization—albeit to varying degrees and according to different time frames in various countries—in the sense that they developed an ethnocentric focus of identity and allegiance and a nationalist base of political legitimacy.

• *Turkey's experience.* The most extensive and thorough secularization, de Islamization, and cultural and political nationalization occurred in post-Ottoman Turkey. Ataturk was a firm believer in Turkey's European destiny and in the theories that attributed to Islam the greatest part of the responsibility for the economic and military backwardness of Muslim countries. Indeed some commentators have suggested that Ataturk wished that Turkey were a Christian country.[32] But because he could not convert the Turks to Christianity, he tried to eliminate Islam's influence in Turkey by various means, including a change of script from Arabic to Latin and a prohibition of the call to prayer in Arabic. He also offered a new ideology, which has come to be known as Kemalism, made up of a mix of ethnic and cultural Turkish nationalism and economic and social progress. Ataturk's de-Islamizing of Turkey was not universally welcomed, and ethnic Kurds offered some armed resistance although the Kurdish

revolts, in addition to their Islamic rationale, had distinct nationalist and separatist connotations.[33] Ataturk, however, did not
have to contend with a strong and independent clerical establishment because, in line with the Sunni tradition of subjecting religion to politics, the Ottoman clerics were nothing more than a
component of the state bureaucracy.

Yet Ataturk's de-Islamization policy was at best only partly
successful: The sociopolitical revival of Islam immediately after
Ataturk's death and, in particular, following the introduction of a
multiparty system in Turkey in 1948 illustrated Islam's resilience
and tenacity.[34] Indeed, from the 1950s onward, Turkey underwent a process of state-supported re-Islamization, when various
parties and governments used their sponsorship of projects to
build mosques and religious schools to gain votes.[35] Nevertheless,
as long as the Turkish economy was developing quickly as it did
between the late 1950s and the late 1960s and the educational
system was expanding, the number of secularized Turks increased and radicalization and politicization of the more Islamically oriented segments of Turkish society did not occur.

In the 1970s, however, Islam emerged as an important political force, battling the growing influence of the Left. During the
1980s the Turkish government, concerned about the contagion of
the 1979 Iranian revolution and the continued challenge of the
Left, actively encouraged the Islamist forces. This strategy was
intended to both co-opt Islam on the side of the government
and use it as a weapon against the leftist forces. This led to the
intensification of an already existing cultural duality in Turkish
society that today is divided along secular-Islamist lines.[36] By
early 1997, however, the Turkish secularists, especially the military, which considers itself to be the guardian of Ataturk's legacy,
had embarked on a strategy of rolling back the process of Turkey's re-Islamization. In February 1997, the Turkish military
warned the Islamist prime minister not to stray from the path of
secularism.[37] The military also demanded the closure of Islamic
schools and a stricter enforcement of the Western dress code.

When the Islamist prime minister, Necmettin Erbakan, re-
sisted the military's pressures, he was forced out of power. The
new government formed under the leadership of Mesut Yilmaz of
the Motherland Party proceeded with a policy of reducing Islam's
influence in the country, including the closure of Islamic schools.
This attitude of the government led to massive demonstrations

on the part of the Islamists, reflecting a further deepening of the cultural divide in Turkey.[38] The latest actions of the Turkish military also reflect its concern over the political appeal of the Islamists, which could challenge the military's own power and privileged position.

• *Iran's experience.* Disruption and disorder in Iran—as its neutrality was violated by all parties to World War I and as it became subject to great power politics, notably British concern it would succumb to revolutionary Russia—led to a change of dynasty. In 1925 Riza Khan was crowned king, inaugurating the birth of the Pahlavi dynasty that was destined to become Iran's last monarchy. The establishment of a new dynasty need not have led to the failure of Iran's experiment with constitutional monarchy because its principles applied equally to the Pahlavis. It nevertheless did.

The purpose here is not to argue whether, given the chaotic conditions of Iran in the period after World War I, a degree of centralization of the state and a firm handling of centrifugal forces were necessary. Nor is it to establish whether these goals could have been achieved through more democratic and less authoritarian methods. The concern here is to establish whether these policies and the methods used to implement them at first enjoyed a degree of popular and elite support, including from the religious establishment. The answer is that they did.

Members of the *Ulema*, in particular, supported Riza Shah at the beginning because they were concerned about Iran's territorial disintegration as a result of domestic turmoil and foreign intervention, as well as about the spread of godless ideologies such as Communism. Moreover, for the first decade of his rule, Riza Shah's policies did not challenge in any serious way the position of the *Ulema* nor the position of the classes that identified, although not completely, with the religious establishment—the merchants and the landowners. Nor was there any change in the Iranian civil law that in matters of personal status, such as family law and inheritance, continued to be based on Islamic principles.

The main area of dispute between the king and the *Ulema* occurred on the cultural level and, in particular, on the issue of the status of women—especially the abolition of the veil in 1937 and the enforcement of that edict by force instead of by leaving it to personal choice, which in the long run might have proved more effective in eliminating the practice of veiling. The forced unveiling of women did cause serious discord between the *Ulema* and the king. Later, during the 1970s under the reign of the second Pahlavi king, the wearing of the veil by a new generation of Iranian female Islamists symbolized opposition to the Pahlavi rule.

At first, however, there was no massive mobilization by the religious establishment against Riza Shah's government. Riza Shah's other policies included the expansion of the modern system of education through the setting up of secular schools and universities, the sending of students to Europe, and the development of a nationalist ideology inspired by Iran's pre-Islamic past, including a near-monotheistic religion, Zoroastrianism, with its highly developed ethical system. It was natural, therefore, that this nationalist ideology should be viewed suspiciously and with apprehension by the clerical establishment because it presented an alternative to Islam as a value system and as a focus of identity and a source of political legitimacy.

Riza Shah and the Pahlavis were not the sole generators of this ideology, however. By the middle of the nineteenth century some revival of interest in pre-Islamic Iran and its traditions had begun. The Pahlavis' policies only intensified these trends. Indeed, throughout Iran's post-Islamic history, these traditions had retained their strength and appeal although many of them were given an Islamic coloration. For several centuries the Iranian Shi'a clerics had not seen serious conflict between attachment to these traditions and their commitment to Shi'a Islam. Some Shi'a *Ulema* such as Muhammad Baqir Majlesi even produced *hadiths* regarding the sayings of the imams, especially the sixth imam, Imam Ja'afar as Sadiq, and the eighth imam, Imam Ali Ibn Musa al Riza, that in matters of faith the Persians are superior to the Arabs.[39] These *hadiths* are of dubious authenticity, but their importance lies in the fact that, by sanctioning Iranian nationalism as being compatible with religious devotion, these *hadiths* legitimized nationalist feelings and resolved the conflict between allegiance to Iran and commitment to Shi'a Islam.

This convergence of Shi'a Islam and Iranian nationalism ended with Iran's gradual modernization and secularization and the identification of Iranian nationalism with secularization. Although the dichotomy between the nationalists and the Islamists was becoming obvious, by the early 1950s mutual fear of the growing influence of the Left prevented open and excessive animosity between the secular-modernists and the Islamic establishment. The antinationalist tendencies among the clergy and other Islamists became politicized and strengthened only in the 1960s, when some of the government reform measures directly affected their economic interests and the basis of their social and political power. This ushered in a new phase of cultural and legal de-Islamization in the context of the shah's so-called White Revolution.

The White Revolution meant massive land reform, granting voting rights to women, and efforts to reform the family law to be less discriminatory toward women. These reforms assailed the religious establishment's material interests just as Iranian nationalism had challenged the establishment's ideological hegemony. These two challenges combined led to a frontal attack on Iran's pre-Islamic traditions and Iranian nationalism by the clergy and other Islamic intellectuals. Murteza Mutahari, a prominent intellectual and professor of Islamic philosophy at Teheran University[40] and one of the intellectual leaders of the Islamic Revolution, tried to undermine the ideological basis of the nationalists by dismissing all virtues attributed to Iran's pre-Islamic civilization and portraying the Sassanid state as socially unjust and morally depraved.[41] Despite these attacks, nationalism remained strong as a cultural and political force well into the early 1970s. Note that until that time, the main challenge to Iranian nationalism had come from the Left, which championed the cause of Iran's ethnic minorities and promoted the theme of their enslavement by the racist Persians.

Since the mid-1980s, however, with growing popular disenchantment with the Islamic government, Iran has experienced a resurgence of nationalism and interest in the pre-Islamic era. Even the government has at times—during the Iran-Iraq War and the Persian Gulf crisis of 1991—resorted to Iranian nationalism to garner support for its policies.

• *The Arab world.*   The Arab World also underwent a process that was more or less similar to the secularization trend of Iran and Turkey. In the Arab world, too, this process was coupled with rising nationalism. The defeat of Sharif Hussain's dream of establishing a united Arab nation and state led to the division of the Ottoman Empire's Arab lands into separate and small territorial and political units. This caused the emergence of territorial nationalisms (in Syria, Egypt, and Iraq, for example) and transnational ideologies such as pan-Arabism. Meanwhile, the European

colonization of Arab lands coupled with the expansion of education had already enlarged the base of the secularized and partially
Westernized elite, thus setting in motion the process of cultural
dualization and polarization of Arab societies that, as everywhere
else in the Muslim world, was accentuated in the following
decades.

The Islamic response to these changes in the Arab world
came more quickly and strongly than they had in Iran and Turkey.
Immediately after the Ottoman defeat in 1919 and continuing well
into the mid-1920s, the idea of restoring the caliphate remained
influential in the Arab world. The Egyptian thinker, Rashid Rida,
was an exponent of keeping the caliphate alive, although he
viewed the new caliphate more as a purely spiritual office and
symbol of Muslim unity than as a political institution. When it
became clear that the caliphate was beyond redemption, Islamic
loyalists created their own organization and developed their own
political thinking. The most important and consequential of these
groups was the Muslim Brotherhood, the *Ikhvan-al-Muslimin*,
which was established in Egypt by Hassan-al-Banna in 1928. The
Brotherhood is significant because it became the nucleus of a
movement that would expand throughout the Muslim world, including non-Arab countries such as Iran, Pakistan, Indonesia,
and Malaysia. Khalil Tahmassebi, who in 1950 assassinated the
Iranian prime minister, General Razmara, was a member of the
Iranian branch—the *Fedaiyan-e-Islam*—of the Muslim Brotherhood.
The Brotherhood was also the breeding ground for later and more
extremist Islamists.

Arab Islamists viewed nationalism as a divisive element and
opposed it. The *Ulema* of Al-Azhar as late as 1928 considered
nationalism a heresy and called on Arabs to "strive for Islamic
unity, rather than allowing themselves to be preoccupied with
Arab unity."[42] The dichotomy, however, between nationalism
and Islamism has never been as strong in the Arab world as in
non-Arab Muslim lands because, first, Arab nationalism that aims
to unite all Arabs cannot be accused of being divisive as can other
nationalisms and, second, as the late Hamid Enayat put it, "The
Arabs cannot promote their identity without at the same time
exalting Islam, which is the most abiding source of their pride."[43]

Thus in Arab societies the Arab nationalists did not threaten
Islam's place as the main component of civilization and identity
as Iranian and Turkish nationalists did in their countries. The

Arab nationalists viewed Islam as an inherently Arab phenomenon that, despite its universalist vocation, was primarily and essentially revealed for them and possesses an Arab character. Abdul Rahman al Bazzaz, an ardent Arab nationalist and Iraq's prime minister in 1965–1966, was an especially strong proponent of the Arabness of Islam; he viewed Islam merely as a refined version of ancient Arab tradition.[44]

Whether or not Arab nationalism and Islam are mutually exclusive or reinforcing, until the late 1960s—to be precise, until 1967 when the Arabs were defeated and East Jerusalem came under Israel's control, thus dealing a severe blow to the credibility of Arab nationalism as an ideology capable of achieving victory for the Arabs—a variety of nationalist and leftist ideas such as Arab nationalism, Arab socialism, and Ba'athism instead of Islamist ideologies dominated the cultural and political landscape of the Arab world.

Emergence of the Left: Impact on Islam. The spread of leftist ideologies and the emergence of leftist, including Communist, parties in most Muslim countries—with varying degrees of strength—made a tremendous impact on the evolution of Islam's political role and on relations between the religious establishments and the new secular elites of the Muslim world. In the history of Islam's interaction with the leftist forces, two distinct periods can be observed.

The first period, roughly from the 1920s to the mid-1960s, was that of Islam's resistance to the Left's challenge and the forging of a kind of Islamic-Nationalist alliance against the leftist forces. In some countries such as Egypt, however, the situation was more complex: Gamal Abd-ul-Nasser in the 1950s and 1960s fought the Muslim Brotherhood although before the 1952 revolution there had been close links between the Free Officers and the Muslim Brothers. The rift between the two seemed to have been caused by the disappointment of the more militant brothers with the slow pace of reform and their growing doubts about the officers' commitment to Islam. The rift culminated in an assassination attempt against President Nasser in 1957, following which the Brotherhood was dissolved and its activities banned. During the 1970s, however, President Anwar as-Sadat legalized the Brotherhood and used it to fight the Communists and the Nasserites.

The second period, which began in the late 1960s and is still continuing, was that of the defeat of the Left (albeit at different rates in different countries), the incorporation of leftist ideas into Islamic discourse, and the emergence of militant and radical Islam. To this underlying pattern must be added the short-lived experience of the Communist Muslims of Russia who, at the time of the Russian Revolution, tried to develop a synthesis between Islam and Communism and to promote National Communism. A major figure behind this intellectual trend was Sultan Galiev.[45]

Underlying this philosophy was the belief that Russia's Muslims had the right to interpret Marxism in light of their own national conditions. For the Muslim Communists this meant reinterpretation in light of their Islamic experience. According to Bennigsen and Wimbush, "Sultan Galiev and his Muslim comrades recognized intuitively that if they were to be successful at promoting Marxism in their societies, they necessarily must integrate its teaching with those of Islam."[46] Because of the Sovietization of Russia's Muslim lands, efforts to synthesize Islam and Marxism came to an end, but decades later in other parts of the Islamic world the leftist forces tried to use Islam to get their message across to the masses.

• *Islamic-nationalist coalition against the Left.* The growing secular and nationalist forces no doubt were a significant challenge to Islam's power and position within Muslim societies and polities. With a few exceptions such as the Kemalist period in Turkey during Ataturk's lifetime, however, secular nationalists were not antireligion. They certainly were not godless themselves, and they did not encourage atheism. The Communists by contrast adhered to—or at least were so perceived—an atheistic and materialistic creed, and they viewed religion, enlightened or obscurantist, as a major source of the backwardness and inequity in all societies. They believed that religion, in the words of Marx, was the opium of the masses, numbing their senses and sapping their energies, thus making them submissive and willing to accept all manner of social and economic injustice and inequity.

As a result, for the leftists, reducing the hold of religion on the masses required that the influence of religious leaders be eliminated. The Communist ideology, particularly during its early decades and before the emergence of nationalist versions of Communism, was also antinationalist. The antinationalism of the Communists was due partly to their universalist aspirations and partly to their belief that class interest and class solidarity should overcome other loyalties if a classless society in the form of a socialist Utopia was to be achieved. In their efforts to undermine their countries' existing governments, however, the Communists manipulated ethnic and linguistic differences and, in fact, promoted local micronationalisms.

Because of their shared need to combat the Left that threatened their interests, the Islamic establishments and secular governments forged a kind of alliance that, although not free of tensions and conflicts of interest, did hold for some time. The secular governments concluded that Islam was basically a conservative force and its influence would be a barrier to the spread of radical ideas such as Communism.

Islamic establishments, for their part, concluded that the existing governments were less evil than godless Communist regimes. Iran from the 1930s to the early 1960s was a good example of an alliance of convenience or, at least, a modus vivendi between the government and the Islamic establishment, with the aim of checking the advance of the Left.[4/] Similar situations prevailed in many Muslim states although the extent of this cooperation depended on specific characteristics of each country, especially the nature of relations between religious establishments and governments and the urgency and seriousness of the leftist threat.

Even at the international level, Islam was used by some countries in the Middle East to combat the influence of the Left. For example, the first impetus for the creation of the Organization of the Islamic Conference (OIC) was the threat that leftist forces—including Arab socialists—posed to the conservative governments of the Islamic World. The OIC made use of Islam to provide an ideological underpinning and basis of legitimacy for an alliance of conservative and pro-Western states that had in common only a fear of radicalism.

• *Radicalization of Islam.*   Traditional and conservative Islam was identified with the local bourgeoisie and, in most instances, with the governments, and because of this it failed to stem the appeal of leftist ideologies for large segments of Muslim populations, especially the poor and the young. Meanwhile, the image of Islam as a conservative and establishment force alienated the young generation of Muslims from their religion. This was particularly true during the 1940s, 1950s, and early 1960s when, in many Muslim countries, there was a tacit alliance among the religious establishments, the moneyed classes, and some Muslim governments. The Iranian Islamo-leftist theorist, Ali Shari'ati, whose reinterpretation of Islam in light of Marxist methodology exerted much influence over his contemporaries in Iran in the 1960s and 1970s, illustrated this common bond with the imagery of the triangular alliance of sword, gold, and the worry bead (*Tigh, zar, va Tasbih*). At least one part of the Islamic establishment reacted with a reinterpretation of Islamic social and economic principles to make them appear to be more in line with the concerns and needs of Muslim youth. Such a reinterpretation, this segment hoped, would show that Islam was a socially progressive, egalitarian creed and a supporter of the weak, which therefore would remove the need for alien radical ideologies.

In Egypt, for example, some of the *Ulema* of Al-Azhar and some Western-educated professors tried to demonstrate that Islam contained all the positive elements of socialism without its negative aspects. In Syria, Mustafa as-Sibai was a prominent exponent of the socialist dimensions of Islam.[48] In the Shi'a world, the prominent leader Imam Mohammed Baqir as-Sadr pioneered in demonstrating Islam's social conscience; his writings on Islamic economics emphasized the egalitarian dimensions of Islam. Indeed, because of the Shi'as' depressed economic conditions in countries such as Iraq and Turkey, Shi'a youth were especially attracted to leftist ideologies, thus posing a more immediate threat to Islam's influence in their respective countries.[49] In their efforts to combat the Left, Muslim religious leaders and scholars borrowed heavily from the Left's terminology and arguments to show the falsity of leftist ideas and Islam's ideological superiority. Some Muslim *Ulema* even became influenced by Marxist theories; one such *alim* was the Iranian ayatullah, Mahmud Taleqani, who became the spiritual leader of the Islamo-leftist Iranian group, the *Mujaheddin-e-Khalq*.[50] The net result was the radicalization of Islamic discourse and the emergence of what could be described as a leftist Islam.

• *Islamization of the Left.* The radicalization of Islam also grew out of what can best be characterized as the Islamization of the Left. Two factors were responsible for this phenomenon. The first was the Left's realization of the continued hold of Islam on the vast majority of Muslim people as well as the revolutionary potential of Islam. The second factor was the success of Muslim governments in dismantling or undermining the structures of the Left coupled with popular disenchantment with the results of homegrown secular leftist ideologies like Nasserism and Ba'athism.

The choice by some leftists of Islam as the basis of their new ideologies certainly had a utilitarian if not an opportunistic dimension because it was done to reach the predominantly Muslim masses. This was the case with the founders of the *Mujaheddin-e-Khalq* movement in Iran and their principal idealogue, Ali Shari'ati. The inability of the leftist Tudeh Party to arouse the masses contributed much to their conclusion.

Shari'ati believed that the Iranian masses and petit bourgeoisie of the late 1960s and the early 1970s were devout and thus like Europeans of the Middle Ages more than Europeans of the French Revolution; Iran, he said, "was neither in the 20th century, nor in the age of the grand bourgeoisie and the industrial revolution, but still in the age of faith in the late feudal era just on the eve of the renaissance. . . . "[51] He therefore recommended that the Iranian intelligentsia should avoid offending the religious sensibilities of the masses but instead should use the medium of religion to get their message across. He and his disciples among the *Mujaheddin-e-Khalq* considered Shi'ism in particular capable of performing such a task for, in the epic resistance of the third Shi'a imam, Hussain Ibn Ali, against the Umayyad despot, Yazid, that culminated in his and his companions death at Karbala, they saw a strong revolutionary potential capable of mobilizing the masses. Muhsen Rezai, one of the founders of the *Mujaheddin*, quite explicitly referred to this potential.[52] Shari'ati himself stated that the message of Hussain's martyrdom was that every man, irrespective of time and place, had the duty to resist oppression; and therefore every month is *Muharam*, every day is *Ashura*, and every place is Karbala. Ali Shari'ati also saw true Shi'ism—which he characterized as that of the first imam, Ali (*Shi'a-e-Alavi*)—as a vibrant and progressive creed unlike official Shi'ism, which he characterized as that of the Safavids (*Shi'a-e-Safavi*). He reinterpreted *Qur'anic* and biblical stories such as Cain and Abel in light of Marxist socioeconomic theories. In Egypt, Hassan Hanafi, whose views traveled beyond Egypt and influenced some groups in Tunisia, represented the Islamic Left.

Intensification of the Dualistic Development of Muslim Societies

The impact of the early reform movements on the traditional so-cioeconomic structures of Muslim societies and on their cultural cohesion and integrity was fairly limited although their political consequences were quite substantial. The consequent impact of these reforms on patterns of social relationships and the balance of power was relatively small. The movement to modernize Muslim societies gathered greater force and momentum in the 1920s and the 1930s, with the process acquiring a more overtly antireligious connotation to different degrees in various coun-tries, with Turkey's reforms the most openly antireligion or, to be precise, anti-Islam.

Because of its intensity and scope, this phase of moderniza-tion profoundly disturbed the patterns of societal relationships and the power equations. Thus the wide-scale secularization of the judicial and educational systems undermined the positions of religious teachers and judges and deprived them of their liveli-hood. Because both the level of accessibility and the attractiveness of the modernizing trend to various segments of population were unequal, it also shattered the cultural unity of Muslim societies.

Alienation between the Elite and the Masses

The cultural divide that emerged was to some degree genera-tional; younger members of even traditional families absorbed modernizing influences. Differences existed, however, even within the modernizing segments of society: By the 1930s, as both mass education and the number of Muslim students studying abroad increased, a division emerged between those who had studied only in their own country in their own language and those who had studied in Europe or America and thus had a command of foreign languages. In the coming decades this divide grew wider. Part of the divide was economic and social in the sense that the modernists, especially those educated in the West who were fluent in Western languages, had more opportunity for upward mobility. Because the ruling elites of most Muslim countries had become Westernized, the majority in Muslim socie-ties became alienated from their rulers. A marginally literate ped-dler from Tangier illustrated this when he said, "Now the Fassis rule as the Christians used to. They have villas, cars and servants. But those of us who toil for a mouthful of bread have gained nothing since independence. And the Fassis and other rich Moroccans have forgotten their religion. *They have become like Christians. Sometimes they speak French among themselves. They send their children to French schools. They marry French women* . . . And even today the Christians still control Morocco [emphasis added]."[53]

That a Western education and familiarity with Western languages ensured preferential treatment and access to better and more remunerative positions was particularly important to the rising political profile of Islam. A comment of the Tunisian Islamist leader Rashid Ghannushi illustrated the impact of this factor: "I am of the generation of *Zaytuna* students during the early years of independence. *I remember we used to feel like strangers in our own country.* We had been educated as Muslims and as Arabs, while we could see the country totally molded in the French cultural identity. For us, the doors to any further education were closed since the university was completely Westernized [emphasis added]."[54]

Empirical evidence shows that a Western education has been important in determining the political tendencies of many African Muslims.[55] In short, the growing cultural chasm within Muslim societies and the increasing sense of alienation and marginalization of the Islamically oriented segments of the society were major factors behind the emergence of the Islamist theories and movements.

Because the existing power elites based their political legitimacy on their modernizing and nationalist philosophies— whether socialist or capitalist—the Islamists countered by delegitimizing their rule and justifying the establishment of an alternative socioeconomic and political system based on Islam. Within the alternative system, those people rooted in the Islamic culture and well versed in Islamic discourse would supplant the Westernized elites. Indeed, this is what happened in Iran after the Islamic revolution in 1979: Inexperienced Muslim youth were given sensitive government jobs with little or no consideration of expertise or competence. Commitment to Islam and to the ideals and goals of the Islamic revolution were given priority. Although the Iranian government has had to pay more attention to technical and professional competence during the past several years, so-called technocrats are still viewed with suspicion by the Islamists. Applicants for university entrance examination are still quizzed regularly on their knowledge of Islamic subjects and failure to perform satisfactorily disqualifies the applicant from pursuing university education even if performance in other subjects is more than adequate. During the past few years, students of secular institutions have complained that religious students receive preferential treatment and are given priority when they apply for jobs. Thus the secularists feel discrimination as did the non-Westernized students during the shah's rule. This illustrates clearly the role that Islamist theories—like any other belief system or ideology—play in the struggle for economic and political power and privilege within Muslim societies and indicates that the rise of the Islamist phenomenon owes more to power and interest-related factors than to the specificity of Islam.

Sociopolitical Consequences of Economic Development

Cultural fragmentation and polarization of Muslim societies have not been the only consequences of the process of modernization, including its economic dimension. Another influential consequence has been large-scale urbanization, resulting more from declining agricultural production and rising population than from massive industrialization, although it, too, has played a role. This particular pattern of urbanization has led to large pockets of urban poverty and a concentration of population in a few large cities, where most of these newcomers maintain their rural and mostly Islamic values and traditions. Some analysts note that the recently arrived urban dwellers have changed the cultural landscape of Muslim cities, leading to a phenomenon that Amira al-Azhari Sonbol has called the "villagization of the cities."[56] They also suffer from an intense sense of alienation from the rest of society. Although not politically activist, these groups nevertheless provide important support for the Islamists.

State-sponsored modernization in most Muslim countries has extended the state's presence and involvement in every aspect of people's and communities' lives, leading to a growing encroachment of government on local freedoms and interests. Those who have felt injured by governmental intrusion have turned against its ideologies as well, and when they have finally decided to challenge the state, they have used Islam as the alternative to the ideology promoted by the state.

Growing Gap between Aspirations and Opportunities.   Muslim societies have experienced the phenomenon of rising expectations. During the early decades of large-scale development, governments were able to absorb their growing work forces and the graduates of newly established universities. When building his Arab socialism in Egypt, Gamal Abd-ul-Nasser guaranteed a government job for every Egyptian university graduate. The legacy of his practice is the present bloated Egyptian bureaucracy. Oil economies, too, in the 1960s and 1970s—and some into the mid-1980s—offered expanding opportunities to their populations, but by the late 1970s and early 1980s rising populations and other difficulties—some growing from the fluctuations of the energy markets—seriously undermined this ability, thus increasing numbers of young and unemployed who felt alienated from governments and political systems that no longer responded to their needs. This alienated and unemployed youth provided the fertile recruiting ground for Islamists in many Muslim countries, notably in Algeria.[57] With falling revenues in the wake of the oil price crash of 1985—1986, the financial burdens of the Persian Gulf War of 1991, and a rising population, even Saudi Arabia has been experiencing a similar phenomenon in the 1990s.

This inability to absorb was not limited to those at the lower end of the economic and educational ladders. In countries such as Iran under the shah, many Western-educated experts with aspirations for power found the system unresponsive. Saad Eddin Ibrahim has pointed out that the Islamist movement is not the result of absolute economic disparity, although that is important, but of "relative deprivation" of both an economic and a political nature. Because Islamism has become "an idiom for expressing profound worldly grievances and the quest for the good life here on earth," Professor Ibrahim also points out that in Europe during the sixteenth century similar worldly concerns were expressed through religious movements.[58] This phenomenon was also observable during early to mid-nineteenth century England, where the so-called dissenting, puritanical movements developed and gained support among the workers of the new industries, especially textile mills. The common thread running through both periods is that they were times of "great fermentation and transformations ushered in by the dramatic geographic explorations, scientific discoveries and sprouting capitalism."[59]

This is why so many U.S.- and European-educated Iranians joined the Islamic revolution and later, with no experience, occupied high positions such as prime minister, foreign minister, and governor of the central bank. Yet this became possible only after massive purges and, as shown later, it entailed heavy costs in terms of the management of the country's affairs. Today a new generation of Iranians finds opportunities for upward mobility limited in Islamic Iran, and many of them are disillusioned with the government and its ideology and are promoting alternative philosophies, including secular ones.

Mass Education and Rising Political Consciousness.   The emergence of the Islamist phenomenon has often been attributed to the failure of the development process in the Muslim world. Although this assessment is certainly true, in particular regarding the continued—and even widened—socioeconomic gap, it only partly explains the Islamist phenomenon. The rise of Islamism, in fact, owes as much to the success of the development experience as to its failures.

Especially important has been progress in the expansion of educational opportunities and the democratization of access to them. As a result, less privileged layers of society have found access to higher education—including study in Western countries through government grants—that before were closed to them. Many of those who benefited from these changes belonged to traditional classes that had retained their strong Islamic convictions. In Iran's case, many students who joined antiregime groups—and this includes the Islamic leftist theoretician, Ali Shari'ati—studied in Europe and America with government funds. In addition, although the democratization and the institutionalization of political life in most Muslim societies has not taken deep root, a process of mass politicization in the sense of bringing the masses "into the political process as participants on a more or less regular basis" has taken place.[60]

Regular elections, periodic referenda, and mass political rallies, even if orchestrated by the state, have become daily staples of political life. Irrespective of the character of the regime, popular will has been accepted as the source of legitimacy and sovereignty in all Muslim states, even if with the qualification that popular will does not contravene Islamic principles. Lay governments in Muslim states have used a variety of nationalist or socialist ideologies to bring the masses into their fight against traditional structures of power. The Islamist phenomenon—like other religiopolitical phenomena—is the consequence of the use of the techniques of mass mobilization by those who, for different reasons, are alienated from the existing structures through the intermediary of religion, which "by providing sacred symbols that acquire political significance" becomes the main agent of mass politicization.[61]

In short, the Islamist phenomenon is but one stage in the political modernization of Muslim countries. Therefore, Islamism is not a fixed and immutable phenomenon but, instead, a point of transition to something else to be determined by different societies' peculiarities. One observer, D. E. Smith, wrote, "Religion helps to produce mass mobilization and then declines politically as increasing numbers of participants come to perceive politics as a relatively autonomous area of human activity."[62]

This is taking place to some degree in Iran after 18 years of Islamic government. The inability of the government to meet the socioeconomic expectations of the people has undermined the credibility and appeal of its ideology based on religion. This gives greater weight to the argument that statecraft is and should be separate from religion. Popular disenchantment with the rule of religious leaders-*cum*-politicians has even generated some popular backlash against religion itself. This development has caused considerable anxiety among members of the traditional clergy about the erosion of the place of religion within Iran and has led them to argue that religious leaders should not be directly involved in politics and government. Eric Rouleau in a June 1995 article quoted Iranian cleric and professor of Islamic philosophy Hudjat-ul-Islam Muhsen Kadivar:

> 98 per cent of more than 80,000 clerics in Iran who are not
> involved in running the state are suffering because of the
> growing unpopularity of the clergy, which is held collectively
> responsible for the mistakes and violations of the few who
> wield power. . . . [63]

There has been a similar reassertion of Iranian nationalism and a revival of interest in Iran's pre-Islamic culture, even among some members of the leadership. The nationalist trend has not yet crystallized into a strong political movement to challenge the regime, but its reassertion illustrates the direct relationship between power and interest and culture and values and identity-related issues.[64] The rise during the Pahlavi regime of Islamist thinking, with its strong antinationalist connotations, was linked directly to the perception by many Iranians that nationalism served the regime and damaged their interests and eroded their power base. Thus they tried to counter it with Islam. Now a reverse process is under way; nationalism is being revived to counter Islamist ideas.

Even more important is the emergence of what can be described as a relativist theory of Islam, and of religion in general, opening up interesting possibilities for some sort of Islamic reformation. This phenomenon is not limited to Iran; in other Muslim countries, notably Egypt, there is a greater tendency to analyze Islam and the Islamic experience in a historical and spatial context. Even left-leaning Islamists such as Hassan Hanafi who in May 1979 wrote "Revolutionary Islam which has triumphed in Iran or is in the process of being born in the Islamic left, is the hope of the future . . . " now talks more about reinterpreting tradition to make it more of a factor of progress, and he has lost most of his enthusiasm for the Iranian revolution.[65]

In Asia, the present deputy prime minister and finance minister of Malaysia, Anwar Ibrahim, is a good example of an Islamist militant turned into Islamic reformer, one who now advocates a middle path, balancing Islamic values with requirements of the modern world.[66]

This methodology of analyzing Islam within historical and spatial contexts inevitably leads to the differentiation between the spiritual essence of Islam, which is divine and unchanging, and Islamic law, which is bounded by time and space and hence is relative and changeable. Because Iran has experimented with an Islamic system with very limited success, because Iranian intellectuals both lay and religious—for example, Ali Shari'ati and the Ayatullah Taleqani—played key roles in developing the conceptual foundations of the leftist version of revolutionary Islam, and because Iran has a long philosophical tradition from Zoroaster to Avicenna and Mulla Sadra Shirazi, the counterreaction and the trend toward innovation has been stronger than in other Muslim countries.

Abdul Karim Surush and the Theory of Islamic Relativism.   During the past several years, views expressed by Abdul Karim Surush have gained much influence and have attracted a considerable amount of attention, both in Iran and abroad. Despite his early enthusiasm for the Islamic revolution, Surush has become the most prominent exponent of Islamic reformation. His views have far-reaching implications for the prospect of Islamic reformation.

Abdul Karim Surush is a thinker well versed in Islamic and Western philosophies, having completed part of his studies in Great Britain as well as being imbued with a sense of Persian mysticism. He was an early supporter of the Islamic Revolution and served on the Council of the Cultural Revolution set up following the establishment of the Islamic Republic.

Surush's philosophy is based on the principle that religion has two aspects: the divine and metaphysical, which constitute its spiritual essence and esoteric dimension; and the exoteric or outward manifestations, which are formed by the characteristics of the different spatial and temporal contexts within which it operates. The divine aspect is constant and absolute, the exoteric is changing and thus relative. In his article "Shari'at va Jameeh-e-shenasi-e-Din" ("Shari'ati and the Sociology of Religion") published in the magazine *Kian*, which is the publication of those Islamic reformists in Iran who have emerged from within the Islamic revolution, Surush expressed his views on the historical and sociopolitical dimensions of religion. According to Surush:

> When the divine inspiration [religion] acquires a concrete and external existence it also acquires a history, it builds societies and civilizations and attracts different peoples to itself. In the history of this actualized religion many wars and peaces, agreements and disagreements, and deviations take place; various sects are created and leaders and clergy emerge . . . later misinterpretations take place. . . . Religion acquires the imprint of different ethnic, intellectual and philosophical trends. . . . The religious order interacts with other orders [and] thus becomes influenced by them and exerts influence over them. . . . *In short, religion becomes a human and earthly organization and like other organizations and orders it becomes an instrument for corrupt and self-serving interests* [emphasis added].[67]

Surush further boldly states that not all religious acts are triggered by religious motives. Referring to the mourning ceremo-

nies in Iran that commemorate the martyrdom of Hussain Ibn
Ali, he states that a group of mourners from, say, the village of
Muhammadabad embark on the mourning ritual "not only for the
sake of God, but also for the sake of Muhammadabad. In order to
assert their identity and triumph over their rivals . . . "[68]
In another part of this important article, Surush states, "The external actualization of a phenomenon is not always at the service
of its essence. Rather, at times it betrays the essence, therefore, it
is the duty of sociologist to demonstrate this betrayal. . . . "[69]

If the outward manifestations of religion are determined by
their spatial and temporal contexts, it naturally follows that they
are representative only of relative, not absolute, truth. Surush
draws the further conclusion that in this form religion must be
subject to the same methods of scientific analysis as applied in
the case of any other political and social philosophy, and not solely
the traditional methods of religious inquiry practiced in religious
seminaries. Surush also argues that anyone with sufficient knowledge and mastery of the methods of scientific inquiry can engage in
this endeavor. Therefore no single interpretation of the religious
phenomenon is valid, and no single individual or particular group
has access to the one true and valid interpretation.

Surush, further relativizing religious interpretations, argues
that such interpretations are conditioned by the interpreter's personal background, socioeconomic condition, and political prefer-
ence.[70] Thus Surush argues that clergy who make their living out
of religion are uniquely disqualified to interpret religious rules
because they will interpret the rules to serve their own parochial
interests.[71] Surush maintains that religion does not offer a plan for
government, and any efforts to derive such a plan are fruitless.
In addition, dealing with social, economic, and political affairs
requires special expertise and therefore must be entrusted to
skilled professionals who are well versed in the modern social
sciences of economics, sociology, and public administration.
Surush states that religion cannot explain these dynamics or deal
with questions raised and problems created by them: there can
be no religious thermodynamics and, by the same token, there
can be no religious politics and economics.[72]

Surush does not prescribe a simple and total separation of
religion and politics. Instead, believing that the politics of each
society reflects—or should reflect—the beliefs of its members, he
argues that in a religious society politics takes a religious form

and this religious form should be the result of a system based on public opinion and participation, in other words, democracy.[73] Surush also opposes the ideologization of religion because of the relationship of religious ideology—like secular ideologies—to power and the use of religion by the holders of power to reduce individual freedom and prevent rational inquiry about religion.[74] Surush believes that all human beings have rights that while compatible with religion are not defined by it.

Surush's theories carry far-reaching implications for the political life of Muslim societies and for the clerical establishment. For clerics, his theory that there is no single authentic interpretation and hence no single interpreter at any one time undermines the basis of the Muslim clergy's power as custodians of the true interpretation of Islam, much as the Protestant Reformation undermined the power of the pope and Rome. Also, some of Surush's Iranian disciples maintain that his theories open the way toward pluralism and the reconciliation of Islam and modernity.[75]

Surush, in his interpretation of Islam, emphasizes the Qur'anic injunction, "La Ikraha Fid Din" ("There is no compelling in faith") and maintains that individuals should choose freely to submit to Islam. To his followers, Surush's view, as well as his rejection of the ideologization of religion and his belief that the political system should reflect public opinion, results in political pluralism and democracy. Surush's conception also clearly disqualifies the clergy from active involvement in politics unless they have the required skills and expertise and are prepared to be subjected to public scrutiny of their performance and questioning of their motives the same as lay politicians.

An additional aspect of Surush's political philosophy bears directly on Islam-West relations: Surush believes firmly that intercultural dialogue is absolutely necessary for all forms of scientific, religious, and economic growth and development and that selective borrowing from Western culture, based on free choice, would benefit the growth and development of Iran and, presumably, that of other Muslim countries. He applies the same rules of selectivity and free choice to the application of the experience of modernity to Muslim societies.[76] In this regard, Surush's views are reminiscent of those of Sir Sayyid Ahmad Khan. This vision certainly does not see a clash of civilizations as inevitable.

It is important to note that Muhammad Khatemi, who was elected to Iran's presidency in mid-1997, also believes that in order to develop a vibrant and dynamic culture, Iranian and other Muslims need to interact with other civilizations, especially the West, and should utilize the positive scientific technological and social accomplishments of Western civilization.

The phenomenon of the new breed of Islamic reformists, notably Surush and his disciples, validates two points: (1) the study of Islam in an abstract and ahistorical manner, outside of specific socioeconomic and political environments, is not adequate to explain its present and future status and functions and its relations with other civilizations; and (2) religion, when it is used as an ideological and political tool to encourage mass mobilization, contributes to political modernization, including the eventual secularization of society, by enhancing the political consciousness of the masses and by subjecting religion to standards of scrutiny and judgment the same as other sociopolitical philosophies. Ideas such as those expressed by Surush plus a series of more liberal interpretations of Islamic principles in Iran (for example, those related to the arts) show that there is nothing in Islam that makes it less amenable to reformation than any other divinely inspired religion.[77]

External Causes of the Rise of the Islamist Phenomenon

It is clear that the rise of the Islamist phenomenon has been directly related to the process of socioeconomic change in Muslim countries. Although socioeconomic development of the various Muslim countries has a number of significant aspects in common, the experience of each country has also been unique, reflecting its particular conditions and characteristics. This explains both the common traits of the Islamist movement and the sharp differences.

External developments, events outside the confines of individual countries, have also deeply affected the course of the development and evolution of the Islamist phenomenon. Some were mentioned earlier: the shock of the first encounter with the military might of the West and the long period of subjugation to colonial or semicolonial rule.

Indeed the impetus behind the first wave of Islamic activism in the last two centuries, reflected in Afghani's activities, was the desire to rid the Muslim world of foreign domination. This motive has continued to be important, but in the last 70 years at least four other factors have played significant roles.

Important since the early days of the rise of an Islamist movement—especially since the creation of the Muslim Brotherhood—have been the Palestinian crisis and the Arab-Israeli conflict. They, in particular, radicalized these Islamic movements. Analysts observe that the Arab-Israeli conflict, which culminated in the Arab general strike of 1936—1939, played a crucial role in transforming the Muslim Brotherhood from a "youth club into a potent political force" and led the brothers to define their ideology in a way "which stressed the ability of Islam to become a total ideology."[78] The 1947 partition of Palestine and the creation of the state of Israel further radicalized the movement and, finally, led to its dissolution in 1948.

The creation of a state, Israel, based principally on religion was of greatest importance because it seemed to make the establishment of an Islamic state in the Muslim lands not only logical but necessary. Muhammad Ghazzali, a Muslim Brother, wrote in 1948 that the Israelis—unlike the Arabs who call their countries after the names of ruling families, such as Saudi Arabia or the Hashemite Kingdom of Jordan—called their country Israel, "which is the symbol of their attachment to their religion and reminiscences, and of their respect for their sacred values." Ghazzali added that despite their many accomplishments and their wealth the Jews "have felt no shame in ascribing themselves to their religion, and have not thought of shirking their responsibilities."[79]

The 1967 Arab-Israeli War and the fall of Jerusalem into Israeli hands had an impact on the development and radicalization of the Islamist movement that was perhaps greater than that of earlier events. This shattering defeat seemed to indicate that more than a century of modernization, Westernization, and relative de-Islamization had done nothing to restore the unfavorable balance of power between the West and the Islamic world. Rather, it had led to a widening power gap and greater foreign encroachment.

This seemed to say to Arabs that Arabism without Islam was an empty vessel, a body without a soul. For some, their defeat appeared as their divine punishment for straying from the path of Islam:

Why did God allow the Christians to rule over the house of Islam? Why did God allow the Jews to take Palestine and holy Jerusalem? Why does God allow the Christians to live like sultans in our land while we are like slaves in their land? This is God's punishment and this is God's test. Muslims have left the path of Islam. . . . [80]

In Iran, meanwhile, the Anglo-American coup d'etat against the nationalist government of Muhammad Mussadeq, the expansion of the American presence in Iran (by 1978 there were 60,000 Americans living in Iran), and the grant by the Iranian government of extraterritorial rights to American military personnel in Iran contributed to the growth of Islamism.

The second development of importance was the oil revolution of the 1970s and the ensuing oil wealth. Some analysts argue that oil wealth contributed to the rise of the Islamist phenomenon by enhancing Muslim self-confidence; however, the impact of any increased self-confidence was fairly limited if not marginal although it might have contributed to the emergence of Islamism. The oil revolution affected the Islamist phenomenon in other ways. First was the active use by Saudi Arabia of its oil money to propagate its brand of Islam—Wahhabism—as an instrument of its foreign policy. This Saudi activism, from Turkey to sub-Saharan Africa to the Indian subcontinent, contributed to an overall Islamization of society through Saudi-financed schools, mosques, charitable organizations, and even Islamic banks, which provided fertile ground for the growth and maturation of militant Islamist tendencies. The oil boom also widened the socioeconomic gap, both within the individual Arab states and among them, and it led to extensive corruption and unreasonable enrichment of the ruling elites. These developments contributed to the rise of the Islamist phenomenon. This was true even in Saudi Arabia although the *Shari'a* is applied strictly there and the ruling dynasty bases its legitimacy on Islam.

The Afghan War, which ended in Soviet defeat and withdrawal from Afghanistan, also played a significant role in the rise of Islamism. The victory of the Western-supported Muslim Afghan mujaheddin over the Soviet army seemed to point to the importance of Islam as a weapon of resistance and victory. If the Arab defeat by Israel in 1967 was the sign of God's wrath toward the Muslims because they had left the path of Islam, then the Soviet defeat must have been the sign of God's renewed mercy because Muslims had rediscovered the straight path—*Sarat-ul-Mustaqim*—of Islam. In addition to the symbolic significance of Afghanistan, the country served as a ground for military training and Islamic indoctrination for large numbers of youth from the Arab and Islamic Worlds, who then disseminated what they had learned among their own peoples. Many Algerian, Egyptian, and Saudi Muslim militants are veterans of the Afghan War and graduates of the Afghanistan training ground.

The fourth factor was the Iranian revolution, although expert opinion is divided over its impact on the growth of the Islamist phenomenon.[81] The Iranian revolution's intellectual and ideological impact on other Islamist movements has been limited.[82] However, the Iranian Islamists' success in bringing down the shah's regime strengthened the belief that a return to Islam would enable Muslims to alter their internal and external conditions and to reverse the long-established pattern of internal oppression and foreign domination. Furthermore, to prevent other Iranian-like revolutions, many Muslim governments tried to co-opt Islamist forces by encouraging greater Islamization of their societies, a policy that contributed to the rise of Islamist movements.

Since 1988, however, the example of Iran has had a dampening effect on the Islamist movement both inside Iran and abroad. The watershed was the humiliating cease-fire that Iran was forced to sign in August 1988 following a more direct American intervention in the Persian Gulf, which included the shooting down of an Iranian passenger airplane. As one Iranian university professor put it, the signing of the cease-fire implied that "God had not triumphed over Satan (Saddam Hussain). . . . "[83] If the Arab defeat of 1967 had illustrated the inefficacy of Arab nationalism as an instrument of redressing wrongs done to Arabs, Iran's relative defeat punctured the new-found Muslim confidence about Islam's potency as a means of overcoming internal and external enemies.

During the 1990s the Persian Gulf War of 1990–1991, the Arab-Western response to Iraq's invasion of Kuwait, and the events in the former Yugoslavia—where the West watched while the Serbs pursued a policy of ethnic cleansing against the Bosnian Muslims—also contributed to the strengthening of Islamist tendencies and the radicalization of some Islamist movements.

Roots of the Islamist Phenomenon's
Anti-Western Dimensions

The West would not have been concerned about the Islamist phenomenon had it not been for the movement's anti-Western views and vocation. In other words, ideological or civilizational incompatibility does not explain the West's concerns. Indeed, if civilizational incompatibility was the West's main preoccupation, the United States and its European allies could not have supported undemocratic and strictly Islamic states—in a cultural and judicial sense—such as Saudi Arabia or Sudan during the last years of Ja'afar Numeiry's rule. Indeed, as one observer has noted, "The greatest hypocrisy in the debate over political Islam is the fact that Americans have fought a war and committed their military and diplomatic power to secure the survival of the most fundamentalist state of all—Saudi Arabia. . . . "[84] Instead, the West's concern derives quite naturally from the fact that Islamists harbor hostile sentiments toward the West and, most particularly, toward the United States—albeit to varying degrees by different groups. This implies that if the Islamists did not have anti-Western sentiments, if they were responsive to Western interests, and if they were willing to accept the West's global preeminence, the West would have been most unlikely to have considered coexistence, and even amicable relations, either impossible or reprehensible despite its abhorrence of certain aspects of Islamists' ideological and civilizational beliefs.

Any judgment on the inevitability or preventability of a civilizational clash between Islam and the West therefore depends on identifying the real causes of the Islamists' anti-Westernism. If it is to be ascribed to Islam's inherent characteristics or to historically rooted animosities, the chances of an Islam-West clash become strong and averting it difficult. But if anti-Westernism is ascribed to more worldly reasons, including certain Western policies, reconciliation and coexistence become more likely although by no means certain.

Western opinion on the causes of the Islamists' anti-Westernism is also divided as between the Neo-Orientalist and Neo-Third Worldist schools described in chapter 2. The Neo-Orientalists see the roots of the Islamists' anti-Westernism in addition to a fundamental civilizational incompatibility in the feelings of humiliation, fear, and envy that the Muslims harbor toward the West. Bernard Lewis maintains that the Islamists' anti-Westernism is in part "due to a feeling of humiliation—a growing awareness among the heirs of an old, proud and long dominant civilization, of having been overtaken, overborne and overwhelmed by those whom they regarded as their inferiors. . . . "[85] Lewis and Daniel Pipes believe the Islamists fear Western culture because of its attractiveness or, as Lewis has put it, its "seductive allure." According to Daniel Pipes, "The more attractive an alien culture, the more fundamentalist Muslims fear it and fight it. A leading Iranian Mullah declared that the main objective of the Islamic revolution is to 'root out' American culture from Muslim countries. He probably never thought of Soviet culture as a comparable threat. . . . "[86]

There are elements of truth in these views. The humiliation factor, in particular, as a consequence of military defeats, colonization, and economic exploitation is certainly a major contributor to the anti-Western dimension of the Islamists' views. In 1988, Iran's then president Ayatullah Khamenei, its spiritual leader at the time of this writing, said to the visiting German foreign minister that Iran's rejection of both the West and the East and its choice of Islam and independence was because of historic insults suffered by Iran during the past 150 years. This statement illustrated how a sense of national humiliation had contributed to the Islamists' anti-Westernism.[87] The envy factor and the attractiveness of Western culture are also important contributors; in fact, many in the Muslim world who have turned against the West have done so because they cannot have access to it and to the benefits that flow from it.

Yet there is a real question: Do these feelings explain the whole phenomenon? And are they only applicable in the case of the Muslims? The answer to both questions is "no." The impact of the so-called seductive lure of the West has been somewhat overplayed. On the contrary, Muslim disenchantment with Western culture has contributed to the Islamist phenomenon. Many of the Islamist leaders and theorists were educated in the West where they found several aspects of Western culture unattractive, a fact that led them to return to Islam. John L. Esposito has written:

In 1949, Sayyid Qutb [the Egyptian Islamist] traveled to the United States to study educational organization. This experience proved to be a turning point in his life. After this visit, he became a severe critic of the West, and shortly after his return to Egypt he joined the Muslim Brotherhood. Although he came to the United States out of admiration, Qutb experienced a strong dose of culture shock which drove him to become more religiously observant and convinced him of the moral decadence of Western civilization.[88]

From the late 1960s to the 1990s, the West's attractiveness as a moral and spiritual model for the Muslims has further declined. The spread of AIDS, the increasing numbers of illegitimate children, and the erosion of family and community coupled with frequent expressions of anxiety by Westerners themselves about the West's loss of a moral and spiritual compass have been partly responsible for this loss of allure. Nor is the fear of cultural contamination limited to the Islamists or even the Muslims. Many secular Muslims who have a keen appreciation for the better aspects of Western civilization—especially its political institutions, its economic dynamism, and its scientific achievements—do not favor the dissolution of their indigenous culture and its replacement by a poor imitation of the worst aspects of Western popular culture. Even individual Western countries are concerned about the maintenance of their cultural authenticity. The French are preoccupied with Anglo-Saxon, especially American, cultural inroads, and they have gone as far as taking legislative measures to protect the French language. French nationalists bemoan globalization, which they equate with Americanization.[89] Even the Canadians are concerned about American cultural influences.

The Muslims are not alone in feeling envy and resentment toward their rivals. Westerners are equally capable of these sentiments. For example, Japan's economic success in the 1980s generated considerable envy and resentment in the West, especially in America. That Japan might have found a better way of running its economy was painful for the West because this challenged the Western sense of cultural superiority. The prospect of China's emergence as a major power is also disconcerting to the West. The debate about whether Asia has anything to teach the West in terms of the management of economies and societies illustrates the difficulty many Westerners have in admitting that they may not always be the best in everything. During the 1970s many

Westerners were even envious of the oil exporting states and viewed them as vulgar nouveaux riches.

Other Western scholars, however, understand that the Islamists' anti-Western sentiments arise from several and more complex sources: the legacy of colonialism, Western domination of the international economic and political systems that discriminate against the weaker states, Western support for unrepresentative and repressive governments in Muslim countries that are subservient to the West, and the selective and discriminatory application of international rules and principles, including in cases of human rights abuses. For many Muslims, particularly Arabs, Western and especially U.S. support for Israel has been a major cause of their animosity to the West. The reason that most Islamists (except for Algerians who look toward their ex-colonial power, France) see the United States as their foremost enemy derives partly from the Israeli factor.

Much of the Islamist animosity toward the United States grows from America's assumption of leadership of the Western world in 1945 and its position as the only global superpower since 1992; with these privileges the United States has also inherited the burden of the West's historic guilt and has become the most intrusive power militarily, politically, economically, and culturally. The West's propensity to retain in power unpopular but subservient governments is a further source of the Islamists' anti-Westernism. Graham Fuller correctly writes, "A residue of considerable anti-Western sentiment will always remain in much of the Third World that still feel anger that colonialism of the past—as well as the present day Western-dominated international political order—often delivered a raw deal to developing countries. . . ."[90] One British diplomat has noted that the Islamists believe that their leadership "had invited the West and was dependent upon it for staying in power."[91] At times the West even has removed a legitimate government because it was not subservient enough. This was certainly the case in Iran when in 1953 an Anglo-American coup d'etat removed Muhammad Mussadeq, perhaps the most popular figure in Iran in modern times.

There is other evidence that civilizational incompatibility is not the principal source of animosity between Muslims and the West, notably the fact that some very strictly Islamic groups have been close collaborators of the West. According to Daniel Pipes,

"As for fundamentalists in power, they divide into two types, conservatives and radicals. The former usually seek good relations with the United States, and keeping the profound differences between their goals and those of the United States in mind, ties should be cultivated. . . . "[92] The West has in fact cultivated relations with conservative Muslims, whether in Saudi Arabia, Pakistan, or Afghanistan. During the Afghan civil war, the United States backed through Pakistan and Saudi Arabia the most extreme and orthodox Islamist group, the Taliban.[93]

Thus the principal, although not the only, cause of the Islamists' anti-Westernism is their resentment of Western domination and a feeling—right or wrong—of having been unfairly treated; hence, the Islamists desire to change the balance of power.

This, however, is not an exclusively Islamist phenomenon. From the 1950s through the 1970s, secular nationalists from Mussadeq in Iran and Arbenz in Guatemala to Nasser in Egypt and Boumedienne in Algeria preached a similar gospel. The West's concern over the Islamists, in turn, is neither their undemocratic nature nor their civilizational incompatibility but rather their temerity to question and challenge Western supremacy. In short, in Graham Fuller's words noted in the introduction, a civilizational clash if there is one "is not so much over Jesus Christ, Confucius, or the prophet Muhammad as it is over the unequal distribution of world power, wealth and influence."[94]

This discussion demonstrates that the emergence of the Islamist phenomenon has been very much part and parcel of the process of the unfolding of the Islamic experience in its various temporal and spatial contexts. As with other aspects of the Islamic experience, this phenomenon has been closely caught up with the social, economic, political, and cultural mutation and transformation of Muslim societies and with the dynamics of their encounter with the non-Muslim world and the forces and ideas emanating from it.

This discussion also illustrates that Islam—in its various interpretations—more often has been used as a tool to explain conditions and situations caused by other forces and as an instrument to deal with them than it has been the force that has triggered these conditions. In the process Islam itself has acquired new meanings and interpretations.

This chapter further shows that despite what is often assumed Islamic principles are flexible and subject to varying interpretations, including both liberal and reformist. The discussion also leads to the conclusion that the rise of the Islamist phenomenon is simply another stage in the development of Muslim societies and will certainly be followed by other sociopolitical and cultural movements. The recent developments in Iran and new thinking among certain Muslim intellectuals in other Islamic countries indicate that the next stage may, indeed, be a greater secularization of Muslim societies and a move toward a synthesis of Islamic precepts and Western concepts.

This chapter illustrates that specific Western policies coupled with the overall disequilibrium in power relationships between the West and the Islamic world are more responsible for the anti-Western dimensions of the Islamists' thinking and behavior than is mere civilizational incompatibility.

3

The Role of Islam in Shaping Foreign Policy: Case Studies of Iran and Saudi Arabia

Chapter 1 demonstrated that the international relations of Muslim states have been determined historically not by Islam but mostly by other dynamics and determinants of state behavior—security, economic needs, ruling-elite interests, and the search for prestige and influence. Commitment to Islam has not been a bond sufficiently strong to allow Muslims to form a united front against the outside world; thus Islam has not prevented conflicts that pit Muslim states against each other. Nor has Islam proved to be an unsurmountable barrier to cooperation between Muslims and non-Muslims. Quite the contrary; the history of the Muslims has been one of internecine conflict, inability to unite even in the face of common enemies, and cooperation with non-Muslims against fellow Muslims.

Two case studies—Iran and Saudi Arabia—demonstrate in more detail the interaction of Islam with other determinants of foreign policy; these studies assess the relative role of Islam in shaping the character of these countries' external behavior. This permits some assessment of the future role of Islam in the external relations of Muslim countries and, most important, the impact of Islam on the character of Muslim governments' relations with the West and whether these relations will be primarily conflictual or cooperative.

Modern Iran

Iran is unique among the Muslim countries because it had 1,500 years of continuous pre-Islamic history as a nation, a country

116

(notwithstanding the conquest by Alexander), and an advanced civilization. Pre-Islamic Iranian civilization included an elaborate philosophical, religious, and ethical system; a sophisticated view of the world; and an elaborate theory of the cosmos, the creation, and the place and destiny of mankind within this cosmic system. Indeed, Iranian-Zoroastrian views and concepts deeply affected Judaism and Christianity and, through them, Islam.

After the conquest by Arab-Islamic armies, Iran was able to escape linguistic and cultural Arabization, and despite the spread of Islam many of its pre-Islamic traditions retained their influence among the people and on the intellectual pursuits of Iranian Muslims. As a consequence, Iran maintained considerable cultural cohesion, and a sense of Iranianness remained strong and affected Iran's post-Islamic cultural and political evolution despite its territorial and political fragmentation. Both the post-Islamic Iranian cultural and political renaissance in the ninth and tenth centuries and the development of what Arnold Toynbee has called the Iranic-Islamic civilization have been direct results of the resilience and tenacity of Iran's pre-Islamic civilization and its sense of cultural distinctness.[1] Moreover, Iranian traditions were adopted by the Arab Muslims and later by the Turks; this has been characterized by some scholars as Iran's "conquest of Islam."[2]

The combination of Iran's Islamization and the survival of its pre-Islamic culture has created an inherent duality in Iran's culture and its sense of collective identity, with at times two rival poles of identification and loyalty: Iran and Islam. A measure of tension between these two poles has always existed. With the increased Shi'aization of Iran, a degree of convergence between Iranian nationalism and Shi'a Islam emerged and, to some degree, mitigated this duality and tension between Iran and Islam.

But this convergence was weakened in the nineteenth century because of emerging nationalism. In the twentieth century, the process of divergence between Islam and Iran accelerated with the rise of nationalism and efforts toward secularization. This dualistic nature of Iran's culture and collective self-identity has had important implications for the conduct of its foreign policy and, in particular, for the role of Islam in determining its content and direction. The fundamental changes that the Islamic revolution of 1979 produced in Iran's social and political life and foreign policy call for an assessment of Islam's role in determining the character and direction of modern Iran's foreign policy within the context of two distinct periods: before the Islamic revolution and after the creation of the Islamic Republic.

The Safavid Dynasty and the Restoration of Iran's Territorial and Political Unity

The territorial and political unity of Iran was shattered by the Arab invasion of A.D. 642, and until 1491 when Shah Ismail Safavi began to reunify the country various parts of Iran were ruled by different Iranian, Turkic, and Turko-Iranian dynasties. The Safavids not only unified Iran but they also restored most of its pre-Islamic borders, albeit in their more truncated state. They also imposed Shi'ism on the population and laid the foundation of a Shi'a religious establishment that over the years became quite independent from the government.[3]

Shi'ism had existed in Iran before the Safavids, particularly in the North. The powerful Buyid dynasty of the tenth century adhered to Twelver Shi'ism and introduced mourning ceremonies for the events of Karbala. Ismailis—Sevener Shi'as—also flourished in Iran.[4] But the massive Shi'aization of the country and the growing identification of Shi'ism with Iranianism occurred during the time of the Safavids.

The Shi'aization of Iran had important political consequences. On the one hand, common adherence to Shi'ism coupled with Iran's other historical and cultural traditions enhanced Iran's sense of national cohesion and helped consolidate the new state, which in turn helped Iran maintain its independence and prevented it from falling under Ottoman control as did many Muslim lands. On the other hand, Shi'aization restricted Iran's access to the predominantly Sunni Muslim world and thus severely limited its ability to expand its influence beyond its frontiers. The limiting impact of this factor, coupled with Iran's linguistic and cultural distinctiveness was, centuries later, felt clearly and strongly in Iran's efforts to export its Islamic revolution to other Muslim countries.

The proselytizing zeal of the Safavids, however, did not extend beyond Iran's borders, and the Safavids did not try to expand the Shi'a faith to the rest of the Islamic World. This reluctance stemmed in part from the existence of the countervailing Ottoman power, but it also derived from the dilution of religious zeal that came with political power. The Safavids thus did not make the propagation of Shi'ism a principal goal of their foreign policy, and ideological and value-related factors played little role in their external behavior. This tendency strengthened in the following decades as the Safavids grew more distant from their Shi'a-Sufi origins and increasingly conducted their foreign policy like secular political leaders.

Their proselytizing zeal subsided even internally although the attitudes of individual Safavid monarchs toward religious minorities was uneven. Some religious minorities fared better than others under the Safavids. They persecuted the Zoroastrians, leading to their large-scale migration to India in the seventeenth century. Large numbers of Christian Armenians who sought refuge from Ottoman persecution in Iran were treated quite well, however, and were allowed to build churches and practice their religion. In Isfahan, Shah Abbas, the Safavid monarch most benevolent toward the Christians, allocated the Armenians a whole district—Julfa. Shah Abbas also permitted various Christian monastic orders, such as the Capucines and the Benedictines, to build monasteries in Isfahan, the Safavid capital.

The fame of Shah Abbas's benevolence toward the Christians reached the European powers. The latter sought to form an alliance with him against the Ottoman Turks, by whom they felt threatened, and sent special envoys to his court. Although little came of these contacts and no Safavid-European alliance against the Turks materialized, the episode is instructive in terms of Islam's role in determining the foreign policy of a Muslim state.

In this particular case, it can be argued that the sectarian differences between Iran and Ottoman Turkey explain why Islamic solidarity did not play a role in Shah Abbas's policy toward Christian Europe and Muslim Turkey. This sectarian difference no doubt explains part of Iran's attitude, but the fact remains that the Sunnis and the Shi'as have had more in common with each other than with the adherents of other religions, and both have been part of the zone of Islamic civilization. Thus if civilizational factors are the most important determinants of behavior, Iran and Ottoman Turkey should have cooperated against the Christian Europeans. Yet this was not the case. Indeed, the history of Ottoman-Safavid relations bears witness to the limited impact of Islam in determining the character and the direction of the foreign policy of two Muslim states toward each other and toward other powers. Thus, instead of any Islamically motivated objectives, the principal goals of those Safavid kings who had sufficient force of character and statesmanship were to protect Iran's borders against foreign invasions, to dislodge those—like the Portuguese in the South—who had already encroached upon Iranian territory and interests, and in the tradition of the times to expand its dominions whenever possible.[5]

The fall of the Safavid dynasty in 1742 was triggered by what at first was a rebellion by the shah's Afghan subjects, resulting from the harsh treatment they had received from the Georgian governor of the shah's Afghan possessions, Gorgin Khan, but it then became a full-blown war. The end of the Safavids ushered in a long period of decline for Iran although Nadir Shah Afshar (1742–1747) attempted a minor revival and a last burst of national effort to restore Iran's historic borders and even expand them. Between the fall of the Safavid dynasty and the consolidation of Nadir's power, an interesting and instructive episode demonstrated the relationship between foreign policy and ideological-civilizational factors, that is, the role of Islam: the entente between Russia and Ottoman Turkey to divide Iran's northern provinces between them.[6] This was another case of a Muslim state cooperating with non-Muslims against a fellow Muslim state.

Nadir's death in 1747 while he was fighting the Lezghis in Dagestan ushered in another period of political instability in Iran. A fierce struggle for power ensued among Nadir's descendants ruling in parts of northeastern Iran, the Zand dynasty established by Karim Khan Zand in southern Iran, and the Qajar tribes until, in 1779, Agha Muhammad Khan Qajar subdued his rivals and established the Qajar dynasty, which lasted until 1925.[7]

The Qajar Dynasty and Foreign Penetration of Iran

Qajar rule coincided with the acceleration and intensification of European imperial expansion into the East, notably into the Muslim world. For Iran, most consequential were Russia's southward thrust to gain access to warm seas and Britain's efforts to protect its newly acquired—and most precious—colony, India, by controlling the land and sea approaches to it.

Russia's southern thrust caused two Russo-Iranian wars in 1804–1812 and 1824–1828. Even before this time, however, during the rule of Queen Anna, Russia had taken advantage of Iran's instability following the collapse of the Safavids and had tried to take over parts of Iran's Transcaucasian possessions and its northern provinces along the Caspian Sea. Hostilities also broke out between Russia and Iran during the time of Catherine the Great and Agha Muhammad Khan. The casus belli was the decision of Georgia's Christian ruler—a vassal of the Iranian kings—to seek Russian protection, followed by Agha Muhammad Khan's decision to bring Georgia back under Iranian control. Hostilities ceased following the deaths of Agha Muhammad Khan in 1789 and Catherine shortly thereafter. On its eastern and southern frontiers, meanwhile, Iran faced the encroaching power of Britain, which also led to the loss of Iranian territory.

Faced with pressures from two expanding imperial powers with strength vastly superior to Iran's, the principal goal of Iran's foreign policy from the early nineteenth century until the late 1960s was the maintenance of its territorial integrity and at least a minimum degree of independence. From the mid-nineteenth century onward, enlisting foreign support for Iran's reform and development efforts also became important to its foreign policy. Achieving these goals at times meant cooperating with one of the competing powers to balance the influence of the other. Sometimes the price of this cooperation was a promise to act against a fellow Muslim state should the need arise. For example, in an 1819 treaty of friendship between the British government and Iran during the reign of Fathalishah Qajar, Iran committed itself to fight against Muslim Afghanistan in the event of a British-Afghan conflict.

Once again Iran and Afghanistan's common adherence to Islam did not prove a hindrance to either Anglo-Iranian cooperation or Iran's commitment to act against a fellow Muslim country. Together with the Russo-Ottoman agreement to divide Iran's northern provinces, this treaty of friendship illustrates that when state interests have required it, Muslims have been willing to enter into alliances with non-Muslim countries. Indeed, as James Piscatori has pointed out, for at least two centuries relations with the non-Muslim powers have come to be actively sought because of "the advantage that they would give in inter-Muslim relations."[8]

The foregoing illustrates that at important moments of Iran's history, security and economic motives not civilizational-ideological considerations determined Iranian policy. Thus Islam played little role in shaping Iran's foreign policy throughout the Qajar period, with one important exception—the second round of Russo-Iranian Wars. In 1824, Iran initiated hostilities largely because of agitation by the Shi'a *Ulema*, who were responding to complaints by the Shi'a population of the Transcaucasus of mistreatment by the Russians. Although the growing penetration of Muslim lands by foreign powers did not change the situation, it did kindle ideas of intra-Muslim cooperation to arrest and reverse the process of foreign domination. Seyyed Jamal ed Din Afghani (see chapter 2) was the strongest spirit behind this trend, but pan-Islamism never won a large following in Iran although some writers such as the Qajar Prince, Abul Hassan Mirza (known as Shaikh ul-Rais), argued in its favor.[9]

The Iranians' sense of their cultural uniqueness coupled with their devotion to Shi'ism were important factors in their lack of receptivity to pan-Islamist ideas. Furthermore, from the latter part of the nineteenth century through 1918, pan-Islamism was used to expand the power and influence of the Ottoman sultan and, consequently, was viewed with suspicion by other Muslim states. As a result, in 1896, when the sultan sent his minister of education, Munif Pasha, to the Qajar court to pave the way for an intra-Muslim rapprochement, nothing much came of these efforts.[10]

Because of the start of a more sustained process of reform in Iran by the mid-nineteenth century, which led to a slow trend toward secularization and the rise of Persian nationalism, Islam's influence as a determinant of Iran's external behavior declined further during the following decades.

The Pahlavi Dynasty and Iranian Foreign Policy

In 1925, Riza Shah's assumption of the throne of Iran ended the rule of the Qajar dynasty and began that of the Pahlavis. The rule of Riza Shah was dominated by two preoccupations: consolidation of the central government's power through the subduing of various tribal warlords and chieftains, and the initiation of Iranian cultural revival and socioeconomic modernization. It is important that this socioeconomic modernization included the secularization of the Iranian educational and judicial systems and the granting to women of certain freedoms, including abolition of the practice of veiling. All these measures tended to erode the role of

Islam in Iranian society and the social and political power of the clergy. At the cultural level, the revival of Iran's pre-Islamic traditions and the promotion of the pre-Islamic symbols of identity undermined the role of Islam—in its Shi'a version—as a component of the Iranians' individual and collective self identity.

Iran's principal foreign-policy preoccupations remained maintaining its territorial integrity, pacifying its frontiers, and achieving a modicum of independence and freedom of action. Riza Shah tried to achieve these goals by pursuing a diplomatic strategy based on the principle of balancing the presence of the great powers, especially Britain and the Soviet Union—which had assumed the traditional role of imperial Russia—by cultivating other powers, especially Germany. This came to be known as the Third Force strategy.[11] Riza Shah also tried to enlist the help of Germany in Iran's economic development. As a result, the Germans agreed to help Iran set up a steel mill, something the British had strenuously tried to prevent. However, because most of the Muslim World was still in one form or another under colonial rule, the scope for intra-Muslim relations was rather limited. As a consequence, the Islamic factor played almost no role in Iran's foreign policy during Riza Shah's era.

During Riza Shah's reign Iran experienced considerable socioeconomic development and saw the foundations of the political and military structures of modern Iran laid. Progress in political institution building and the development of a modern civil society remained very limited, however, because of Riza Shah's authoritarian tendencies and Iran's great problems of internal instability, which required giving priority to establishing law and order and strengthening the role of the state.

Riza Shah's modernizing policies created inevitable contradictions and fissures within Iranian society. In particular, his policies caused the gap to widen between the secular nationalists and the loyalists to Islamic traditions. The far-reaching consequences of this division would be felt a full half century later during the Islamic revolution. For nearly another four decades, however, the secular nationalist trend dominated Iran's politics and policies, both internally and externally.

Muhammad Riza Shah: Acceleration of Modernization and Widening of Societal Divide.   Riza Shah's reign ended abruptly in 1941 as a result of the dynamics set in motion by the start of World

War II. When the war began in 1939, the Iranian government declared its neutrality as it had during World War I. Because of Iran's geostrategic situation, the allied powers did not respect its neutrality; and, using the pretext of German presence in the country, they occupied Iran in 1941. Riza Shah was deposed and sent into exile in South Africa, and his young son assumed the throne. From 1941 to 1946, when Russian troops finally left Iran and the Soviet-created Democratic Republic of Azerbaijan was dismantled, Iran's greatest preoccupation was again the safeguarding of its territorial integrity, and all its efforts in foreign policy were focused on this central priority. Thus relations with the great powers, not with the Muslim states, were of the utmost importance to Iran.

From 1947 to 1953, after the departure of the occupation forces until Britain and the United States engineered a coup d'état to remove the nationalist government of Muhammad Mussadeq, Iran was caught in a nationalist fervor and a desire to end the intervention of foreign powers in its internal affairs. Iran's desire to gain control over its economic and political destiny led to Mussadeq's decision to nationalize the Anglo-Persian Oil Company and expel British officers from the country, a decision that ultimately resulted in his own ouster.

Mussadeq's theory of negative equilibrium—in fact, the forerunner of the NAM—outlined a way for Iran to cope with its geostrategic predicament and dependent situation within the international political system. Its essence was the denial of any special advantages to any major power. At this time, some religious figures such as Ayatullah Abulqassem Kashani who were active in politics suggested that the Islamic countries should form a united front to serve as the Third Force between East and West.[12] In the age of nationalism, however, his ideas had little impact either in Iran or in other Muslim countries. Nor, because of their politically and economically dependent state, would the Muslim countries have been capable of achieving unity, even if other conditions had been propitious.

The Islamic factor had a very limited effect on Iran's foreign policy during this period. It did have a determining role on one occasion: During the passage of the United Nations resolution on the division of Palestine and the creation of the state of Israel in 1948, Iran, mindful of the sensitivity of Islamic sentiment on this issue, voted against the partition of Palestine. Later Islamic sentiment contributed to Iran's refusal to establish full diplomatic relations with Israel although it maintained very close, but clandestine, ties with the Jewish state.

Despite some changes and fluctuations, Iran's foreign policy from 1954 to 1971 was essentially driven by two fundamental concerns: the need to cope with the security threat posed by the Soviet Union and its regional allies; and, partly deriving from that security threat, the need to protect its strategic alliance with the United States. Islam entered very little into the foreign policy calculations of the Iranian government, except as a potential weapon to combat the ideological and security threat of socialism and its local variants, especially Arab socialism. In other words, ideology was to be put at the service of achieving security. Thus Islam was used as an ideological cover and a unifying theme to cement cooperation among the pro-Western governments of Iran, Saudi Arabia, and Tunisia when they formed the coalition that later became the Organization of the Islamic Conference (OIC).

Beyond Iran's two fundamental security-related objectives, the themes of independence and Third Worldism helped to determine the nature of its foreign policy. Iran wanted to change the international political and economic system to improve, within the system, the economic and political position of the developing countries, including itself, thus giving them a greater role in shaping the international rules of economic and political conduct that affected their destinies. As a result, Iran joined the Organization of Petroleum Exporting Countries (OPEC), was active during the 1960s in the decolonization committee of the UN, and it spoke in favor of improving the terms of trade of the developing states.

The other factor that influenced the direction and content of Iran's foreign policy was a desire to improve the margin of its independence, albeit within the limits permitted by Iran's dependent status within the international system and its alliance with the United States.[13] There was also a domestic dimension behind this desire for a more independent foreign policy. The deep-rooted nationalist feelings in the country, the overdependence of the Iranian regime on the United States, and Iran's perceived subservience to American interests were becoming a domestic liability and were beginning to undermine the regime's legitimacy. This led the shah to proclaim his so-called national independent foreign policy (*Siasat-e-Mustaqil-e-Milli*) to try to dispel these perceptions.

After tacit cooperation with the religious establishment throughout the 1950s, the shah and the ruling Iranian elite from 1962 onward accelerated the secularization of Iranian society and government, increasingly resorting to pre-Islamic Iranian traditions as the basis of the regime's legitimacy and the justification for their policies. Even in his foreign policy the shah at times resorted to pan-Aryan themes rather than to themes of the common bonds of Islam: he sought to explain his efforts to forge closer ties between Iran and India, Pakistan, and Afghanistan and help the latter countries resolve their differences and develop closer relations among themselves in terms of Aryan brotherhood. He told the Indian journalist R. K. Karanjia that his goal in expanding Iran's relations with India and Pakistan was to bring about "a renascent Aryan brotherhood . . . to hold high the torch of a glorious, humanitarian, and moralistic civilization."[14]

The shah's use of pan-Aryan symbols, the growing rivalry between Iran and Saudi Arabia for influence in the Middle East and South Asia, and Saudi Arabia's use of Islam as an instrument of its foreign policy caused Iran to increase its distance from the OIC while Saudi Arabia's role grew more dominant.

Between 1973 and 1978, the oil revolution and the dynamics it set in motion caused Iran's foreign policy to acquire both a more independent streak and a more Third-Worldist tone. Thus the shah became a major voice in the North-South dialogue of the 1970s and a major supporter of a fundamental reform of the international system and the creation of a new international economic order (NIEO), while the Islamic factor became less and less significant as a determinant of the direction of Iran's foreign policy and as an instrument for rationalizing and legitimizing it.

In sum, the role of Islam was negligible in determining the foreign policy of Iran from its reunification at the beginning of the sixteenth century until the Islamic Revolution in 1979.

Islam and the Foreign Policy of the Islamic Republic of Iran

The Islamic revolution, or more exactly, a broader-based revolution that increasingly acquired an Islamic flavor, occurred because a variety of forces with divergent socioeconomic and political ideologies came together. Included were diverse elements such as the Communist Tudeh Party, the Islamo-socialist *Mujaheddin-e-*

Khalq, the Marxist *Fidaeian-e-Khalq*, the Islamo-nationalists such as Abol-Hassan Bani-Sadr and Mehdi Bazargan, and liberal nationalists in the tradition of Mussadeq such as Karim Sanjabi. Each group had specific and divergent views, about both the internal organization of Iran's socioeconomic and political system and the direction of its foreign policy. Thus the Islamo-nationalist Mehdi Bazargan wanted to pursue a variant of Mussadeq's strategy of negative equilibrium by establishing balanced relations with both superpowers and a greater measure of independence from the United States. He also wanted Iran to acquire a more nonaligned posture on regional and other international issues, again in conformity with a longstanding tendency within the Iranian population. But at no time did he envisage a full-scale confrontation with the United States or an activist policy of promoting revolutionary change in the region.[15] Even figures such as Bani-Sadr and Sadeq Qutbzadeh, who competed with Bazargan and with each other for the highest political office, did not foresee total estrangement from the West or even from the United States.

Leftist groups, meanwhile, favored a closer relationship with the Soviet Union. Even religious forces were divided along several lines. The first division was between the supporters of the Ayatullah Ruhollah Khomeini and the supporters of the more traditional clergy, for example, Ayatullah Kazim Shariatmadari. The basic distinction between the groups was that supporters of the traditional clergy did not envisage a direct political role for the clergy in actual government operations. Nor did members of this group depart from the traditional Shi'a view on politics and government; they continued to view the role of the religious establishment as supervisory, more or less along the lines of the 1906 constitution. They wanted to ensure that secular legislation was compatible with Islamic legal and ethical rules and, in general, promote an Islamic moral code of conduct in society. This group favored a free market economy, and they certainly opposed socialist tendencies.

Even the followers of Ayatullah Khomeini were divided into a hard-line and a pragmatic faction. Considerable philosophical differences on both domestic issues and foreign policy existed between the two groups; many still exist and continue to affect Iran's internal developments and foreign policy. In broad terms, the hard-liners had a more socialist interpretation of Islam and favored an essentially state-controlled economic system, massive nationalizations, and the development of a more egalitarian society. The pragmatists favored a greater role for the private sector and a less rigid social code.

In foreign policy, the hard-liners were viscerally anti-Western—especially anti-American. They also favored the export of the revolution, advocated the establishment of close ties with other non-Muslim revolutionary governments and movements, and supported a foreign policy based on a so-called people-to-people strategy. The hard-liners, however, were not averse to cooperation with the Soviet Union despite the fact that Soviets subscribed to the atheistic creed of scientific materialism. Indeed, between 1979 and 1982, there was tacit cooperation between the hard-liners and the Iranian Communist Party, the Tudeh. For example, the Tudeh Party supported the taking of the American hostages in November 1979 because, as the secretary general of the party, Nureddin Kianuri, told Eric Rouleau, "As long as the hostages are in Iran, normalization of relations with the United States . . . will not be possible."[16]

The pro-Soviet sympathy of some of the Islamic hard-liners and their socialist leanings were so considerable that the Iranian foreign minister, Ali-Akbar Velayati, accused them of being "leftists with an Islamic veneer,"[17] which indicates that the Islamic hard-liners' anti-Westernism had to do more with militant Third-Worldism and the influence of leftist ideas than with Islam. The pragmatists, by contrast, favored a less confrontational foreign policy at both the regional and international levels.

It is not surprising that the ideological differences among various supporters of the revolution, coupled with individual personal power ambitions, led to fierce struggles for power among factions and individuals. These struggles and their outcomes affected greatly the conduct of Iran's foreign policy and, to some degree, they still do.

Because the Islamists ultimately triumphed over their liberal and leftist rivals, it is their view of the nature of the international political system, the dynamics of interstate relations, and the principles that should guide Iran's foreign policy that need to be discussed here. It is nevertheless important to determine the extent to which their views have been shaped by Islam and to what extent by other influences related to Iran's historical experience and to political and ideological trends prevalent throughout the Third World. Most important has been the process whereby these ideological views have been diluted by the influence of internal and external factors and by the reassertion of requirements of Iran's security and other needs and interests, thus leading to the adaptation of Iranian foreign policy to external realities, albeit not yet sufficiently.

Khomeini's World View.   Because all Iranian Islamist forces— pragmatist or hard-line—claim to draw their inspiration and guidance from Ayatullah Khomeini, his views on the nature of the international system and the dynamics of interstate relations need to be analyzed carefully.

• *A polarized vision.*   Khomeini's world view is polarized along several lines, the first of which is power. Khomeini believed the world is divided into two camps: those who have power and use it to exploit and dominate others—the arrogant powers or *Mustakberin*, and those who do not have power and hence are subjected to domination and exploitation—the downtrodden *Mustazefin*. Khomeini preached that the so-called oppressor camp consisted of the two superpowers and a few other great powers pitted against the camp of the downtrodden composed of the Muslim countries and the rest of the Third World. International organizations including the UN all belonged to the oppressors' camp because they were dominated by the arrogant powers and served as instruments for perpetuating their global economic and political dominance.

The second division is along ideological lines, between those who followed the East (the Soviet bloc) and those who followed the West (the United States and its allies). Khomeini was convinced that there were no truly independent countries except Islamic Iran because the NAM was merely a sham; in reality its members belonged to either the Western or the socialist camp.

The third division is according to what could be characterized as moral or spiritual criteria. Khomeini held that the world is divided into those who follow the right path, the path of God and belief, and those who follow the corrupt path of Satan and disbelief.[18] The right path, in Khomeini's vision, is that of Islam and the *Qur'an*. The corrupt path is that of the arrogant powers and those whom the Ayatullah considered their lackeys.

Khomeini's perception of the international system was certainly and importantly influenced by the traditional Islamic division of the world into *Dar-ul-Islam* and *Dar-ul-Harb*, although this does not represent the totality of the traditional Islamic world view. It is important, however, not to underestimate the impact on Khomeini and his disciples of other non-Islamic and purely Iranian traditions, Iran's recent experiences with the great powers, and ideas prevalent in the Third World. The dualism of Khomeini's vision also partly reflects the dualistic pre-Islamic Iranian view of the entire world, creation, and the cosmic order, based on the principle of an existential battle between the forces of light and darkness, good and evil. His view also reflects the essential bipolarity of the post-World War II international political system that was divided between the Western and the socialist camps.

Iran's experience with the great powers since the beginning of the nineteenth century also contributed to the development of this polarized vision of a world divided into the powerful and the meek, illustrated in the aforementioned comment by then Iranian president Ali-Akbar Khamenei to the visiting West German foreign minister. Khamenei explained that the insults suffered by Iran in the last 150 years at the hands of the great powers had led the Iranian people to welcome slogans of independence and the philosophy of "neither East nor West."

Khomeini and the hard-line group of his disciples, however, were more hostile to the West than to the East. For 50 years the West had been the dominant foreign power in Iran and was identified with the Pahlavi regime, whose policies were seen as detrimental to both the role and the place of Islam in Iranian society and damaging to the parochial interests of the clerical establishment. The West's identification with Israel contributed also to the Islamists' greater hostility toward the West as compared with the Soviet Union although, from a religious and civilizational point of view, the agnostic West was less an enemy of Islam than the atheistic Soviet Union.

These factors also explain why many lay intellectuals in Iran have had a similar vision of the international political system and the principal dynamics of interstate relations. Jalal Al-Ahmad, author of *Garb Zadeghi* (*Westoxication*), wrote that the world is divided into two sets of countries, those that have mastered the machine (his metaphor for technology) and those that have not. For Al-Ahmad, this divide determines the essence of relationships between the two groups, the latter's dependency on the former. He argued that the advanced countries try to maintain this state of dependency to ensure their own continued supremacy. Al-Ahmad viewed international organizations as new tools to perpetuate what are essentially colonial relationships between the great powers and the less powerful countries; he wrote that the great powers do not wear the colonial hat anymore and do not represent themselves as *Sahib* and *Memsahib*; rather they come as advisers or "representatives of UNESCO."[19]

Many non-Muslim intellectuals shared Al-Ahmad's views from the 1950s to the 1980s, and his views still have some adherents. Similar ways of thinking were at the root of efforts by Third World countries to change the character of the international economic system to make it more responsive to the needs and concerns of the developing countries.

Ayatullah Khomeini's belief that international law and international organizations are mere instruments at the service of the great powers also is not purely Islamic or even Iranian. It has long been shared by most Third World intellectuals. A representative Third World view of the international system, with some affinities with those expressed by Khomeini, was expounded by the Guatemalan leader Juan Jose Arevalo. His work focused on the relationship between the United States and Latin America and on the legal and political foundation of the inter-American system. Yet many of his ideas also apply to the global order. In his book *The Shark and the Sardines*, wherein the shark represents the great powers and the sardines the weak states, Arevalo referred to "the imperial origins" of law and law's allegiance to the shark: "The shark smiled, because at this moment he discovered the deepest secret of law—its imperial origin . . . its Mephistophelian function, *its allegiance to the sharks* [emphasis added]."[20]

Khomeini also professed great suspicion of the post-Westphalian territorial nation-state in general and, even more, its impact on the unity of the Muslim world. He considered the spread of nationalist ideas into the Muslim world and the breakup of the Ottoman Empire to have been conspiracies by the European powers to weaken the Muslim world and thus facilitate domination according to the maxim of "divide and rule."

Yet there is nothing in Khomeini's writings or speeches that sanctions the elimination of the existing nation-states in the Islamic world and the creation of a single Muslim community. On the contrary, Khomeini recognized the reality of the territorial state and the attachment of peoples to their homelands, and he indicated clearly that he did not oppose nationalism if it meant the love of one's country and the desire to defend its borders. He opposed nationalism only if it became a source of discord among the Muslims and thus diluted their sense of unity.[21] Thus at no point did he advocate the creation of a single Islamic state or the restoration of the caliphate, even as a spiritual office. Despite his use of Islamic symbols and language, Khomeini in fact was more a Third World militant than an Islamic political thinker and theorist in the mold of his predecessors (see chapter 1).

Other Iranian officials have more explicitly accepted the existing international political system based on the nation-state and the basic rules that govern it, such as respect for the territorial integrity of other states and noninterference in their external affairs; like many other government leaders, however, they have not always refrained from interference. These beliefs help explain why Islamic Iran's assimilation into the international system accelerated beginning in 1984 and why Iran's foreign policy is now geared toward this system.

In short, what Khomeini desired was a Muslim spiritual unity that would, in turn, enable believers to resist the pressures of the so-called arrogant powers, redress the balance of power between the Muslims and the great powers, safeguard Muslim rights, and spread Islamic values—without, however, altering existing state boundaries.

• *Iran the international standard bearer.* The views of Khomeini and his disciples about Iran's international role and mission have evolved during the past two decades. Nevertheless elements of the vision prevalent at the outset of the revolution linger and affect Iran's foreign policy. It is important to determine the extent to which this vision was affected by Islam and to what extent it was shaped by other factors.

Khomeini and his disciples believed that Iran is the only true Islamic and independent country and the only depository of the essence and message of Islam. Khomeini felt that this imposed special duties on Iran, especially to help other Muslim states achieve a similar status. However, Khomeini and his disciples did not limit their assistance and cooperation in combating the so-called arrogant powers just to the Muslim states. Instead they advocated the unity of all so-called oppressed peoples. Khomeini's trans-Islamic and Third-Worldist attitudes are illustrated by his comments to Nicaragua's minister of education who visited Iran during the Sandinista period: "As you say, your country is very similar to our country . . . *we should all try to create unity among the oppressed, regardless of their ideology and creed. Otherwise the two oppressors of East and West will infect everyone like a cancerous tumor . . .* [emphasis added]"[22] In other words, Iran had to assume the role of standard bearer for all oppressed peoples. This example clearly illustrates that, in Khomeini's vision, Iran's main role was to lead the oppressed, irrespective of their religious creed, rather than to spread Islam as a religion. What he wanted to spread was the revolutionary spirit, not a particular religion.

Because Khomeini's true independence would be impossible without limiting the power and influence of the arrogant powers and this could be achieved only by forging a close cooperation among all the oppressed countries, Iran had to be in the vanguard of a global antiarrogance revolution, spread its message, and develop a coalition of oppressed peoples. But this goal had to be achieved without resort to violence. Instead, Iran should set an example attractive to other Muslims as well as to other oppressed people. In Khomeini's words, addressed to a group of Iranian diplomats: "It does not take swords to export this ideology. The export of ideas by force is no export. We shall have exported Islam only when we have helped Islam and Islamic ethics grow in those countries."[23]

Khomeini insisted also that revolution should be exported without the use of force and certainly without the initiation of aggressive wars: "When we say we want to export our revolution we mean we want to export this spirituality which dominates Iran . . . we have no intention to attack anyone with swords or other arms. . . ."[24] This statement has deep roots in the Shi'a theory of war and peace: Wars for the spread of Islam can be waged only by the Imams; and since the Shi'a world (Twelver Shi'ism) has been without an Imam since the occultation of the twelfth Imam, no expansionist wars can be waged.[25]

Islamic Impulse or Revolutionary Zeal? Important questions need to be asked at this point. To what extent does this activist, change-oriented dimension of Khomeini and his disciples' world view and their vision of Iran's regional and international role stem from an activism inherent in all revolutionary movements at a certain stage of their development? And to what extent do they reflect the influence of Islam and its inherently proselytizing and expansionist tendencies? Furthermore, to what extent does this activism reflect a security need common to all states irrespective of their ideology—namely, to create a nonthreatening political and strategic environment and a milieu congenial to their interests?

It is clear that a particular interpretation of Islam—shaped partly by Iran's experience as a nation and partly by the life experiences of Khomeini and some of his disciples—formed an important component of their world view and their vision of Iran's special role. However, Islam alone does not explain the activist and anti-status-quo dimension of this vision. Rather, a streak of Third World militancy and revolutionary zeal—especially a determination to change the international equation of forces that has long been detrimental to the weaker states—has been at the heart of Khomeini's and his followers' confrontational style and opposition to the established order. In this respect the Islamists have not been much different from their secular counterparts.

In addition, a direct relationship existed between these activist tendencies and the security needs of the Islamic regime, as perceived at the time. This relationship is reflected in statements of the nonclerical figures during the early years of the revolutionary regime. For example, writing in his journal *Enghlab-e-Islami* (*Islamic Revolution*) about whether Iran should become active in southern Lebanon, the Islamo-nationalist leader Abol-Hassan Bani-Sadr urged the Iranians to become engaged there: "If we don't go out of Iran to keep the revolution, others will come to our country to plot against us. . . . "[26] Bani-Sadr was in fact saying that, if Islamic Iran did not create a congenial security environment for itself, its survival could be in danger. Thus in addition to reflecting the proselytizing zeal of a revolutionary movement in its early stages, Bani-Sadr's view reflected another common propensity of states: to seek a political milieu that is congenial to their political views and aspirations, based on the often mistaken assumption that states that have similar ideological views and values do not threaten each other. This is why, during the post-World War II period, both the Soviet Union and the United States emphasized the creation and maintenance of a congenial international environment by spreading their respective ideologies and by other means. Other countries, including those in the Middle East—Egypt under Nasser, Ba'athist Iraq, and Qadhafi's Libya—have tried to enhance their security by spreading their particular ideologies. Even Iran under the shah tried to prevent the spread of radical ideologies into surrounding areas because of fear of the impact of these ideas on Iranian security. However, as the Sino-Soviet dispute and Syria-Iraq conflict illustrated, ideological affinity is no guarantee of interstate amity.

Adjusting Revolutionary Goals to External Realities.   The impact of Iran's revolutionary ideology on the formulation and conduct of its foreign policy has varied greatly during different periods of the new republic's life. Similarly, this ideology has affected with greater force some aspects of Iranian foreign policy than others. These fluctuations have reflected the impact of four factors: (1) the reassertion of the influence of more traditional determinants of Iran's external behavior; (2) the realization of the limits of Iran's ability to achieve its ideological goals; (3) the reaction of other countries and international institutions, in the form of policies of containment and the implementation of punitive measures, toward Iran's revolutionary challenge; and (4) the revision and alteration of Iran's ideological outlook as a result of internal developments, external events, and domestic consequences of external reactions. In light of the foregoing, the impact of Islamic ideology on the external behavior of the Islamic republic of Iran should be analyzed and assessed in the context of three distinct phases.

• *The domination of ideology, 1979–1984.*   Between the fall of the shah's regime in February 1979 and 1984, a fundamental shift influenced by ideological forces unleashed by the revolution occurred in the character and direction of Iran's foreign policy. Between 1979 and 1981, the Iranian political scene was characterized by fierce ideological and power struggles among a wide spectrum of political forces. During the premiership of Mehdi Bazargan (February 1979–November 1979), the official government espoused a mild form of nonalignment based on the principle of maintaining an equal distance from both superpowers, a policy similar to Mussadeq's negative equilibrium, as well as a foreign policy less active both regionally and internationally than that pursued by the shah from the late 1960s until his downfall. As a result, Iran officially withdrew from the Central Treaty Organization (CENTO) even though the alliance had been effectively dead for nearly a decade. It also severed ties with South Africa because of the policy of apartheid.

The Bazargan government did not favor confrontation toward either the United States and other Western countries or the

Soviet Union. Nor did it favor the aggressive export of revolution and interference in neighbors' internal affairs. Bazargan wanted to establish a nonhostile working relationship with the United States; thus he and his foreign minister, Ibrahim Yazdi, agreed to meet with U.S. secretary of state Cyrus Vance and Zbigniew Brzezinski, national security adviser to President Carter, during the funeral of Algerian leader Houari Boumedienne in 1979. This fateful meeting contributed to the 1979–1980 hostage crisis and the downfall of the Bazargan government. In short, as far as Bazargan and his colleagues were concerned, Islam played no role in shaping a suitable foreign policy for Iran.

Bazargan and his colleagues had only incomplete control over the government apparatus; a number of revolutionary committees undermined their authority. A loose and tacit coalition of leftist and Islamist forces (although these groups had different philosophies regarding Iran's foreign policy orientation, all shared hostility toward the West, especially the United States, and a streak of revolutionary activism) tried to bring down his government. The multiplicity of centers of power resulted in a nonfocused and contradictory foreign policy and the emission of contradictory signals from a variety of sources.

Between the fall of the Bazargan government in November 1979 and the downfall of Bani-Sadr's presidency in 1981, power struggles among groups and personalities affected the direction of Iran's foreign policy. Both the leftists and the militant Islamists used the American hostage crisis to give a radical and anti-Western tone to Iran's foreign policy. Iranian conduct during the hostage crisis was a clear by-product of the melding of views of leftists and Islamists who perceived the United States as the archenemy of Muslims and other so-called oppressed peoples. They used the hostage crisis to humble the United States and, by doing so, to relieve the burden of national humiliation accumulated during nearly two centuries of foreign domination.

It is important to determine how much of this behavior can be attributed to Islam and how much to other factors. Iran's own historical experience had a great deal to do with its desire to defy the most powerful country on Earth to relieve its sense of national humiliation. It did not seem important at the time to calculate the costs to Iran's long-term interests.

On other occasions, too, and without the added influence of Islam, similar impulses motivated Iran's behavior. The best example was Mussadeq's nationalization of the Anglo-Persian Oil Company, his expulsion of its officials from Iran, and his adamant refusal later to accept a settlement, policies that proved fatal to the Mussadeq government and damaging to Iran both economically and politically. But at the time they provided intense emotional satisfaction to the Iranians who, for 150 years, had resented the British policy of weakening and dominating Iran. The control by the Anglo-Persian Oil Company of Iran's most important natural resource, oil, symbolized this domination. Mussadeq's policies thus helped to ease Iranian humiliation.

The Islamic dimensions of the Islamist elements' ideology also played an important role in determining the new regime's behavior during this period. The Islamists resented the United States as the protector of the shah's regime and secularization drive, which undermined their own power and position. The United States was also perceived to be the main force behind the creation of the state of Israel and the main supporter of what Islamists believed to be its anti-Islam policies. They also viewed the United States as the main propagator of a culture that is anathema to Islam's ethical teachings. In a sense there was an element of cultural and civilizational clash in the Iranian Islamists' animosity toward the West, especially the United States, but the Islamists also resented what they perceived to be the U.S. ambition for global domination or, as Ayatullah Khomeini called it, America's "world devouring" propensities plus its support for corrupt and repressive governments, of which the shah's regime was but one example.

Besides the issue of Israel—Jerusalem, in other words—there is nothing particularly Islamic about these views. The Islamists' views regarding the nature of the United States and the local regimes supported by it are almost identical to those of the leftists and even liberal nationalists. Even in regard to Israel, the Islamists, leftists, and other Third World militants hold common views. All see a worldwide conspiracy by the so-called forces of global imperialism, international Zionism, and their regional lackeys to rob the oppressed of the world, especially Muslims, of their natural resources, territory, culture, and honor. The propaganda of Iraq's Ba'athist regime during the Persian Gulf War emphasized and highlighted this interaction.[27]

The Islamic factor did play an important role in Iran's conduct of the war with Iraq, which began with the Iraqi invasion of

Iranian territory in September of 1980 and lasted until August 1988. In their conduct of the war, Iranians were was deeply affected by the Islamic Republic's Islamist ideology and revolutionary character. The regime cast the conflict not in terms of territorial or national dispute but in terms of a battle between truth and falsehood (*Haq Va Batil*), Islam and blasphemy, which had important consequences for the war's resolution for it followed that the war could end only after the destruction of the symbol of falsehood and blasphemy, namely Iraq. Therefore, in 1982, after expelling Iraq from its territory, Iran refused to come to an advantageous agreement to end the conflict. It chose instead to push for the ouster of Saddam Hussain.

Iran's decision to continue with the war reflected its desire to propagate its ideology and to encourage the development of similar revolutionary movements in other Muslim countries. These ideological goals were in clear conflict with Iran's more parochial interests as a territorial nation-state. That ideology was given priority over national interests demonstrated the impact of the Islamist factor. In short, the conduct of the Iran-Iraq War was a clear case of ideological-civilizational factors exerting a degree of influence greater than other determinants of foreign policy.

Not every aspect of Iran's behavior during this phase of the war was determined by ideological principles. A number of Iranian actions reflected more parochial interests and demonstrated the ability and willingness of the Islamists to compromise on their ideological principles when other interests demanded it. For example, Iran continued to maintain its friendship with Syria even after the Ba'athist regime of Hafiz Al-Assad put down the rebellion of Syrian Islamists in Hamam in 1982 and killed nearly 30,000 people. Iran even accused the Syrian Islamists of being the agents of Iraq and Zionism.

In a similar manner, despite Iran's violent anti-Israel and anti-Zionist sentiments, Iran did not refuse to buy Israeli arms, which reached Iran clandestinely. One secular explanation and one Islamic interpretation can be offered for Iran's behavior. The secular explanation: as a general rule, when the survival of a state or a government is at stake, ideological goals and principles are relegated to second place. The Islamic regime was no exception. The Islamic interpretation: the concept of *Masalahat* (general interest and good) leads believers to conclude that when the general interest and overall good of Muslims are at stake, Islamic governments can and should show flexibility in the application of Islamic injunctions. Iran believed friendship with Syria was compatible with the general good of the Iranian Muslims and thus was sanctioned by *Masalahat*.

Iran's involvement in Lebanon after Israel invaded it in 1982 is another example of foreign policy being driven by ideology. Iran had no compelling security interest or any other interest for engaging in Lebanon. Although Iran has had close historical links with Lebanon's Shi'a community, these links were not sufficient reason for an involvement as extensive as Iran's in the 1980s. In fact, Iran's motives in Lebanon were purely ideological and revolutionary; Iran took advantage of the opportunity provided by the Israeli invasion to create a foothold in Lebanon and use it to radicalize the Lebanese Shi'as and other Muslims, thus creating an environment propitious for an Islamic revolution like Iran's, which could then be a catalyst for similar revolutions in other Arab and Islamic states. Even when it became clear that the involvement in Lebanon, which included entanglement in hostage-taking operations, was harming rather than helping Iran—by stiffening the resolve of the Western countries to help Iraq in its war with Iran—the Iranian government did not alter its policy toward Lebanon.

In sum, between 1979 and 1984, Iran's revolutionary impulse and ideological zeal prevailed over limited national goals and pragmatic and prudent considerations and motivations. Islam did not cause this zeal and mode of behavior, either wholly or even largely. Most of it reflected the radicalism and militancy common to many Third World countries during the 1960s and the 1970s. Iran caught the fever in the 1980s.

• *Consolidation of the Islamic state, greater pragmatism, and persistence of ideology, 1984–1988.* Several developments produced a significant change in Iran's approach to the conduct of its foreign policy. This was first officially signaled in a speech by Ayatullah Khomeini in October 1984. Although he did not state clearly that Iran accepted the existing international order and the system of interstate relations, he did indicate a tacit acceptance of both with important exceptions. Khomeini noted first that the prophet Muhammad had considered it necessary for Muslims to have relations with other countries and peoples; this contradicts the repeated assertion that *Dar-ul-Islam* should not have anything to do with *Dar-ul-Harb* except to wage *jihad* against it. Khomeini asserted that not having relations with other countries is against Islamic precepts, a point of view (discussed in chapter 1) that affirms Islam's acceptance of the territoriality and the plurality of states, including Muslim states, and their underlying legitimacy.[28]

Ayatullah Khomeini also criticized the proponents of people-to-people diplomacy, characterized their views as irrational, and said that such an approach would end only in extinction and annihilation. He then set some stringent conditions under which Iran should establish state-to-state relations. He insisted first and foremost that Iran's new relations "must be friendly, rather than that between a master and his servant," a clear reference to the relationship that, in the Islamists' view, the shah's government had with the United States. The second condition was that under no circumstances should Iran pursue state-to-state relations if such relations undermined Islam and its influence, either in Iran or internationally. Third, the ayatullah ruled out relations between Iran and three countries: the United States, Israel, and South Africa.

From that time onward Iran began to talk about wanting improved relations with nearly all countries on the basis of mutual respect for the sovereignty, independence, and territorial integrity of the parties and noninterference in one another's internal affairs. The speeches of many Iranian officials, especially those of the foreign minister and his colleagues, became replete with references to the UN charter although at times they were critical of some of its provisions such as the veto power of the Security Council's permanent members. Emphasis was shifted from people-to-people diplomacy to South-South relations, a mantra well known in the 1970s. Iran also became more active in the NAM, which initially Khomeini had dismissed as a sham. Iran changed its behavior because of

• the experience of the revolutionary leaders in governance within the context of an international order dominated by the nation-state. The Iranian leaders came to realize that for Iran and the regime to survive they had to operate within the existing international political system, notwithstanding its unfair and unjust character. They also had learned that some rules and regulations of this system could be useful to Iran.

• other countries' and peoples' lukewarm responses to Iran's revolutionary appeal and the resilience and strength of the existing Muslim governments. Given the ease with which the shah's regime was dismantled and the fact that the Islamists attributed this collapse solely to the strength of Islam and the force of popular protest, they had believed that if the peoples of other Muslim states were mobilized they, too, could bring down their corrupt governments. Contrary to the revolutionaries' expectations, however, the response of most Muslims (especially the Sunnis) was less than enthusiastic or, if revolutionary Iran garnered any sympathy and attraction, was not strong enough to propel others into action. Also through policies that combined repression of dissent and co-optation of Islamists, other Muslim regimes succeeded in protecting themselves and their countries from the disruptive consequences of Iran's revolutionary activities.

• the Iran-Iraq war and its consequences. The way the Iran-Iraq war started, its evolution, and the position of outside forces toward it had the deepest impact on both Iran's internal evolution and its conduct of external relations. First, the Iran-Iraq war led to a reassertion of Iranian nationalism, forcing the Islamic regime to relent on its antinationalist campaign, which inevitably led to a dilution of the Islamic component of its ideology. The regime tried to gain additional support for its war efforts with appeals to national sentiment. The government's shift was a grudging, tacit admission of the role played by factors other than Islam in shaping the character of the Iranians' collective identity. For similar reasons the regime had to appeal to the Shi'a sentiments of the population and manipulate Shi'a symbols, although this undermined the universalist, nonsectarian pretensions of the Iranian revolution.

Second, the war demonstrated the strength of both ethnocentric nationalism and sectarianism in other Muslim countries. Although the leaders of the Islamic republic denigrated Iranian nationalism and Iran's pre-Islamic culture and de-emphasized its Shi'a character, the outside world saw Iran as a Persian Shi'a entity and questioned its Islamic credentials. The absence, in the meantime, of the much expected—and dreaded—mass Shi'a uprising in Iraq illustrated the strength of ethnocentric nationalism in the Arab world. The prevalence of ethnocentrism over Islam was made clear by the attitude of Arab countries, the majority of which supported Iraq. It is interesting that the only two Arab countries to support Iran—Syria and Libya—were extreme Arab nationalists that suppressed their own Islamists, as Syria did when its army massacred the people of Hamam. Their common animosity toward the West, toward Israel, and toward conservative Arab regimes—not common loyalty to Islam—prompted them to side with Iran. Indeed, the reaction of various Muslim countries to the Iran-Iraq War illustrated clearly the strength of non-Islamic factors in determining the individual and collective self-identities of the Muslims and in motivating their behavior. It also highlighted the fragmented state of the Islamic world.

Third, the reaction of the international community to the Iraqi invasion and its overall support for Baghdad despite the fact that it was the clear aggressor demonstrated the heavy cost of Iran's revolutionary activism to its more important interests, especially the maintenance of its territorial integrity. After the 1988 confrontation between Iran and the United States over the shooting down of an Iranian passenger plane by the USS *Vincennes* in the Persian Gulf, a number of Iranian leaders including the speaker of the Iranian parliament who later became president, Ali Akbar Hashemi Rafsanjani, admitted that Iran's excessive revolutionary zeal had created enemies unnecessarily.

Despite the gradual adjustment of the rhetoric and practice of Iran's foreign policy to the realities of international life, ideological motives and impulses continued to affect key areas of Iranian foreign policy. The most important manifestation of the lingering impact of ideology was Iran's refusal to settle the war with Iraq, which ultimately led to greater direct American involvement and Iran's humiliating consent to a cease-fire in August 1988.

Second in importance was Iran's continued involvement with Lebanon and the problem of Western hostages there, issues that were extremely complicated and were linked to Syrian designs and policies in Lebanon and in the Middle East generally. Thus Iran alone was not capable of disentangling the entire affair. Nevertheless Iran did have a good deal of influence over the hostage takers and, had it wished to, it might have been able to settle the problem earlier than it finally did.

Third, Iran refused to enter into direct and open negotiations with the United States despite the fact that this refusal was highly damaging to Iran's interests. Thus, during this period of adjustment, Iran's foreign policy acquired a dual character: One aspect was conducted in line with normal state practices and was motivated by national interest more than by ideological impulses, but another aspect was still dominated by ideological and revolutionary zeal.

• *Growing pragmatism and lingering traces of ideology, 1988–1997.* The August 1988 cease-fire in the Iran-Iraq War was a watershed in the evolution of Iran's foreign policy. The cease-fire, in effect an admission by Iran of relative defeat that left some Iranian territory under Iraqi occupation, dealt a heavy blow to the ideological foundations of the regime. More important, it shook the faith of many Iranians in the justness of their cause and hence in their ultimate victory. After suffering more than one million casualties—500,000 dead—Iran began to ask itself a basic question: If Iran's cause was just, why did God not help defeat the satanic Saddam Hussain and his equally satanic Western and Arab allies?

The war with Iraq demonstrated clearly to the Iranians that victories on the battlefield and elsewhere cannot occur solely with faith, revolutionary commitment, and a spirit of sacrifice. Instead, sophisticated weaponry and sufficient material and diplomatic support were needed to prevail over one's enemies. When a large number of Iranians realized this, it severely undermined the credibility of the Islamists' theory of international relations and the conduct of Iran's foreign policy. It also undermined the influence of the hard-liners within Iran although they later recovered much of their lost influence.

The death of Ayatullah Khomeini in June 1989, by contrast, had a more contradictory impact on the process of the deideologization of Iran's foreign policy. On the one hand, the death of the man who, it can be argued, was the most Islamist of Iran's revolutionary figures has enabled the regime to pursue a more conventional and pragmatic foreign policy. On the other hand, Khomeini's death also eliminated the one authoritative figure whose edicts could not be challenged and who could take difficult and controversial decisions such as resolving the American hostage crisis and agreeing to a cease-fire with Iraq. Thus it became impossible for the Iranian government to resolve some difficult issues in its foreign relations. For example, despite its need and its desire for improved relations with the industrialized European states, the Iranian regime has not been able to rescind Khomeini's death order against the British author of Indian origin, Salman

Rushdie; yet the Western countries have made this a necessary precondition for improved relations with Iran. Had he been alive, Khomeini could have done so himself and no one would have disputed his decision. Also Khomeini could have ruled easily that, because the *Masalahat* (interest and welfare) of the Islamic republic required it, Iran should resume diplomatic relations with the United States.

With Khomeini gone, no truly authoritative force remains to interpret his ideological legacy. With each competing faction claiming to act according to his guidance, the government has proved incapable of adjusting certain aspects of its foreign policy although this is costly in terms of Iran's interests. By contrast, on most other important issues of foreign policy, Iran has behaved in a pragmatic and nonideological manner. Nothing better illustrates this than Iran's stance toward the Persian Gulf War of 1990–1991 and its policy toward developments in the Soviet Union between 1988 and 1991 and toward the Soviet successor states since 1992.

• *Iran and the Persian Gulf crisis of 1990–1991.*   Immediately after the cease-fire in August 1988, Iran's paramount preoccupation was how to secure the withdrawal of Iraqi troops from parts of its territory, gain implementation of UN Security Council Resolution 589, and force Iraq to accept the 1975 Algiers agreement as it applied to the Shat-al-Arab. Despite Iran's efforts, however, neither the UN Security Council nor the major powers was willing to pressure Iraq into accepting Iran's demands. Quite the contrary, until early 1990 major Western powers including the United States sought Iraq as a potential ally and new pillar of their security structure in the Persian Gulf. Thus they rebuffed Iran's overtures, which were low key and discreet in any case, to secure Western support for the withdrawal of Iraqi forces from Iranian territory and for the principle of the division of the Shat-al-Arab in exchange for greater Iranian efforts to resolve the Lebanon hostage crisis and in general to improve relations with the West. After Iraq invaded Kuwait in August 1990 and withdrew its troops from Iranian territory, Iran breathed a sigh of relief.

Iraq's attack on Kuwait demonstrated to the Persian Gulf Arabs and to the West, which had bankrolled part of Iraq's war effort against Iran, that Saddam Hussain was the more serious threat to Persian Gulf security. The Iraqi invasion of Kuwait also posed serious security dilemmas and difficult policy choices for Iran. An Iraqi victory, the absorption of Kuwait into Iraq, and the establishment of an effective Iraqi hegemony in the Persian Gulf would have degraded Iran's security environment. And after Kuwait, Iraq almost certainly would have turned its attention once again to Iran's province of Khusistan and perhaps to its other coastal provinces—Iraq at times has called them the Northern Arab Emirates—thus threatening Iran's territorial integrity. But a Western coalition victory over Iraq—to Iran, a U.S. victory—would expand and consolidate the American presence in the Persian Gulf and lead to a deterioration in Iran's security environment. In fact, since the 1991 Desert Storm victory, the U.S. military presence in the Persian Gulf has dramatically increased, which, given the strained nature of U.S.-Iran relations, has exacerbated Iran's security concerns and reduced its policy options.

In 1990 Desert Shield contenders considered Iran's decisions important. Despite its war-battered economy and military, Iran's size, resources, sensitive geographic position, and influence with segments of Gulf Arab and Muslim populations guaranteed that its attitude toward the conflict would have significant implications for the war's conduct and outcome. An Iranian decision to side with Iraq could have made it difficult for some Muslim countries to join the anti-Saddam coalition. As a consequence, both Iraq and the anti-Saddam forces tried to win over Iran.

To gain Iran's cooperation, Iraq appealed to its Islamic and anti-American sentiments, warned of the dangers to Islam from the presence of the American forces in Islam's holy lands, and urged joint Iran-Iraq action against the United States to protect Islam. These Iraqi strategies were not without some impact in Iran. Small-scale demonstrations were held in Iran in support of Iraq. Some clerics such as Ayatullah Khalkhali called for Iran to join Iraq in resisting U.S. presence in the region. But these minority views lacked broad support within the population and among the leadership. The Iranian people's suffering during the eight-year war with Iraq made repugnant the thought of cooperating with Saddam Hussain. The leadership understood the negative security implications and the critical risk that Iran's support for Iraq would have rendered Iran vulnerable to punitive measures, including military strikes, by the anti-Saddam coalition.

But given the ideological and political constraints, joining the U.S.-led international coalition against Saddam Hussain was also not a realistic option for Iran. Therefore Iran adopted a position of neutrality with a certain degree of anti-Iraq bias. For example, Iran complied with the UN-imposed embargo on Iraq, condemned its invasion of Kuwait, and defended Kuwait's territorial integrity. To justify its policy, Iran minimized the Islamic character of Saddam's conflict with the United States. Thus, while broadcasts of Baghdad radio resorted to Islamic slogans and its language came to resemble the speeches of Ayatullah Khomeini, Iran's spiritual leader, Ayatullah Khamenei, stated that, because the Persian Gulf War was not a battle between Islam and disbelief, the Iranian people had no Islamic duty to support Saddam Hussein. President Hashemi Rafsanjani meanwhile appealed to the Iranians' national sentiments and asked whether Iranians wanted Saddam Hussein to turn the Persian Gulf into a true Arabian Gulf.

Iran's policy toward the Persian Gulf War reflected the flexibility of Islamic ideology: its capacity to accommodate the requirements of security and national interest and its continued restraining effect on Iran's ability to act solely on the basis of its national interest. For example, Iran desperately needed financial and other assistance for its reconstruction effort and could have obtained a good deal of help, perhaps including the release of most of its U.S.-held assets, if it had joined the anti-Saddam coalition. But that would have undermined Iran's Islamist credentials beyond any level acceptable to the regime, especially its hard-line factions. More important than ideological rigidity, however, was the excessive anti-Americanism of certain personalities in the regime, notably Ayatullah Khamenei, which made inconceivable Iran's joining any coalition led by the United States.

• *Iran and the Soviet successor states: Triumph of pragmatism.* Iran's approach toward the Persian Gulf War demonstrated both the growing importance of national security calculations in the formulation of Iran's foreign policy and the continued influence of its Islamist ideology. This contrasted with Iran's policy toward the USSR and, later, toward the Soviet successor states, especially Russia, a policy that provides an even more convincing case of the triumph of pragmatism over Islamist ideology.

By the time the disintegration of the Soviet Union gathered momentum in the late 1989, Iran had laid the foundation for close relations with the USSR. The first stage of Soviet-Iranian rapprochement was the meeting between the Soviet foreign minister, Eduard Shevardnadze, and Ayatullah Khomeini in February 1989, followed by Rafsanjani's visit to Moscow in June 1989, shortly after Khomeini's death. Between January 1990 and December 1991, when the Soviet Union was dismantled, Iran needed to shield itself from the potentially disruptive consequences of events in the USSR and to avoid conflict and tensions with Moscow.[29]

Thus throughout 1989 when interethnic tensions in the southern republics of the former Soviet Union increased, Iran maintained a hands-off policy. Several times the Iranian foreign ministry stated that these interethnic disputes were the Soviet Union's internal affairs. Iran even remained silent when, in January 1990, Mikhail Gorbachev sent Soviet troops to Baku to quell Azeri-Armenian clashes; this despite the fact that Gorbachev accused Iran of fomenting Islamic fundamentalism. Some influential clerical figures objected to and criticized the Teheran government's passivity toward the events in Azerbaijan. Ayatullah Mussavi Ardabili, the chief justice of Iran at the time, warned the government that its noninvolvement in Azerbaijan left the field open to the Turks and the Egyptians to influence the Azerbaijani Shi'as.

After the southern republics of the Soviet Union gained their independence, Iran continued its nonideological and pragmatic approach to relations with them. The Islamic factor has played only a marginal role in shaping Iran's approach toward the Soviet successor states; the motivating factors have been security and economics. In the Transcaucasus, because of security considerations, Iran has established much warmer relations with Christian Armenia than with mostly Shi'a Azerbaijan, going as far as surreptitiously assisting the Armenians in the Nagorno-Karabakh conflict with Azerbaijan. In Central Asia, too, Iran's objectives have been to protect its security and to increase its economic involvement in the region rather than to spread revolutionary Islam. Thus, despite the war of the government of Immamali Rahmanov in Tajikistan against that country's armed Islamic opposition, Iran has tried to establish good relations with the Rahmanov government.[30] Iran has also played an important role in efforts to end the Tajik civil war.

An even more obvious example of this nonideological policy toward the Soviet successor states has been Iran's eagerness to strike a strategic partnership with Russia despite frequent

Russian statements that Islamism is the main threat to Russian security and other interests.[31] Not even Russia's war against the Muslim Chechens has dissuaded Iran from its policy of rapprochement. The Iranian press criticized Russia's behavior in Chechnya but there were no widespread calls for Iran to help the Chechen cause. The Iranian government adopted the position that the war in Chechnya was an internal concern of Russia.

Iran's Policy toward Israel and the Arab-Israeli Conflict: The Predominance of Ideology. In contrast with its policy toward the Soviet successor states, Iran's policy toward Israel and the Arab-Israeli conflict has been determined for the most part by ideological factors and Islamist tendencies at the expense of Iran's security and other interests. None of the traditional causes of interstate conflict can explain the Iranian government's hostility toward the Jewish state: Iran does not have common borders with Israel, it has no territorial conflicts with it, and the two countries have never been at war with each other although, since 1982, Iran has been engaged in an indirect conflict with Israel brought on by Iran's links with Lebanon's Shi'a militant Islamist groups.

Iran in the meantime faces irredentist claims to its territory from a number of Arab states, including the Iraqi claim to Iran's Khusistan province and the United Arab Emirate claim to the Persian Gulf islands of Abu-Musa, Greater Tunb, and Lesser Tunb, and the prevailing Arab desire to give a wholly Arab character to the Persian Gulf. Nor has there been any historic feud between the Iranian and the Jewish peoples; on the contrary, the history of the two peoples has been marked by friendship more than by hostility. In the early days of the Iran-Iraq War, rumors of Israeli arms reaching Iran were explained away in the Iraqi press as transactions reflecting the age-old Jewish-Persian alliance.

More important, many Palestinians share these Arab claims toward Iran. The Palestine Liberation Organization (PLO), which supported Iraq during the Iran-Iraq War, reflected and underlined this basic Arab view. From Iran's national security perspective, the presence of Israel in the Middle East creates a counterweight to Arab power and thus serves Iran's strategic interests; in short, there is no nationalist reason for Iran's animosity toward Israel. The Islamic Republic's animosity toward Israel derives from its Islamist ideology and pure Islamic motives; the Iranian leadership perceives Israel as the usurper of Jerusalem and the number one enemy of Islam. The Islamic motivation is strength-ened further by the old and now discarded Third World militancy that perceived Israel as an agent of imperialism in the heart of the Third World.

Iran's inability to approach the question of Israel in a prag-matic, nonideological manner has damaged a range of Iran's in-terests, including its internal economic development. By refusing to recognize the legitimacy of the state of Israel and by opposing the peace process between Israel and its Arab neighbors, Iran has effectively cut itself off from international sources of capital and is excluded from all regional schemes that involve the countries of the Middle East or the former Soviet Union. Iran's ideological stand on Israel has antagonized the major powers and diminished Iran's strategic options, forcing it to deal with its neighbors and other countries such as China and Russia from a position of stra-tegic disadvantage.

Iran's inability to approach this central issue of its foreign policy pragmatically shows that the Iranian regime

• has not yet completed the process of adjusting to the inter-national system and to the equation of power within it. Iran is still to a degree change-oriented and aims at altering the equation of power;
• intermingles certain foreign policy issues with domestic matters such as power struggles within the regime; and
• lacks an adequately authoritative figure to reinterpret Ayatullah Khomeini's foreign policy views.

It would be a mistake, however, to attribute Iran's policies on relations with the United States and Israel and its opposition to the Arab-Israeli peace process solely to these three factors. U.S. policies toward Iran between 1988 and 1997 and the regional policies of the United States and Israel have also contributed to shaping Iranian attitudes and have made it difficult for Iran to break from ideological constraints.

The following will help to explain these points. After the Iran-Iraq cease-fire of August 1988, the position of the pragmatists within the leadership improved. Coupled with Iran's eagerness to obtain the removal of Iraqi troops from its soil, this prompted Iran to seek improved relations with the West. Although Iran's domestic politics did not allow it to admit to reaching out to the

United States, messages expressing a desire to reduce the hostile tone toward the United States were transmitted through intermediaries such as Turkey, Pakistan, and Japan. The U.S. policymaking community believed that the end of the Cold War had caused Iran lose its strategic value whereas the large oil reserves in Iraq and the Gulf Arab states had increased their worth to the West. As a result, U.S. policymakers decided to try to cement an alliance with Iraq.

Meanwhile both the United States and Israel hoped that Iraq could be persuaded to join the peace camp and abandon its rejectionist attitude toward the Arab-Israeli peace process. As a consequence, Iran's overtures were ignored and Washington repeated that it would only speak openly to official representatives of the Iranian government. By the autumn of 1988, the hard-liners in Iran had recouped some of their influence and elicited from Ayatullah Khomeini the edict sanctioning Salman Rushdie's death. Under these circumstances it was natural that no Western country could take positive steps toward Iran. The impact within Iran, however, was a discrediting of the pragmatists' strategy of overtures to the West.

Iraq's invasion of Kuwait opened another opportunity for conciliation between Iran and the West. Iran's neutral stand facilitated the task of the anti-Saddam coalition, and, using its influence in Lebanon, Iran succeeded in gaining the freedom of Western hostages. Contrary to Iranian expectations, Western (especially U.S.) policy toward Iran hardened: The United States did not change its attitude on the question of Iranian assets, nor did it change its position on denying loans to Iran from other Western countries and multilateral agencies; and America vetoed Iranian participation in the many schemes under discussion for a postwar security structure involving the Gulf Cooperation Council (GCC) in the Persian Gulf—for example, the GCC plus Egypt, or the GCC plus Egypt, Syria, and others, notably Turkey and Pakistan.

The fall of the Soviet Union in December 1991 led Washington to adopt an even more stringent policy of isolating Iran, which was further refined in the context of the Clinton administration's Dual Containment strategy. Meanwhile, the threat of Iran common to both conservative Arabs and Israel was used by Israel to encourage the Arab states to make peace. The combined effect of these policies was a growing belief in Iran that once the Arab-Israeli peace was completed the U.S. policy of containment would change into active intervention to unseat Iran's regime. The Iranians thus concluded that the success of the Arab-Israeli peace process would threaten their security. In short, Islamist ideology notwithstanding, secular earthly reasons also contributed greatly to this aspect of Iranian foreign policy.

Conclusion

Since Iran was Islamized by the Arab Conquest, Islam has been only one of the influences shaping Iranian cultural and political evolution and, until the Islamic revolution, was not the most important. In Iran, as elsewhere in the Muslim world, Islamic universalism has not conquered parochial notions of individual and collective identity and loyalty and hence has not been capable of subduing nationalism. In Iran the dichotomy between Islam and pre-Islamic Iranian traditions has been especially marked and only partly mitigated by the country's Shi'aization. The process of accommodating Islamic principles to external realities, which has occurred in other parts of the Muslim world throughout history, has also taken place in Iran. Until the advent of Iran's Islamic revolution, Islam played a minor role in determining Iran's relations with the outside world; even after the Islamic revolution, other influences have remained strong and have asserted themselves gradually over Iranian external behavior. The anti-Westernism of Islamic Iran has roots other than merely the cultural incompatibility of Islam and the West. To some degree a cultural clash has affected the Iranian Islamists' view of, and attitude toward, the West.

Saudi Arabia: A Different Kind of Islamic State

Few countries in the Muslim world adhere to Islamic rules and regulations as strictly as the kingdom of Saudi Arabia. The Saudis state openly that the *Qur'an* is their constitution. The rules of the *Shari'a* are applied rigorously—from the *hudud* (punishments that include the amputation of hands, beheading, and stoning) for crimes such as theft and murder to the prohibition of alcohol and the veiling of women.

The Saudi leadership bases its legitimacy on its role as the guardian of Islam's holy places, and the Saudi king is referred to as the guardian of Mecca and Medina. Nowhere else is the fusion of religion with politics and government more complete, acknowledged, and undisputed than in Saudi Arabia. Nowhere else is the clash of culture between the West and an Islamic country more glaring than in Saudi Arabia. Yet there are few countries in the Islamic world that have as close a relationship with the Western powers, especially the United States, as does Saudi Arabia.

The close Saudi-Western relationship cannot be reconciled with the thesis that civilizational clash between Islam and the West is the major source of discord between the two. The Western powers do not find the mixing of religion and politics objectionable when it comes to Saudi Arabia. Nor do they protest against the Saudi application of *hudud*, including the stoning of women for adultery. There are no resolutions before the UN Commission on Human Rights that condemn the disregard for basic human rights in Saudi Arabia.

In sum, it seems that the West does not see a clash of civilizations with Saudi Arabia. This forbearance is reciprocated by Saudi Arabia. The Saudi leadership's embrace of the West seems unhindered by the many Western practices and values that oppose those recommended by Islam. Nor as the guardians of Islam's holy places are the Saudis inhibited by the support of the West—especially the United States—for the state of Israel, which claims sole possession of Jerusalem, the third holiest place in Islam and the first to which the early Muslims prayed.

Yet Saudi behavior fits well with the customary pattern of behavior of other Muslim countries; and the West's behavior regarding the impact on external behavior of value and belief systems—both religious and secular—is in line with that of other states.

The outwardly strict adherence to Islamic rules of the Saudi leadership and political class has not shielded the leaders from being challenged from those who question the sincerity of their commitment to Islam and who see merely a cynical exercise of the legitimization of their power and position. The opposition in Saudi Arabia uses Islam as justification for opposing the present Saudi leadership, which is natural and illustrative of the functions of a belief system as a means of delegitimizing power as well as justifying it. Since the establishment of the kingdom of Saudi Arabia, power and interest-related factors and nonideological motives have shaped the external relations of Saudi Arabia. Islam has justified policy and has been used to advance other policy goals.

Wahhabi Islam and the Emergence of the House of Saud

Like Iran, Saudi Arabia has several features that give it a unique character. Most important is the identification of the country not with an ethnic group, a distinct culture or language, or a historic political existence but with a family, the House of Saud. The only country in the Muslim world similar to Saudi Arabia in this sense is Jordan, which is identified with the Hashemites and is known officially as the Hashemite Kingdom of Jordan. The implication of this identification of the state with a particular family is that, without the House of Saud, Saudi Arabia in its present shape and form does not and cannot exist. This suggests that Saudi Arabia's sense of national identity is weak compared with its sense of monarchical identity, which blurs the boundary between national interest and monarchical interest.

Also, Saudi Arabia is distinguished by the birth of Islam within its current territory, which is the source and only justification of its claim to greatness. Because the Saudi territory of today had a comparatively less advanced pre-Islamic culture, there are no cultural rivals to Islam in Saudi Arabia. As a consequence, Islam is the very core of the Saudi Arabs' collective identity.

The third feature that distinguishes Saudi Arabia is the symbiotic relationship between the Wahhabi brand of Islam and the House of Saud. Indeed, since 1744 when Muhammad Ibn Sa'ud, a minor prince of Najd and the ruler of Al Dar'iya, decided to champion the religious revival preached by Muhammad Ibn Abd-ul-Wahhab, the fortunes of the House of Saud and of Wahhabi Islam have become inextricably linked.[32]

All these special features would seem to argue for a close link between Islam and Saudi Arabia's external relations and the fashioning of Saudi behavior according to Islamic principles. Yet, since the beginning in the eighteenth century, Islam has been at the service of the House of Saud rather than the reverse.

By the late eighteenth century in what is now Saudi Arabia, orthodox Islam—especially among the Bedouins of Najd—had given way to superstitious practices and paganism, such as the cult of trees and stone worship.[33] Abd-ul-Wahhab, in response, preached a return to the true teachings of Islam, based on the *Qur'an* and the *Sunna*, as interpreted by the strict *Hanbali* school. With the support of Ibn Sa'ud, Abd-ul-Wahhab converted the Najdis and the two set out to spread both true Islam—Wahhabism—and the power of the House of Saud to the rest of Arabia. Wahhabi Islam provided the ideological underpinning and the legitimizing force behind the territorial and political ambitions of the House of Saud. When Muhammad Ibn Saud contested the power of his rivals the Hashemite family who ruled in Hijaz on behalf of the Ottoman Turks, for example, he argued that the Hashemites had fallen away from true Islam and hence were no longer fit for the guardianship of Islam's holy places.

The first thrust of the combined Saudi-Wahhabi forces for the political and spiritual mastery of Arabia failed when, in 1819, Ottoman forces destroyed the Wahhabi capital, Al-Dar'iya.[34] It was one century later when the House of Saud, under the leadership of Abdul-Aziz Ibn Saud, could once more begin its quest for the unification of all of Arabia under its rule. The first step was the capture of Riyadh in 1902; the conquest was completed in 1925 with the capture of Mecca and Medina and the end of the rule of the Hashemites in Arabia.

Islam and Saudi Foreign Policy: The Era of Abdul Aziz,
1902–1953

The foundations of Saudi Arabia's future foreign policy were laid during the expansion and consolidation of the power of the House of Saud throughout the regions that now form the kingdom of Saudi Arabia. The Wahhabi Islam from this early period became the ideological underpinning of the new state, serving as the basis of legitimacy for its new leader and as an instrument for advancing the goals and ambitions of the House of Saud, rather than the force defining and shaping these ambitions.

The most important determinant of the foreign policy of the House of Saud has always been dynastic interests—the extension of the power of the House of Saud to all parts of Arabia. To achieve this, Abdul Aziz did not exclude any means, including the support and cooperation of Western Christian powers. Thus he asked for Britain's support against his Muslim rivals, the Hashemites and the Ottoman Turks, even at "the risk of upsetting his religiously conservative supporters. . . . "[35] But he appealed to Islam whenever it suited his interests and served his ambitions. Thus, like his ancestor, he "regularly denounced the Turks and the Hashemites for their distortions of true Islam" and he portrayed the House of Saud as the only defender of true Islam.[36] Saudi rulers have continued this practice ever since.

After establishing control over what is now called Saudi Arabia, Abdul Aziz's main concern was gaining international recognition for his dominions, even if the first state to accord it was the godless, Communist Soviet Union. But whenever there was no incompatibility between the Saudis' dynastic interests, Islamic injunctions, and the state Abdul Aziz had established, considerations rooted in Wahhabi Islam did influence policy. Even in these cases, however, worldly considerations more often than not were the main determinants of policy. To illustrate, King Abdul Aziz did not establish diplomatic relations with Egypt, for example, ostensibly because the Wahhabis disapproved of the manner in which the Egyptians performed the ceremony of covering the Ka'aba, but in fact the early estrangement between Saudi Arabia and Egypt was caused by dynastic rivalry. King Abdul Aziz believed that the Egyptian royal house, like the Hashemites, had ambitions of reestablishing the caliphate under its own leadership, which would challenge Abdul Aziz's authority and independence.[37]

Since that early time the prevention of the emergence of a single country or group of countries that could dominate the Arab world—and challenge or threaten Saudi Arabia's interests—became the cornerstone of Saudi foreign policy that guided the approach of King Abdul Aziz and his successors to the dominant themes of intra-Arab politics: Arab nationalism and pan-Arabism, Arab economic and political integration, and the Palestinian problem. The Saudi approach to these issues was guided from the beginning by political realism and was determined on the basis of the strategy that would best serve Saudi interests.

Whenever Islam could be an instrument for deflecting challenges from other Arab states or for justifying a particular policy, it was used as such. In his opposition to the move for a strong Arab league in 1945, King Abdul Aziz used an Islamic argument: "The attempt to unify educational and constitutional methods in Arab countries is to be praised. However, the Saudi Arabian Kingdom, whose territory includes certain holy places, thereby claims a special status and cannot sanction any educational or constitutional program that is not consistent with the tenets and traditions of Islam. . . . "[38]

Safeguarding the territorial integrity of the new kingdom and consolidating the power of the House of Saud would not remain Saudi Arabia's only objectives. By the mid-1960s, an important part of Saudi foreign and security policy became the extension of Saudi influence, in its immediate neighborhood in the Persian Gulf and the Red Sea regions and in the more distant periphery such as South Asia—notably Pakistan and Afghanistan—plus the rest of the Arab world and Muslim Africa. The expansion of Saudi Arabia's sphere of influence came to be seen as necessary for achieving more fundamental national and dynastic security interests. Saudi Arabia used a range of instruments including Islam and its position as the home of the Muslim World's holiest places to achieve this goal.

Islam versus Arab Radicalism and Communist Penetration

Two developments, in the Middle East and around the world, that began in the mid-1950s and gathered momentum in the following two decades were largely responsible for the Saudi leadership's more systematic use of Islam as an instrument of its foreign and security policy. The first development was the rise of Arab nationalism and Arab socialism, various versions of which came to be called Nasserism and Ba'athism. The other development was the intensification of the Cold War and the Soviet drive for influence in the Middle East.

Since the very beginning of its life, the Saudi kingdom has been wary of any Arab unification schemes, first, because it has felt that it would occupy a secondary place within such a pan-Arab scheme and, second, because the kingdom has feared the spread of ideas that could be potential threats to the power base and the legitimacy of the House of Saud. The Saudis have not been mistaken. The views and the plans of the new breed of Arab nationalists, who first burst on the Arab political scene in the late 1940s, had the potential to damage Saudi interests far more than the dynastic ambitions of Egypt or the Hashemites. The Arab nationalists believed, for example, that the oil of Saudi Arabia and other oil-rich Arab states belonged to the Arab nation and not only to the oil producers and should be used for Arab economic development and be at the service of achieving its other goals.[39] In addition, the new Arab nationalists viewed the conservative Arab monarchies—the reactionary powers, as they called them— as one of the two significant hurdles on the way to achieving Arab goals and safeguarding Arab rights; the other hurdle was imperialism. Thus the Arab radicals posed an existential threat to Saudi Arabia, a threat made more serious because of the support they received from the Soviet Union and other Communist countries. From the mid-1950s until the end of the 1980s, the prevention of Communist inroads in the Arab world and nearby regions was an overriding objective of Saudi foreign policy.

Islam—not only Wahhabi Islam—increasingly came to be seen as an ideological counterweight to both Arab radicalism and to Communism and a convenient framework for an antiradical coalition. During the 1962 *hajj* ceremonies, Saudi initiative helped establish the Muslim World League, which was justified as a way of defeating the serious plots the enemies of Islam tried to use to draw Muslims away from their religion and destroy their unity and brotherhood. This initiative is a good example of the use of Islam for antiradical coalition building.

An initiative that began in the mid-1960s to form an Islamic coalition culminated in 1972 in the establishment of the OIC. Two of Saudi Arabia's earliest collaborators in this scheme were the Iranian Shi'a Pahlavi monarchy and the secular government of Habib Bourguiba of Tunisia. Ironically, at this time the shah of Iran was challenged by Islamic forces, notably the exiled Ayatullah Khomeini and his disciples, for pursuing anti-Islamic policies, and these Islamic groups were supported financially and morally by Nasser's socialist Egypt, which was waging a relentless war against the Egyptian Muslim Brothers.

In short, instead of Islam setting the objectives and the policies, the Saudi leadership used Islam to advance goals and policies that had been developed on the basis of other concerns and priorities. In the years following the establishment of the OIC, it would become an important tool for expanding Saudi influence throughout the Muslim World; yet at no time did King Faisal, under whose stewardship the OIC was established, or his successors consider turning the OIC into a supranational or semisupranational pan-Islamic organization that would have the potential to limit Saudi Arabia's freedom of action in foreign policy.

*The Oil Revolution of 1973: Saudi Arabia's Islamic and
Riyal Diplomacy*

The 1973 Arab-Israeli War and the ensuing Arab oil embargo and
the revolution that they produced in international oil markets
turned Saudi Arabia into a potent financial and political force,
regionally and internationally. The consequences for the content
and the style of Saudi Arabia's diplomacy were important. Saudi
foreign policy had hitherto been primarily defensive and aimed at
protecting the country and its leadership from external and internal threats. During the 1970s it became more activist and aimed
at producing change and shaping events to serve Saudi interests
rather than to merely respond to them or to try to contain their
disruptive potential. Second, the field of action for Saudi foreign
policy expanded greatly and began to encompass Asia and Africa
in addition to the Arab world and Saudi Arabia's non-Arab neighbors such as Iran, Turkey, and Pakistan. Third, Saudi Arabia
began a determined effort to acquire the spiritual and political
leadership of the Arab and Islamic worlds.

The main vehicle for achieving these ambitious foreign policy
goals was Saudi Arabia's new wealth. The kingdom embarked on
a large foreign aid program through a variety of bilateral, pan-
Arab, and pan-Islamic channels, which resulted in, for example,
the establishment of the Islamic Development Fund with its head-
quarters in Jiddah.[40] In addition, Saudi Arabia worked to spread
Wahhabi Islam through a large-scale effort to finance mosques,
Islamic schools, and other institutions throughout the Muslim
world. In addition to the influence that money buys, the Saudi
effort to propagate Wahhabism was based on the assumption
that religious—in other words, ideological—affinity between the
Saudis and other Muslims would support and enhance the kingdom's claim to the leadership of the Islamic World.

In certain areas, such as Pakistan and Afghanistan, this policy was also designed to undermine Saudi Arabia's regional rivals, notably the shah's Iran, that had much more extensive historical, cultural, and linguistic ties with these countries than did
Saudi Arabia. It is interesting that the shah at this time was using
pan-Aryan themes to expand Iranian influence into the Indian
subcontinent while Saudi Arabia was spreading Wahhabism for
the identical purpose. Although Iran and Saudi Arabia had coop-

erated in the past to ward off Communist and Arab radical threats in the Middle East and in South Asia, the Saudis considered Iran a principal rival and disliked Iran because of its Persian and, especially, Shi'a character because to Wahhabis the Shi'as—even Arab Shi'as—are worse than infidels.

Saudi Arabia also aided other Islamic movements, including those in Turkey, to gain a lever of influence. This Saudi strategy succeeded best in Pakistan. Pakistan's relations with Saudi Arabia, and with other Gulf Arabs, dated to the early 1960s; Pakistani military officers, for example, had trained the Saudi and Gulf militaries. One such officer was General Zia ul-Haq who, in 1976, through a military coup d'état, unseated Zulfiqar Ali Bhutto and ruled Pakistan until his death in 1988. Zia ul-Haq embarked on an extensive Islamization of Pakistan along strict Sunni lines. Although Zia's policy exacerbated Pakistan's sectarian divisions, it also contributed to closer Saudi-Pakistani ties and led to the cooler relations between Pakistan and Iran, whose influence Saudi Arabia had long wanted to curtail in Pakistan.[41]

Following the downfall of the Afghan regime of Muhammad Zahir Shah in 1972 as a result of a coup d'état by his cousin Daoud and Daoud's efforts to distance Afghanistan from Russia, Saudi-Iranian competition for regional influence extended to Afghanistan also. Here, too, Saudi Arabia gained influence by using Wahhabi Islam in conjunction with its riyal diplomacy. The adepts that Saudi Arabia gained in Afghanistan later became close cooperators in the fight against Soviet occupation in the 1980s. The war against the Soviet Union offered additional opportunities for Saudi Arabia to use Wahhabi proselytizing as an instrument of influence.

In sum, during the 1970s, security concerns and the quest for greater regional and international influence and prestige determined Saudi foreign policy, but the spread of Wahhabi Islam became closely interconnected with the achievement of the secular objectives. Despite its increased financial resources and the concomitant enhanced political influence, Saudi Arabia challenged neither the West nor the existing balance of international power. Thus its efforts to spread its version of Islam and to use it as a lever of power were not perceived in the West as negative or threatening. On the contrary, the West viewed Saudi-style Islam as a convenient antidote to both Communism and Arab radicalism, and it considered the spread of Saudi influence as enhancing Western power because, ultimately, Saudi Arabia was and is a client-state of the West.

The Iranian Revolution and the Challenge of Militant Islam

In the early 1960s most experts on the Middle East region and on political development agreed that as a social and political force Islam had no future. No serious observer predicted that Islam could become a radical and change-oriented force, challenging the power status quo that prevailed within Muslim states or regionally and internationally. This appraisal did not change in the 1970s despite the surfacing of small radical Muslim groups—one in Egypt attacked the military academy in 1974—the growing activism of the Lebanese Shi'as, and the emergence of politically active but mostly clandestine Islamic groups and organizations in Iran.

Thus the Islamic revolution in Iran in 1979 was both a surprise and a challenge, for which neither Muslim governments nor Western countries were prepared. The challenge of the rise of radical Islam was especially difficult for Saudi Arabia because its entire political system and the legitimacy of its ruling elite rested on Islam. Although it was easy for Saudi Arabia to counter secular radicalism and Communism as being anti-Islam, godless, and hence illegitimate, the kingdom did not know how to deal with a creed that claimed to represent the true Islam, challenged the very Muslimness of Saudi Arabian leadership, and accused the Saudis of representing American Islam—an Islam subservient to the West and hence estranged from its essence.

Saudi Arabia's strategy during most of the 1980s was a mix of counterattack against Iran's militant brand of Islam and co-optation of the less radical and more conservative groups in other Muslim countries. When they counterattacked Iran, the Saudis stressed Iran's Shi'a character, implying its heresy and hence its illegitimacy. The Saudis also highlighted Iran's Persian character, again implying that the Iranian revolution and its ideology were the expression of its Shi'a-Persian character and had little to do with true Islam. With Saudi roots deep in Arabia and in the Arab culture, King Fahd called on Iran to stop trying to export its

Shi'a-Persian ideology, which he said was alien to Islam and to the Arab world.

Meanwhile, the Saudis doubled their efforts through financial assistance, training, and indoctrination to gain a controlling influence over other Islamic groups in the Arab world, particularly in the Afghan training camps in Pakistan's North West Frontier Province in and around the city of Peshawar. One Islamic group, the Islamic Salvation Front (FIS), which received considerable Saudi financial support, operated in Algeria and in the late 1980s became a potent political force. The FIS challenge to the Algerian military-ruled political establishment led finally to a military takeover in 1992 and to large-scale civil strife that, as late as 1997, had not been eliminated.[42]

The other part of Saudi Arabia's strategy was to draw closer to other Arabs, including those regimes with which Saudi Arabia had been at odds in the past, including the Ba'athist regime of Saddam Hussein in Iraq, and to Western allies. This strategy was manifested in the formation of the GCC in 1981, financial and political support for Iraq in its war with Iran (1980–1988), and close cooperation with the United States.

In sum, during the 1980s Islam's role in determining the nature and direction of Saudi Arabia's external behavior remained minimal. At the same time, Saudi use of Islam as an instrument of policy and as a tool to achieve Saudi Arabia's security and political objectives continued to be important.

The Persian Gulf War: Limits of Islam-Based Strategy

By the end of the 1980s, the Saudis could look with a good deal of satisfaction at the results of their foreign policy strategy. Iran had been defeated in the war with Iraq without Iraq becoming a clear and undisputed—and threatening—victor; the Soviets were preparing to leave Afghanistan, opening the way for Saudi Arabia and Pakistan to put their Muslim allies in power in Kabul; and Communism itself appeared to be on the verge of collapse, leaving the Saudis' Western patrons the undisputed masters of the world.

Saudi complacency did not last long, however; it was shattered by the Iraqi invasion of Kuwait on August 2, 1990. Among the myriad events associated with that invasion and the ensuing Gulf War, the most relevant to this study was that Islamist groups such as the FIS, which for years had benefited from Saudi largesse, sided with the regime in Baghdad. Saddam Hussain's regime had no Islamic credentials even though, during the crisis, Baghdad appealed to Islamic solidarity to gain support among the Arab and other Muslim masses while Saudi Arabia claimed the leadership of the Muslim world. Thus the conduct of groups like the FIS is instructive in terms of Islam's role as a determinant of Muslim political behavior: The Islamists supported Iraq not because of the Islamic character of the regime but because they perceived that Iraq was standing up against the West and for the restoration of what they considered to be Arab rights, especially in Palestine. That Saddam Hussain was not a good Muslim and did not apply the Islamic *Shari'a* in Iraq influenced them little; that he was an Arab militant standing up against a great power was enough.

Saudi Arabia's conduct following Iraq's invasion of Kuwait, although in line with its traditional foreign policy, is also instructive: when their security was in danger, the Saudis did not hesitate to allow foreign troops to enter Islam's sacred lands, over which they claim to be the guardian. Saudi conduct validated the age-old pattern of behavior on the part of Muslim governments— their propensity to collaborate with non-Muslims against fellow Muslims whenever it has suited their interests. Indeed, the Persian Gulf War is the most glaring example of the limited role that Islam plays in determining the behavior of Muslim states among one another or toward non-Muslim countries.

Post-Gulf-War Diplomacy: A Reduced Role for Islam as a Policy Instrument

Islam has not played a very important role in determining Saudi Arabia's external behavior, but as an instrument to legitimize and justify policy and as a tool to achieve security and other goals and to gain influence, Islam's impact has been quite significant. However, because of the disillusion over the reaction of the Islamist groups to Iraq's behavior toward Kuwait and toward the anti-Saddam coalition coupled with the strategic and financial consequences of the Gulf War, Saudi Arabia's regional role and Islam's position as an instrument for performing this role have been diminished.

The conclusion of the Gulf War and the collapse of the Soviet

Union eliminated the traditional barriers and inhibitions to a direct Western presence in the Persian Gulf region. Unhindered by fear of Soviet reaction, the United States has since 1992 assumed direct responsibility for the Persian Gulf region, which in turn has reduced the need for regional surrogates—influentials, they were called in the 1970s. Nevertheless, Saudi Arabia and other selected Gulf and Arab countries such as Bahrain and Jordan retain their importance as bases for U.S. military operations. This more extensive and direct U.S. security role in the regions of concern and of interest to Saudi Arabia also reduces the need for direct Saudi action and, hence, the need to use Islam as an instrument of policy.

A second and equally important factor is Saudi Arabia's disappointment with the results of its Islamic diplomacy. It became clear during the Gulf War that those Arab Muslims who were trained with Saudi money in Pakistan and were imbued with Wahhabi notions turned against the Saudi monarchy and supported Saddam Hussain. A third factor is the financial cost of the Gulf War and the reduction in Saudi Arabia's monetary assets that have led to a contraction in the sphere of Saudi diplomacy and, hence, to a diminution of the role of Islam as one instrument of its foreign policy.

Perhaps even more important is the emergence within Saudi Arabia of a more widespread Islamic opposition to the existing leadership. This development has highlighted three basic facts. First, the mere application of Islamic rules is no guarantee against social and political opposition if other causes of dissent are not eliminated. Second, Islam as an instrument of legitimization of political power is a double-edged sword; it can be used by the opponents of the existing power structure to challenge and delegitimize it, as it has been used during the history of the Muslim world. Third, Islamic dissent has to do with worldly socioeconomic and political issues more than with the observance of religious rules.

This is indeed what has happened in Saudi Arabia, especially since the Gulf War; thus it undermines what Hrair Dekmejian aptly characterized as "the symbiosis between royal power and religious puritanism."[43] Although tensions between some Wahhabi puritans and the Saudi kings had existed as early as 1929, they largely reflected the inevitable incompatibility between the aspirations of ideological purists—lay and religious—and the

requirements of policymakers for maintaining power and governing. Despite these growing tensions, the underlying and mutually supporting alliance between Wahhabi Islam and the Saudi
monarchy is still alive although the post-Gulf War Islamist wave
has weakened this alliance and divided the Wahhabis into supporters and opponents of the Saudi kingdom.

The case studies of the foreign policies of Iran and Saudi
Arabia—one represents a conservative and the other a revolutionary Muslim country—show that factors unrelated to Islam, in
other words, noncivilizational determinants of state behavior, are
most influential in shaping their external relations.

In Saudi Arabia, Islam has served as a useful tool for rationalizing policies adopted out of other considerations, and it has
served as an effective instrument for expanding Saudi influence.
In Iran since the establishment of the Islamic Republic, factors
related to Islam have played important roles in determining aspects of its foreign relations, especially during the first half of the
republic's life; however, Islam-related factors have been increasingly subordinated to other state interests in the long-established
Islamic practice of subordinating religious principles to *Masalahat*,
or to what is made necessary by the requirements of the common
good. The anti-Westernism of the Islamic Republic's policies has
resulted more from revolutionary zeal, Third World militancy,
and the bitter legacy of Iran's encounter with the great powers
and factional politics than from Islam.

These case studies show that, irrespective of whether there is
civilizational incompatibility between Islam and the West, factors
other than religious ones will have most influence on the state of
relations between Muslim and Western countries.

Conclusions and Outlook for Islam-West Relations

This volume has provided a basis for examining the future state of relations between Islam and the West through its analysis of the unfolding of the Islamic experience in its spatial and temporal context—especially the development of various schools of Islamic political thought and the Islamic world view. It has also analyzed the impact that these views have had on the behavior of Muslim states both toward one another and toward non-Muslims.

Several conclusions flow from this work. First, despite the widespread belief in the specificity of Islam because of an assumed fusion of politics and religion, in reality the fusion—of the spiritual and the temporal—has not been greater in Islam than in other religions. Therefore the slower pace of secularization in Muslim countries cannot be attributed to Islam's specificity. All religions at least in theory put religious laws and codes of conduct above those of man, and all believe that every aspect of human life should be organized in light of these principles.

If these principles have not been observed either in Western countries or in Muslim communities during modern times, it is because religion—defined as a divinely inspired system of belief, values, and rules—has lost the battle to the secular creed. In most secular societies, however, the contest between secularism and faith is continuing and, unless one takes an absolutely linear view of the evolution of ideas in the future, a change in the balance between religious and secular systems of value and belief cannot be ruled out.

Historically, the change in the balance between secularism and religion has been due to economic, social, and political developments—especially the growth of industrialization and urbanization. Thus if the Muslim world in general is less secularized than the West, it is not because of the peculiar quality of its creed but because its social and economic development is less advanced. Most Muslim societies have remained largely rural and traditional and hence more religion minded. Urbanization in the Muslim world has not been the result of industrialization but of flight from rural poverty; thus the proportion of the Islamic world's urban population that has retained its rural values and character is larger than the West's. From a cultural perspective, most of the Islamic world is at the preindustrial, even feudal, stage of development, when religion has a great hold on the society and the people; this also prevailed in Europe during its preindustrial times.

Second, throughout Islam's history, religion has been held in an unfavorable position in relation to politics. Assuming that in the Christian West religion and politics have always been separate—itself a dubious assumption—in Islam, by contrast, religion has been subordinated to politics and to its requirements, whether in the running of the internal affairs of Muslim countries or in determining their behavior toward other Muslim and non-Muslim states.

Third, Islamic civilization is a hybrid and a syncretic phenomenon that developed from early Islam's encounter with other regions and civilizations in the course of its historical expansion; the notion of Islamic civilization as a unique and coherent phenomenon does not reflect reality. Like all civilizations, Islamic civilization is a living, evolving organism, constantly responding to new realities and circumstances. In the process, it is being affected by them and, in its turn, is having an impact upon them. This process takes place within Muslim societies and in the context of their external relations. Thus an assessment of the impact of civilizational factors on the behavior of Muslim states must describe clearly the specific Islamic civilization and its temporal and territorial context.

Fourth, the absence of unity and uniformity in the Muslim world is also great at the political level. Islam has not eliminated ethnic, cultural, and other particularisms from the Muslim world.

In addition, modern notions of nationalism have taken firm root in the Islamic world, fragmenting it further. The ideal of creating a single unified Muslim nation and entity remains as elusive as ever.

That the ideal remains elusive has had important implications for the Muslim sense of individual and collective identity, focus of loyalty, belief and value systems, and hence for Muslim behavior toward other states. The most important consequence of unrealized Muslim unity has been that Islam is only one component of the Muslim sense of identity and values and very often it is not the most important. Even if one were to ascribe a significant role to civilizational factors as determinants of Muslim behavior, one must realize that Islam is only one element of the culture and civilization of different groups of Muslims and, as such, its role is limited.

The second consequence has been the great importance of parochial components of identity—ethnicity and language, among others—and focus of loyalty in the Muslim world, which has meant that national, dynastic, sectarian, and other parochial interests rather than impulses and motives derived from Islam have to a large extent determined the external behavior of Muslim collectivities and states. In addition, the Muslims have seldom been able to act in unison, and Muslim unity has remained an elusive goal. The so-called Muslim world has thus never become a coherent political entity and a single actor on the international level. Compared with the Islamic world, the Western countries have been more successful in their efforts to integrate and act in unison. European countries have produced the European Union (EU), which, once it completes its expansion eastward early in the next century, will include nearly all the European states. In parallel with its integration and expansion, the EU has set a goal of creating a common foreign and security policy (CFSP), so it can be a single actor on many international issues. In the security arena, the North Atlantic Treaty Organization, spanning Western Europe and North America has acted with a degree of unity rarely achieved by the Muslims. Yet even in the Western world it is impossible to speak of a single actor in terms of dealing with other countries, including the Muslim states.

This lack of total coherence among both Muslim and Western countries implies both that approaching relations between them at the level of contending civilizations is unrealistic and that evaluating the state of their relations at the level of the Islamic and the Western worlds is also unproductive. At the civilizational level, the conflict is not so much between Islam and Western liberalism as it is between faith and secularism. Absolute secularism—or what Carla Power characterized as secular radicalism and John Esposito as secular fundamentalism—is as much at odds with Christianity or Judaism as it is with Islam.[1] At the political level, talk of relations between the Islamic world and the West as though each were a coherent and unified entity is also unjustified. The only realistic and productive way of dealing with these relations is instead at the level of individual Muslim states and Western countries.

Fifth, the role of Islam within each Muslim society, as well as in the context of intra-Muslim relations and their ties with non-Muslim states is similar to the roles of other religions and secular belief systems. In this sense Islam's role is directly linked with struggles for power, influence, and legitimacy within Muslim societies and in the context of their interaction with the outside world; thus Islam is used by various groups to acquire or maintain power and to legitimize and delegitimize existing power structures. At the intra-Muslim and the international levels, Islam, like any other belief system, is used to galvanize support for one's own policies, to undermine policies of one's enemies, and to rationalize policies that are adopted on the basis of security, political, or economic considerations.

Within Muslim societies as well as internationally, Islam's role has evolved in response to socioeconomic and political developments and the dynamics they set in motion. During the past two centuries, the process of socioeconomic modernization, the changes that it has triggered, and Islam's encounter with the West have influenced most strongly the evolution of Islam's social and political role, including the emergence of a new brand of militant ideology. Indeed, Islam's increased political salience during the past few decades has been the direct consequence of shifts in the relative power and position of various elements of society, and the efforts of those who suffered as a result of these shifts to redress the balance, using Islam to rationalize and justify their actions. The same factors have also been the main impetus behind a reformist trend within Islamic countries.

Seventh, the causes of discord between some Muslim and

Western states as well as the sometimes strident anti-Westernism of Islamist elements have been inextricably linked to change within Muslim societies and to the massive intrusion of the West into Muslim countries, leading to their loss of independence, a drastic shift of international power in favor of the West by the nineteenth century, and Muslim efforts to redress the unfavorable balance of global power. These factors and specific actions by Western states—their support for unpopular governments in the Muslim world—have been the main causes of discord, not any civilizational incompatibility deriving from Islam's specificity. At the interstate level the most important sources of discord between the Muslim countries and the West have not been disagreements rooted in civilizational incompatibility. Instead, discord has grown from the efforts of Muslim governments, including governments that espouse a secular philosophy and agenda, to increase their margin of independence, to challenge the supremacy of the West, and to pursue policies contrary to Western interests.

Implications for Future Relations

These conclusions contain a number of important implications for the future of relations between Muslim and Western countries. First, as in the past, motives rooted in Islam will continue to have much less influence on the behavior of Muslim states, toward one another or toward non-Muslims, than will other determinants of state behavior such as security considerations, economic requirements, and interests of the elite. Thus despite periodic shows of outward unity it is highly unlikely that Islam will bridge the differences among the Muslim states and enable them to act as a unified Muslim entity. As in the past, some Muslims will entertain better relations with non-Muslims than with fellow Muslims, or they will form alliances with non-Muslims against other Muslims. The latest example of this phenomonon is the military alliance forged between Israel and Turkey in 1997.

Second, these relations will be of an uneven character in the sense that while a number of Western countries will have strained relations with some Muslim states, other Western and Islamic states will enjoy cooperative and even cordial ties in accordance with the historical pattern of Islam-West relations.

Third, because the social, economic, and political transformation of Muslim societies, including their gradual secularization, is not complete, the character of their external relations will be changeable and unstable, reflecting their underlying internal volatility. Even a complete secularization of Muslim societies and their adoption of important aspects of Western civilization would not guarantee perpetual amity between the Western and the Muslim countries, however, as long as other sources of discord remain, especially the Muslim countries' desire to redress the unfavorable balance of power vis-à-vis the West.

Fourth, as in the past, the level of amity or enmity between the Muslim world and the West will depend greatly on the attitude of Western countries on issues of importance to the Muslims, in terms both of their own internal development and their relations with the outside world. A good example of the impact of Western attitudes on Muslim behavior is the question of Muslim rights in Jerusalem. However, the impact of this factor on the behavior of individual Muslim states will differ depending on the extent to which this question is linked to their more worldly interests.

Fifth, in the future as in the past, a degree of competition and rivalry will remain between the Western states that want to maintain their global economic and political superiority and their influence in the Muslim world and those Muslim states that want to enlarge their own margin of independence and influence.

Sixth, the possible emergence of a new, viable economic and political counterweight to Western power, which would provide Muslim states with a potential ally and a source of assistance, could encourage their competitive tendencies toward the West and induce them to challenge Western supremacy. By contrast, the lack of such counterweight is likely to elicit a more accommodating Muslim attitude.

In the future as in the past, relations between Muslim states and Western countries, like other interstate relations, will remain a combination of conflict and cooperation. Other dynamics of interstate relations, not civilizational factors, will principally determine the underlying character of these relations.

Notes

Introduction

1. John Buchan, *The Greenmantle* (Hertfordshire, England: Wordsworth Classics, 1994), 5–6.

2. Charles Krauthammer, "The Foreign Policy President," *Washington Post*, April 16, 1993.

3. Quoted in Daniel Pipes, "The Muslims Are Coming! The Muslims Are Coming!" *National Review* 19 (November 1990): 28.

4. Bernard Lewis, "The Roots of the Muslim Rage," *Atlantic Monthly* (September 1990): 60.

5. Francis Fukuyama, *The End of History and the Last Man* (New York: The Free Press, 1992).

6. See Norman Cohen, *Cosmos, Chaos, and the World to Come: The Ancient Roots of Apocalyptic Faith* (New Haven: Yale University Press, 1993), 77–104, 220–226.

7. Georg Wilhelm Friedrich Hegel, *The Philosophy of History* (New York: Dover Publications, 1956), 173–174.

8. Samuel P. Huntington, "The Clash of Civilizations," *Foreign Affairs* 72, no. 3 (Summer 1993).

9. Richard E. Rubenstein and Farle Crocker, "Challenging Huntington," *Foreign Policy*, no. 96 (Fall 1994): 118.

10. Huntington, "Clash of Civilizations," 40–41.

11. Clifford Geertz, *The Interpretation of Cultures* (New York: Basic Books, 1973), 93.

12. *American Heritage Dictionary of the English Language*, 3rd ed. (Boston: Houghton Mifflin, 1992).

13. Geertz, *Interpretation of Cultures*, 89.

14. Henry Louis Gates, "Blood and Irony," *Economist* (September 11–17, 1993): 38.

15. See John Lancaster, "Non-Orthodox Israelis Are Bracing for a 'Culture War,'" *International Herald Tribune*, June 7, 1996; see also Patrick Cockburn, "Israel's Fundamentalists Get Ready to Call in Their Dues," *Independent on Sunday*, June 16, 1996. Indications are that this culture war is already under way. For example, a number of Orthodox rabbis and judges of religious courts have asked airlines to ban movies on flights to and from Israel and to assign only male attendants to male passengers; see "Rabbis Demand Modest Travel," *International Herald Tribune*, September 27, 1996.

16. See Odon Vallet, "La France n'est plus laïque," *Le Monde*, May 11, 1996.

17. Ariane Chemin, "Sur 'le chemin de croix des laïques' 7000 personnes defile contre la visite papale," *Le Monde*, September 24, 1996.

18. See Joan Biskupic, "Justice Scalia: Defender of the Faith," *International Herald Tribune*, April 11, 1996; see also Robert A. Sirico, "Scalia's Dissenting Opinion," *Wall Street Journal Europe*, April 22, 1996.

19. Quoted in Rubenstein and Crocker, "Challenging Huntington," 118.

20. Quoted in Ibid.

21. Extract from a speech delivered by the Tunisian Islamist leader at a conference in Teheran in October 1991; obtained by the author.

22. See Jim Hoagland, "Driving a Wedge between the Dominant Branches of Islam," *International Herald Tribune*, April 29, 1996.

23. See Leslie Gelb, "The Free Election Trap," *New York Times*, May 29, 1991; see also Amos Perlmutter, "Wishful Thinking about Islamic Fundamentalism," *Washington Post*, January 19, 1992; Bernard Lewis, "Islam and Liberal Democracy," *Atlantic Monthly* 275 (February 1993).

24. Quoted in Rubenstein and Crocker, "Challenging Huntington," 118–119.

25. See Vallet, "La France n'est plus laïque."

26. See Graham Fuller, "The Next Ideology," *Foreign Policy*, no. 98 (Spring 1995): 150.

27. Shireen T. Hunter, "The Rise of Islamist Movements and the Western Response: Clash of Civilizations or Clash of Interests," in *The Islamist Dilemma*, ed. Laura Guazzone (Reading, England: Ithaca Press, 1995), 329.

28. Geertz, *Interpretation of Cultures*, 205.

29. See Hans J. Morgenthau, *Politics among Nations* (New York: Alfred A. Knopf, 1958), 92.

30. See Zbigniew Brzezinski, *Ideology and Power in Soviet Politics* (Westport, Conn.: Greenwood Press, 1976), 4–5.

31. F. S. Northedge, "The Nature of Foreign Policy," in *The Foreign*

Policies of the Powers, ed. F. S. Northedge (London: Faber & Faber, 1968), 13.

32. On Turkey's serious human rights abuses as reported by Amnesty International, see "Amnesty Castigates Turkey," *Financial Times*, October 2, 1996.

33. See Robert H. Ferrell, ed., *Off the Record: The Private Papers of Harry S. Truman* (New York: Harper and Row, 1980), 53. During World War II, of course, ideological incompatibility did not hamper cooperation with Stalin's Soviet Union although there was a need to humanize him as "Uncle Joe" to try to make ideology consistent with state interests.

34. Melyn P. Leffler, "Inside Enemy Archives: The Cold War Reopened," *Foreign Affairs* 75, no. 4 (Summer 1996): 135.

35. Ibid.

36. Irving Kristol, "A Post-Wilsonian Foreign Policy," *Wall Street Journal Europe*, August 7, 1996.

Chapter 1

1. These were, in chronological order, Abu Bakr, Omar, Osman, and Ali.

2. See Bernard Lewis, "Politics and War," in *The Legacy of Islam*, ed. Joseph Schacht and C. E. Bosworth (Oxford: Oxford University Press, 1979), 156.

3. See Norman L. Zucker, "Secularization Conflicts in Israel," in *Religion and Political Modernization*, ed. Donald E. Smith (New Haven: Yale University Press, 1974), 96.

4. Donald E. Smith, "Religion and Political Modernization: Comparative Perspectives," in ibid., 14.

5. Zucker, "Secularization Conflicts in Israel," in ibid., 96.

6. For a more detailed analysis of these issues, see Montgomery Watt, *Islamic Political Thought: The Basic Concepts* (Edinburgh: Edinburgh University Press, 1968).

7. On the Constitution of Medina, see ibid., 485–486; and for an elaboration of these issues, see Nazih Ayubi, *Political Islam: Religion and Politics in the Arab World* (New York: Routledge, 1991), 6.

8. Ibid., 6.

9. Some Shi'as believe that a verse in the *Qur'an*, later removed by Ali's opponents, proclaimed Ali's successorship. This theory is of course refuted by the Sunnis as a Shi'a fabrication.

10. On the question of the impact of Arab tribal traditions on the development of Shi'ism, see S. Hussain M. Jafri, *Origins and Early Development of Shi'a Islam* (London: Longman, 1979).

11. There were other differences of a doctrinal and tribal character between the Kharijites and other Muslims; for details, see Watt, *Islamic Political Thought*, 54–57.

12. The terms are borrowed from James Bill; see his "Resurgent Islam in the Persian Gulf," *Foreign Affairs* 63, no. 1 (Fall 1984): 108–127.

13. Ayubi, *Political Islam*, 8.

14. Watt, *Islamic Political Thought*, 68.

15. Ibid.

16. Mujtaba Minovi, ed., *Nameh-e-Tansar* (Teheran: Kharazmi, 1354 [1975]), 53.

17. Anne K. S. Lambton, "Islamic Political Thought," in *Legacy of Islam*, ed. Schacht and Bosworth, 417.

18. Ibid.

19. Ibid., 418.

20. Ibid., 420–421.

21. Ayubi, *Political Islam*, 24.

22. Watt, *Islamic Political Thought*, 82–83.

23. Ayubi, *Political Islam*, 22.

24. Lambton, "Islamic Political Thought," in *Legacy of Islam*, ed. Schacht and Bosworth, 408.

25. Ibid., 409.

26. Ayubi, *Political Islam*, 9.

27. Ibid., 127.

28. See Hamid Enayat, "Iran and the Arabs," in *Arab Nationalism and a Wider World*, ed. Sylvia Haim (New York: American Association for Peace in the Middle East, 1971), 13–25.

29. Ibid.

30. Hamid Enayat, *Modern Islamic Political Thought* (Austin: University of Texas Press, 1982), 19.

31. Ibid., 26.

32. Ibid., 27.

33. For an elaboration of these issues see Fazlur Rahman, *Islam and Modernity: Transformation of an Intellectual Tradition* (Chicago: University of Chicago Press, 1982).

34. For example, Adda Bozeman maintains that Islam is inimical to the "core idea of the state." Bozeman and Elie Kedourie also assert that the modern nation-state cannot emerge from among the Muslims. See Adda B. Bozeman, "Iran, U.S. Foreign Policy, and the Tradition of Persian Statecraft," *Orbis* (Summer 1979): 389; and Elie Kedourie, ed., *Nationalism in Asia and Africa* (London: Weidenfeld & Nicolson, 1970).

35. See Bernard Lewis, *The Middle East and the West* (Bloomington: Indiana University Press, 1964), 135–136.

36. For a more detailed discussion of these issues, see James P.

Piscatori, *Islam in a World of Nation States* (Cambridge: Cambridge University Press, 1986), 44.

37. Mamoun Fandy, "Tribe Versus Islam: The Post-Colonial Arab State and the Democratic Imperative," *Middle East Policy* 48 (1994): 40–51.

38. Piscatori, *Islam in a World of Nation States*, 69.

39. Watt, *Islamic Political Thought*, 91.

40. Fandy, "Tribe Versus Islam," 48.

41. This was developed by the Sha'fi school.

42. For example, according to Ibn Taymiyya, "because of Islam's essential religious unity, it need not have only one political regime." According to Ibn Khaldun, the factual rise and decline of political units is entirely natural and, by implication, in accord with Islam. See Piscatori, *Islam in a World of Nation States*, 47.

43. For views of modern Muslim intellectuals on the international system, see ibid., 77–115.

Chapter 2

1. Works by John L. Esposito, James P. Piscatori, Francois Burgat, and Gill Kepel are among the best in the field, as well as R. Hrair Dekmejian, *Islam in Revolution* (Syracuse: Syracuse University Press, 1985) and Shireen T. Hunter, ed., *The Politics of Islamic Revivalism: Diversity and Unity* (Bloomington: Indiana University Press, 1988).

2. Martin Kramer, "Islam versus Democracy," *Commentary* (January 1993).

3. Amos Perlmutter, "Wishful Thinking about Islamic Fundamentalism," *Washington Post*, January 19, 1992.

4. Among such scholars are John L. Esposito and John O. Voll; see "Islam's Democratic Essence," *Middle East Quarterly* (September 1994): 3–11; also their *Islam and Democracy in the Muslim World* (New York: Oxford University Press, 1996).

5. Francois Burgat, *l'Islamisme en face* (*Confronting Islamism*) (Paris: Editions La Decouverte, 1995), 107.

6. Quoted in "Les Islamists En Europe," *l'Express*, May 6, 1994.

7. Francois Burgat, *l'Islamisme en face* [author's translation], 267.

8. Fereydoun Adamiyat, *Andisheh-e-Taraghi va Hokoumat-e-Ghanoun: Asr-e-Sepah Salar* (*The Idea of Progress and the Rule of Law: The Era of Sepah Salar*) (Teheran: Entesharat-e-Kharazmi, 1354 [1975]).

9. For Iqbal's views, see Hafeez Malik, ed., *Iqbal: The Poet-Philosopher of Pakistan* (New York: Columbia University Press, 1971).

10. Alexandre Bennigsen and Chantal Lemercier-Quelguejay, *Islam in Russia* (New York: Praeger, 1967), 35.

11. Quoted in L. R. Gordon-Polanskaya, "Ideology of Muslim Nationalism," in *Iqbal: The Poet-Philosopher of Pakistan*, ed. H. Malik, 113.

12. Hafeez Malik, *Sir Sayyid Ahmad Khan and Muslim Modernization in India and Pakistan* (New York: Columbia University Press, 1980), 175.

13. Ibid.

14. Afghani's dissimulation of his ethnic and sectarian origin was due to the existence of widespread anti-Persian and anti-Shi'a bias in the Ottoman Turkish empire and among its Arab subjects, where he wanted to gain adepts and mobilize the population. For details of Afghani's Iranian birth and upbringing, see Nikki R. Keddie, *Sayyid Jamal ed-Din Afghani: A Political Biography* (Berkeley: University of California Press, 1972).

15. Ibid., 16–17.

16. Elie Kedourie, *Afghani and Abduh: An Essay on Religious Unbelief and Political Activism in Modern Islam* (London: Frank Cass & Co., Ltd., 1966), 42–43.

17. Ibid., 42.

18. Ibid., 44.

19. Ibid., 45.

20. Keddie, *Jamal ed-Din Afghani*, 18.

21. Kedourie, *Afghani and Abduh*, 45.

22. Keddie, *Jamal ed-Din Afghani*, 138.

23. Quoted in Kedourie, *Afghani and Abduh*, 3.

24. Ibid.

25. Albert Hourani, *Arabic Thought in the Liberal Age* (Oxford: Oxford University Press, 1970).

26. Keddie, *Jamal ed-Din Afghani*, 138.

27. On the Ottoman reforms, see Kemal H. Karpat, *Turkey's Politics: The Transition to a Muslim Multi-Party System* (Princeton: Princeton University Press, 1959), 3–98. On the Iranian experience, see Fereydoun Adamiyat, *Andisheh-e-Taraghi va Hokoumat-e-Ghanoun: Asr-e-Sepah Salar* (*The Idea of Progress and the Rule of Law: The Era of Sepah Salar*) (Teheran: Entesharat-e-Kharazmi, 1354 [1975]) and Fereydoun Adamiyat, *Amir Kabir va Iran* (*Amir Kabir and Iran*) (Teheran: Chapkhaneh-e-Payam, 1323 [1944–1945]).

28. Malik, *Sir Sayyid Ahmad Khan*, 126–127.

29. Ibid.

30. Edward A. Allworth, *The Modern Uzbeks* (Stanford: Hoover Institution Press, 1990), 103–141.

31. For details see Vanessa Martin, *Islam and Modernism: The Iranian Revolution of 1906* (London: Tauris, 1989), 66.

32. Philip Robins, *Turkey and the Middle East* (London: Pinter Publishers/Royal Institute of International Affairs, 1990), 7.

33. Michael M. Gunter, *The Kurds in Turkey* (Boulder, Colo.: Westview, 1990), 11.

34. Feroz Ahmad, *Turkish Experiment in Democracy* (London: C. Hurst and Company, 1977).

35. Feroz Ahmad, "Islamic Reassertion in Turkey," *Third World Quarterly* 10, no. 2 (April 1988): 749–769; and Binnaz Toprak, *Islam and Political Development in Turkey* (Leiden: E. J. Brill, 1981).

36. For more details see Shireen T. Hunter, *Turkey at the Crossroads: Islamic Past or European Future?* (Brussels: CEPS Paper No. 61, 1995).

37. James M. Dorsey, "Turkey's Military Advises Premier to Toe Secular Line," *Wall Street Journal Europe*, March 3, 1997; Christopher Dickey, "Tired of Waiting?" *Newsweek* (April 28, 1997): 16–17.

38. John Barham, "Ankara Stamps on Islamic Schools," *Financial Times*, July 23, 1997; John Barham, "Riot Police Battle Turkish Islamists," *Financial Times*, July 30, 1997.

39. Enayat, "Iran and the Arabs," in *Arab Nationalism and a Wider World*, ed. S. Haim, 13–25.

40. Enayat, *Modern Islamic Political Thought*, 123.

41. Ibid., 123–124.

42. Ibid., 117–118.

43. Ibid., 112.

44. Ibid., 112–114.

45. Alexandre Bennigsen and S. Enders Wimbush, *Muslim National Communism in the Soviet Union* (Chicago: University of Chicago Press, 1979).

46. Ibid., 50. Some Tatar and other Central Asian Communists maintained that dialectical materialism, which they called energetic materialism, was developed in the East by the Mongols: Ibid., 49.

47. Shahrough Akhavi, *Religion and Politics in Contemporary Iran. Clergy, State Relations in the Pahlavi Period* (Albany: SUNY Press, 1980).

48. For details of these arguments, see Enayat, *Modern Islamic Political Thought*, 148–152.

49. Chibli Mallat, "Iraq," in *The Politics of Islamic Revivalism*, ed. S. T. Hunter, 71–87.

50. Ervand Abrahamian, *Radical Islam: The Iranian Mojahedin* (London: I. B. Tauris and Co., Ltd. 1989), 82.

51. Quoted in Abrahamian, *Radical Islam*, 113.

52. Ervand Abrahamian, "The Guerrilla Movements in Iran, 1963–1977," *MERIP Report*, no. 86 (March/April 1980): 3–21.

53. Quoted in Henry Munson, "Morocco," in *The Politics of Islamic Revivalism*, ed. S. T. Hunter, 141.

54. See Norma Salem, "Tunisia," in ibid., 162.

55. See Sulayman S. Nyang, "West Africa," in ibid., 204–225.

56. See Amira Al-Azhari Sonbol, "Egypt," in ibid., 26.

57. See Shireen T. Hunter, *The Algerian Crisis: Origins, Evolution and Lessons for the Maghreb and Europe* (Brussels: CEPS Paper No. 63, 1996). On Saudi Arabia, see Douglas Jehl, "Challenges to a Monarchy Festers Below the Surface," *International Herald Tribune*, November 6, 1996.

58. Saad Eddin Ibrahim, "Islamic Activism: A Rejoinder," *Security Dialogue* 25, no. 2 (1994): 193.

59. Ibid., 194.

60. See Donald Eugene Smith, "Religion and Political Modernization: Comparative Perspectives," in *Religion and Political Modernization*, ed. D. E. Smith, 17.

61. Ibid.

62. Ibid., 18.

63. Reproduced under the title of "Iran: Paradoxes and Contradictions in a Changing Society," *Civil Society* 4, no. 47 (November 1995): 13. (The magazine is published by the Ibn Khaldoun Center for Development Studies in Cairo.)

64. Hooshang Amirahmadi, "Emerging Civil Society in Iran," *SAIS Review* 16, no. 2 (Summer/Fall 1996): 18.

65. Hassan Hanafi, "Des Ideologies Modernistes a l'Islam Revolutionnaire," *Peuples mediterraneens*, no. 21 (October–December 1982): 13; also Peter Waldman, "Leap of Faith: Some Muslim Thinkers Want to Reinterpret Islam for Modern Times," *Wall Street Journal Europe*, March 15, 1995.

66. Edward Mortimer, "On the Middle Path," *Financial Times*, July 10, 1996; for more on the prime minister's views, see Peter Montagnon and James Kynge, "A Modern Man in the Wings," *Financial Times*, November 8, 1996.

67. See *Kian* (author's translation from the Persian original) 3 (Third Year), no. 13 (June–July 1994): 5.

68. Ibid.

69. Ibid.

70. "An Iranian Martin Luther Preaches Islamic Reform," *Christian Science Monitor*, April 20, 1995.

71. "Abdul Karim Surush: Views and Reactions," FBIS/NES-95-421-5 (December 15, 1995): 12.

72. Ibid.; see also Valla Vakili, *Debating Religion and Politics in Iran: The Political Thought of Abdol Karim Soroush*, Occasional Paper Series, no. 2 (New York: Council on Foreign Relations, 1996), 19.

73. Abdul Karim Surush, *"Jameeh-e-Payambar Pasand"* ("Society Approved by the Prophet"), *Kian* 3 (Third Year), no. 17 (1994): 21.

74. For more details, see Vakili, *Debating Religion and Politics in Iran*, 12–14.

75. See "Iranian Martin Luther Preaches Islamic Reform"; also "Iran: Kiyan on Religious, Political Pluralism," FBIS-NES-96-123-S (June 25, 1966): 1–34.

76. Ibid.

77. See "Culture Comes Out of the Closet," *Middle East Economic Digest* (May 31, 1996): 7–8. For example, according to the director of the Islamic Propagation Organization's (IPO) Arts Center, the reason that for one thousand years the Shi'as did not deal with arts was "not because the arts were un-Islamic," but because they were the purview of illegitimate rulers; thus "the arts were originally considered good but because their practice was left in the hands of the *Taghout* (the religiously corrupt), they became *haram* (religiously forbidden)."

78. See Enayat, *Modern Islamic Political Thought*, 86.

79. Ibid., 87–88.

80. Quoted in Munson, "Morocco" in *Politics of Islamic Revivalism*, ed. S. T. Hunter, 140.

81. John L. Esposito, ed., *The Iranian Revolution: Its Global Impact* (Miami: Florida International University Press, 1990).

82. Shireen T. Hunter, "Iran and the Spread of Revolutionary Islam," *Third World Quarterly* 10, no. 2 (1988): 730–749.

83. Quoted in Eric Rouleau, *Le Monde*, April 18, 1980.

84. Leon T. Haddar, "What Green Peril?" *Foreign Affairs* 72, no. 2 (Spring 1993): 39.

85. Lewis, "Roots of the Muslim Rage," 62.

86. Daniel Pipes, "Fundamentalist Muslims between America and Russia," *Foreign Affairs* 64, no. 5 (Summer 1986): 948.

87. Foreign Broadcasting Information Service, FBIS/ME/SA (July 24, 1984): 2–4.

88. John L. Esposito, *Islamic Threat: Myth or Reality* (Oxford: Oxford University Press, 1992), 127.

89. Christian Chambeau, "Le Front National designe le mondialisme a la Vindicte des Travailleurs," *Le Monde*, May 3, 1996.

90. Graham Fuller, "Islamic Fundamentalism: No Long-Term Threat," *Washington Post*, January 13, 1992.

91. Hugh Leach, "Observing Islam from Within and Without," *Asian Affairs* 21, part 1 (February 1991): 13.

92. Pipes, "Fundamentalist Muslims," 959.

93. See William Maley, "Taliban Triumphant," *World Today* 52, no. 11 (November 1996); see also Thomas W. Lippman, "U.S. Relinquishes Hope of Stable Taleban Rule," *International Herald Tribune*, November 5, 1966.

94. Fuller, "The Next Ideology," 150.

Chapter 3

1. Arnold Toynbee, *A Study of History* (Oxford: Oxford University Press, 1963).
2. Adda B. Bozeman, "Iran: U.S. Foreign Policy and the Tradition of Persian Statecraft," *Orbis* (Summer 1979): 392.
3. On the Safavids, see R. K. Ramazani, *The Foreign Policy of Iran: A Developing Nation in World Affairs 1500–1941* (Charlottesville: University Press of Virginia, 1966).
4. The stronghold of one of the most important figures of the Ismaili faith, Hassan Sabbah, was the fort of Alamut near Qazvin, a city near Teheran.
5. Shah Abbas managed to expel the Portuguese from the port of Gumbrun, which is the present Bandar Abbas (named after the king) and from the island of Hormuz with the help of Great Britain, which was competing with Portugal for mastery of the Persian Gulf.
6. From 1736 to 1742, when he declared himself king, Nadir acted on behalf of Shah Tahmasseb II to try to rid Iran of its enemies. See Ramazani, *The Foreign Policy of Iran.*
7. Ibid.
8. Piscatori, *Islam in a World of Nation States*, 55.
9. Enayat, *Modern Islamic Political Thought*, 122.
10. Jacob M. Landau, *The Politics of Pan-Islam* (Oxford: Clarendon Press, 1994), 45. Munif Pasha was a Syrian Arab who, according to Landau, had been "the initiator of the policy to strengthen the international authority of sultan-caliph via pan-Islam."
11. R. K. Ramazani, *Iran's Foreign Policy 1941–1973: A Study of Foreign Policy in Modernizing Nations* (Charlottesville: University Press of Virginia, 1975).
12. Richard Cottom, *Nationalism in Iran* (Pittsburgh: University of Pittsburgh Press, 1979), 153.
13. For an analysis see R. K. Ramazani, *Iran's Foreign Policy 1941–1973*; also see Shahram Chubin and Sepehr Zabih, *The Foreign Relations of Iran* (Berkeley: University of California Press, 1976) and Shireen T. Hunter, *OPEC and the Third World: Politics of Aid* (Bloomington: Indiana University Press, 1984), 106–113.
14. R. K. Karanjia, *The Mind of a Monarch* (London: George Allen and Unwin, 1977), 236.
15. For more details, see Shireen T. Hunter, *Iran and the World: Continuity in a Revolutionary Decade* (Bloomington: Indiana University Press, 1990), 54–56.
16. *Le Monde*, April 18, 1980.
17. "Iranian Minister Defends Policy," *Washington Post*, November 27, 1986.

Dekmejian, R. Hrair. *Islam in Revolution: Fundamentalism in the Arab World*. Syracuse, N.Y.: Syracuse University Press, 1985.

Dessuki, Ali E. Hillal and Alexandre S. Cudsi. *Islam and Power*. Baltimore, Md.: Johns Hopkins University Press, 1981.

Djait, Hisham. *La Grande Discorde: Religion et Politique dans l'Islam des Origines*. Paris: Editions Gallimard, 1989.

Enayat, Hamid. *Modern Islamic Political Thought*. Austin: University of Texas Press, 1982.

Esposito, John L. *Islam and Development: Religion and SocioPolitical Change*. Syracuse, N.Y.: Syracuse University Press, 1980.

_____. *Islam and Politics*. Syracuse, N.Y.: Syracuse University Press, 1984.

_____. *Islamic Threat: Myth or Reality*. New York: Oxford University Press, 1992; 2nd ed. 1995.

_____, ed. *Voices of Resurgent Islam*. New York: Oxford University Press, 1983.

_____, ed. *The Iranian Revolution: Its Global Impact*. Miami: Florida International University Press, 1990.

Esposito, John L., and John O. Voll. *Islam and Democracy in the Muslim World*. New York: Oxford University Press, 1996.

Feroz, Ahmad. *Turkish Experiment in Democracy*. London: C. Hurst & Company, 1977.

Fukuyama, Francis. *The End of History and the Last Man*. New York: The Free Press, 1992.

Geertz, Clifford. *The Interpretation of Cultures*. New York: Basic Books, 1973.

Guazzane, Laura, ed. *The Islamist Dilemma*. Reading, England: Ithaca Press, 1995.

Gunter, Michael M. *The Kurds in Turkey*. Boulder, Colo.: Westview, 1990.

Habib, John S. *Ibn Saud's Warriors of Islam: The Ikhvan of Najd and Their Role in the Creation of the Saudi Kingdom, 1910–1930*. Leiden: E. J. Brill, 1978.

Haim, Sylvia, ed. *Arab Nationalism and a Wider World*. New York: American Association for Peace in the Middle East, 1971.

Hegel, Georg Wilhelm Frederich. *The Philosophy of History*. New York: Dover Publications, 1956.

Hirst, David. *Oil and Public Opinion in the Middle East*. London: Faber & Faber, 1966.

Hourani, Albert. *Arabic Thought in the Liberal Age*. Oxford: Oxford University Press, 1970.

Hunter, Shireen T. *OPEC and the Third World: Politics of Aid*. Bloomington: Indiana University Press, 1984.

_____. *Iran and the World: Continuity in a Revolutionary Decade.* Bloomington: Indiana University Press, 1990.

_____. *Iran after Khomeini.* New York: Praeger/CSIS, 1992.

_____. *The Transcaucasus in Transition: Nation-Building and Conflict.* Washington, D.C.: CSIS, 1994.

_____. *Turkey at the Crossroads: Islamic Past or European Future?* Brussels: Center for European Policy Studies (CEPS) Paper No. 61, 1995.

_____. *Central Asia since Independence.* Westport, Conn.: Praeger/CSIS, 1996.

_____. *The Algerian Crisis: Origins, Evolution and Lessons for the Maghreb and Europe.* Brussels: Center for European Policy Studies (CEPS) Paper No. 63, 1996.

_____, ed. *The Politics of Islamic Revivalism: Diversity and Unity.* Bloomington: Indiana University Press, 1988.

Huntington, Samuel P. *The Clash of Civilizations and the Remaking of World Order.* New York: Simon & Schuster, 1996.

Jafri, S. Hussain M. *Origins and Early Development of Shi'a Islam.* London: Longman, 1979.

Karanjia, R. K. *The Mind of a Monarch.* London: George Allen and Unwin, 1977.

Karpat, Kemal H. *Turkey's Politics: The Transition to a Muslim Multi-Party System.* Princeton: Princeton University Press, 1959.

Keddie, Nikki R. *Sayyid Jamal ed-Din Afghani: A Political Biography.* Berkeley: University of California Press, 1972.

Kedourie, Elie. *Afghani and Abduh: An Essay on Religious Unbelief and Political Activism in Modern Islam.* London: Frank Cass & Co. Ltd., 1966.

_____. *Nationalism in Asia and Africa.* London: Weidenfeld and Nicolson, 1970.

Kepel, Gilles. *Le Prophete et Pharaon: Les Mouvements Islamistes dans l'Egypte Contemporaine.* Paris: Editions La Decouverte, 1984.

_____. *La Revanche de Dieu, Chretiens, Juifs et Musulmans a la reconquete du monde.* Paris: Editions du Seuil, 1991.

Landau, Jacob M. *The Politics of Pan-Islam.* Oxford: Clarendon Press, 1994.

Lewis, Bernard. *The Middle East and the West.* Bloomington: Indiana University Press, 1964.

_____. *Islam and the West.* New York: Oxford University Press, 1993.

Malik, Hafeez. *Sir Sayyid Ahmad Khan and Muslim Modernization in India and Pakistan.* New York: Columbia University Press, 1980.

_____, ed. *Iqbal: Poet-Philosopher of Pakistan.* New York: Columbia University Press, 1971.

Malley, Robert. *The Call from Algeria: Third Worldism, Revolution, and the Turn to Islam.* Berkeley: University of California Press, 1996.

Martin, Vanessa. *Islam and Modernism: The Iranian Revolution of 1906*. London: Tauris, 1989.

Mazrui, Ali. *Africa's International Relations: The Diplomacy of Dependency and Change*. Boulder, Colo.: Westview, 1977.

Minovi, Mujtaba, ed. *Nameh-e-Tansar (Book of Tansar)*. Teheran: Kharazmi, 1354 (1975).

Moadel, Mansoor. *Class, Politics and Ideology in the Iranian Revolution*. New York: Columbia University Press, 1993.

Morgenthau, Hans J. *Politics among Nations*. New York: Alfred A. Knopf, 1958.

Munson, Henry J. R. *Religion and Power in Morocco*. New Haven: Yale University Press, 1993.

Northedge, F. S. *The Foreign Policies of the Powers*. London: Faber & Faber, 1968.

Pipes, Daniel. *In the Path of God: Islam and Political Power*. New York: Basic Books, 1983.

Piscatori, James P. *Islam in a World of Nation States*. Cambridge: Cambridge University Press, 1986.

_____. *Islamic Fundamentalism and the Gulf Crisis*. Chicago: The American Academy of Arts and Sciences, 1991.

_____, ed. *Islam in the Political Process*. Cambridge: Cambridge University Press, 1983.

Quandt, William B. *Saudi Arabia in the 1980s: Foreign Policy, Security and Oil*. Washington, D.C.: The Brookings Institution, 1981.

Rahman, Fazlur. *Islam and Modernity*. Chicago: University of Chicago Press, 1982.

Rajaee, Farhang. *Islamic Values and World View: Khomeini on Man, the State and International Politics*. Lanham, Md.: University Press of America, 1983.

Ramazani, R. K. *The Foreign Policy of Iran: A Developing Nation in World Affairs 1500–1941*. Charlottesville, Va.: University Press of Virginia, 1966.

_____. *Iran's Foreign Policy 1941–1973: A Study of Foreign Policy in Modernizing Nations*. Charlottesville, Va.: University Press of Virginia, 1975.

Raoudja, Ahmed. *Les Freres et la Mosquee. Enquete sur le Mouvement Islamiste en Algerie*. Paris: Karthala, 1990.

Robins, Philip. *Turkey and the Middle East*. London: Pinter Publishers/ Royal Institute of International Affairs, 1990.

Said, Edward. *Orientalism*. New York: Vintage Books, 1978.

Salem, Norma. *Habib Bourguiba, Islam and the Creation of Tunisia*. London: Croom Helm, 1984.

Schacht, Joseph and C. E. Bosworth, eds. *The Legacy of Islam*. Oxford: Oxford University Press, 1979.

Sivan, Emmanuel. *Radical Islam: Medieval Theology and Modern Politics.* New Haven: Yale University Press, 1985.

Smith, Donald E., ed. *Religion and Political Modernization.* New Haven: Yale University Press, 1974.

Toprak, Binnaz. *Islam and Political Development in Turkey.* Leiden: E. J. Brill, 1981.

Toynbee, Arnold. *The Study of History.* New York: Oxford University Press, 1963.

Von der Mehden, Fred R. *Religion and Nationalism in Southeast Asia.* Madison: University of Wisconsin Press, 1986.

Waardenburg, J. D. *L'Islam dans le Miroir de l'Occident.* Paris: Mouton, 1963.

Watt, Montgomery. *Islamic Political Thought: The Basic Concepts.* Edinburgh: Edinburgh University Press, 1968.

Articles

Abrahamian, Ervand. "The Guerrilla Movements in Iran, 1963–1977." *Middle East Research and Information Project (MERIP) Report* 86 (March–April 1980).

Amirahmadi, Hooshang. "Emerging Civil Society in Iran." *SAIS Review* (Summer–Fall 1986).

Batatu, Hanna. "Iraq's Underground Shi'a Movements: Characteristics, Causes and Prospects." *Middle East Journal* 35, no. 4 (Autumn 1981).

Bill, James. "Resurgent Islam in the Persian Gulf." *Foreign Affairs* 63, no. 1 (Fall 1984).

Bozeman, Adda. "Iran, U.S. Foreign Policy, and the Tradition of Persian Statecraft." *Orbis* (Summer 1979).

Dekmejian, R. Hrair. "The Arab Anatomy of Islamic Revival: Legitimacy Crisis, Ethnic Conflict, and the Search for Islamic Alternatives." *Middle East Journal* 34, no. 1 (Winter 1980).

_____. "The Rise of Political Islamism in Saudi Arabia." *Middle East Journal* 48, no. 4 (Autumn 1994).

Esposito, John L., and John D. Voll. "Islam's Democratic Essence." *Middle East Quarterly* (September 1994).

Esposito, John L., and James P. Piscatori. "Democratization and Islam." *Middle East Journal* 45, no. 3 (Summer 1991).

Fandy, Mamoun. "Tribe versus Islam: The Post-Colonial Arab State and the Democratic Imperative." *Middle East Policy* 48 (1994).

_____. "Egypt's Islamic Group: Regional Revenge?" *Middle East Journal* 48, no. 4 (Autumn 1994).

18. Farhang Rajaee, *Islamic Values and World View: Khomeini on Man, the State, and International Politics* (Lanham, Md.: University Press of America, 1983), 45–46.

19. Jalal Al-Ahmad, *Garb Zadeghi* (*Westoxication*) (Islamic Students' Association of Europe, U.S., and Canada, 1979).

20. Juan Jose Arevalo, *The Shark and the Sardines* (New York: E. L. Stuart, 1961), 84.

21. Rajaee, *Islamic Values and World View*, 86.

22. *Keyhan*, May 12, 1983.

23. R. K. Ramazani, "Khumayni's Islam in Iran's Foreign Policy," in *Islam in Foreign Policy*, ed. Adeed Dawisha (Cambridge: Cambridge University Press, 1983), 19.

24. Rajaee, *Islamic Values and World View*, 83.

25. Ibid., 88–91.

26. Abol-Hassan Bani-Sadr, *Sad Magaleh* (*Hundred Essays*, a collection of articles), (1359 [1979]), 84.

27. According to Ali Mazrui, Israel is a piece of the West deposited in the heart of the Third World; see his *Africa's International Relations: The Diplomacy of Dependency and Change* (Boulder, Colo.: Westview, 1977).

28. Hunter, *Iran and the World*, 45.

29. For an analysis of these issues, see Shireen T. Hunter, *The Transcaucasus in Transition: Nation-Building and Conflict* (Washington, D.C.: CSIS, 1994), 170–176.

30. For details, see Shireen T. Hunter, *Central Asia since Independence* (Westport, Conn: Praeger/CSIS, 1996), 129–134.

31. Shireen T. Hunter, "Closer Ties for Russia-Iran," *Transition*, 1, no. 24 (December 29, 1995): 42–45.

32. Al Dar'iya is located approximately 10 miles north of present-day Riyadh, the capital of Saudi Arabia.

33. See John S. Habib, *Ibn Sa'ud's Warriors of Islam: The Ikhvan of Najd and Their Role in the Creation of the Sa'udi Kingdom, 1910–1930* (Leiden, The Netherlands: E. J. Brill, 1978), 3.

34. Ibid., 4.

35. James P. Piscatori, "Saudi Arabia," in *Islam in Foreign Policy*, ed. Adeed Dawisha, 34.

36. Ibid.

37. Ibid., 35.

38. Ibid., 36.

39. On the relationship between oil and Arab nationalism, see David Hirst, *Oil and Public Opinion in the Middle East* (London: Faber & Faber, 1966); also see Emile Bustani, *Marche Arabesque* (London: Robert Hale Ltd., 1961).

40. For a detailed study of the impact of aid on diplomacy, see Hunter, *OPEC and the Third World*, 123–132.

41. During the past few years, Shi'a-Sunni strife has reached alarming proportions in Pakistan, and the Wahhabi-influenced Sunni group *Sepah-e-Sahaba* regularly attacks and kills Shi'as. On Zia ul-Haq's Islamization policy, see Mumtaz Ahmad, "Pakistan," in *Politics of Islamic Revivalism*, ed. Hunter, 229–246.

42. Hunter, *The Algerian Crisis*.

43. R. Hrair Dekmejian, "The Rise of Political Islamism in Saudi Arabia," *Middle East Journal*, 48, no. 4 (Autumn 1994) 627.

Conclusions

1. Carla Power, "Secularist Radicalism," *Newsweek* (July 16, 1997): 2, and Robert H. Pelletreau, Daniel Pipes, and John Esposito, "Symposium: Resurgent Islam in the Middle East," *Middle East Policy 3*, no. 2 (1994): 12.

Select Bibliography

Books

Abir, Mordechai. *Saudi-Arabia in the Oil Era: Regime and Elites, Conflict and Collaboration*. London: Croom Helm, 1988.

Abrahamian, Ervand. *Radical Islam: The Iranian Mojahedin*. London: I. B. Tauris & Co. Ltd., 1989.

_____. *Iran between Two Revolutions*. Princeton: Princeton University Press, 1992.

Adamiyat, Fereydoun. *Amir Kabir va Iran (Amir Kabir and Iran)*. Teheran: Chapkhaneh-e-Payam, 1323 (1944–1945).

   . *Fakr-e-Azadi va Nehzat-e-Mashrutiat (The Idea of Liberty and the Constitutional Movement)*. Teheran: Entesharat-e-Sokhan, 1340 (1962).

_____. *Andisheh-e-Taraghi va Hokoumat-e-Ghanoun: Asr-e-Sepah Salar (The Idea of Progress and the Rule of Law: The Era of Sepah Salar)*. Teheran: Entesharat-e-Kharazmi, 1354 (1975).

_____. *Fakr-e-Democracy-e-Ejternai dar Nehzat Mashrutiat-e-Iran (The Idea of Social Democracy in the Constitutional Movement of Iran)*. Teheran: Payam, 1354 (1975).

Adams, Charles C. *Islam and Modernism in Egypt: A Study of the Modern Reform Movement Inaugurated by Muhammad Abduh*. New York: Russel and Russel, 1968.

Akhavi, Shahrough. *Religion and Politics in Contemporary Iran: Clergy, State Relations in the Pahlavi Period*. Albany, N.Y.: SUNY Press, 1980.

Al-Ahmad, Jalal. *Gharbzadeghi (Westoxication)*. Islamic Students Association of Europe, U.S., and Canada, 1979.

Algar, Hamid. *Religion and State in Iran 1785–1906*. Berkeley: University of California Press, 1968.

Algar, Hamid, ed. *Islam and Revolution: Writings and Declarations of Imam Khomeini.* Berkeley, Calif.: Mizan Press, 1981.

Allworth, Edward. *The Modern Uzbeks: From the Fourteenth Century to the Present.* Stanford: Hoover Institution Press, 1990.

Arevalo, Juan Jose. *The Shark and the Sardines.* New York: E. L. Stuart, 1961.

Ayubi, Nazih N. *Political Islam: Religion and Politics in the Arab World.* New York: Routledge, 1991.

Bani-Sadr, Abol-Hassan. *Sad Mageleh (Hundred Essays).* Organization of Iranian Students in the United States, 1359 (1979).

Batatu, Hannah. *The Old Social Class and the Revolutionary Movements of Iraq.* Princeton: Princeton University Press, 1978.

Beling, William A., ed. *King Faisal and the Modernization of Saudi Arabia.* Boulder, Colo.: Westview, 1980.

Bennigsen, Alexandre, and Chantal Lemercier-Quelguejay. *Islam in Russia.* New York: Praeger, 1967.

Bennigsen, Alexandre, and S. Enders Wimbush. *Muslim National Communism in the Soviet Union.* Chicago: University of Chicago Press, 1979.

Binder, Leonard. *Religion and Politics in Pakistan.* Berkeley: University of California Press, 1961.

_____. *Islamic Liberalism: A Critique of Development Ideologies.* Chicago: University of Chicago Press, 1988.

Brzezinski, Zbigniew. *Ideology and Power in Soviet Politics.* Westport, Conn.: Greenwood Press, 1976.

Buchan, John. *The Greenmantle.* Hertfordshire, England: Wordsworth Classics, 1994.

Burgat, Francois. *L'Islamisme au Maghrebe: La Voix du Sud.* Paris: Editions Karthala, 1988.

_____. *l'Islamisme en Face.* Paris: Edition la Decouverte, 1995.

Bustani, Emile. *Marche Arabesque.* London: Robert Hale Ltd., 1961.

Chubin, Shahram, and Sepehr Zabih. *The Foreign Relations of Iran.* Berkeley: University of California Press, 1974.

Cohen, Norman. *Cosmos, Chaos and the World to Come: The Ancient Roots of Apocalyptic Faith.* New Haven: Yale University Press, 1993.

Cottom, Richard. *Nationalism in Iran.* Pittsburgh, Pa.: University of Pittsburgh Press, 1979.

Daniel, Norman. *Islam and the West: The Making of an Image.* Edinburgh: Edinburgh University Press, 1958.

_____. *Islam, Europe and Empire.* Edinburgh: Edinburgh University Press, 1966.

Dawisha, Adeed, ed. *Islam in Foreign Policy.* Cambridge: Cambridge University Press, 1983.

Dekmejian, R. Hrair. *Islam in Revolution: Fundamentalism in the Arab World*. Syracuse, N.Y.: Syracuse University Press, 1985.

Dessuki, Ali E. Hillal and Alexandre S. Cudsi. *Islam and Power*. Baltimore, Md.: Johns Hopkins University Press, 1981.

Djait, Hisham. *La Grande Discorde: Religion et Politique dans l'Islam des Origines*. Paris: Editions Gallimard, 1989.

Enayat, Hamid. *Modern Islamic Political Thought*. Austin: University of Texas Press, 1982.

Esposito, John L. *Islam and Development: Religion and SocioPolitical Change*. Syracuse, N.Y.: Syracuse University Press, 1980.

_____. *Islam and Politics*. Syracuse, N.Y.: Syracuse University Press, 1984.

_____. *Islamic Threat: Myth or Reality*. New York: Oxford University Press, 1992; 2nd ed. 1995.

_____, ed. *Voices of Resurgent Islam*. New York: Oxford University Press, 1983.

_____, ed. *The Iranian Revolution: Its Global Impact*. Miami: Florida International University Press, 1990.

Esposito, John L., and John O. Voll. *Islam and Democracy in the Muslim World*. New York: Oxford University Press, 1996.

Feroz, Ahmad. *Turkish Experiment in Democracy*. London: C. Hurst & Company, 1977.

Fukuyama, Francis. *The End of History and the Last Man*. New York: The Free Press, 1992.

Geertz, Clifford. *The Interpretation of Cultures*. New York: Basic Books, 1973.

Guazzane, Laura, ed. *The Islamist Dilemma*. Reading, England: Ithaca Press, 1995.

Gunter, Michael M. *The Kurds in Turkey*. Boulder, Colo.: Westview, 1990.

Habib, John S. *Ibn Saud's Warriors of Islam: The Ikhvan of Najd and Their Role in the Creation of the Saudi Kingdom, 1910–1930*. Leiden: E. J. Brill, 1978.

Haim, Sylvia, ed. *Arab Nationalism and a Wider World*. New York: American Association for Peace in the Middle East, 1971.

Hegel, Georg Wilhelm Frederich. *The Philosophy of History*. New York: Dover Publications, 1956.

Hirst, David. *Oil and Public Opinion in the Middle East*. London: Faber & Faber, 1966.

Hourani, Albert. *Arabic Thought in the Liberal Age*. Oxford: Oxford University Press, 1970.

Hunter, Shireen T. *OPEC and the Third World: Politics of Aid*. Bloomington: Indiana University Press, 1984.

_____. *Iran and the World: Continuity in a Revolutionary Decade.* Blooming-ton: Indiana University Press, 1990.

_____. *Iran after Khomeini.* New York: Praeger/CSIS, 1992.

_____. *The Transcaucasus in Transition: Nation-Building and Conflict.* Washington, D.C.: CSIS, 1994.

_____. *Turkey at the Crossroads: Islamic Past or European Future?* Brussels: Center for European Policy Studies (CEPS) Paper No. 61, 1995.

_____. *Central Asia since Independence.* Westport, Conn.: Praeger/CSIS, 1996.

_____. *The Algerian Crisis: Origins, Evolution and Lessons for the Maghreb and Europe.* Brussels: Center for European Policy Studies (CEPS) Paper No. 63, 1996.

_____, ed. *The Politics of Islamic Revivalism: Diversity and Unity.* Bloomington: Indiana University Press, 1988.

Huntington, Samuel P. *The Clash of Civilizations and the Remaking of World Order.* New York: Simon & Schuster, 1996.

Jafri, S. Hussain M. *Origins and Early Development of Shi'a Islam.* London: Longman, 1979.

Karanjia, R. K. *The Mind of a Monarch.* London: George Allen and Un-win, 1977.

Karpat, Kemal H. *Turkey's Politics: The Transition to a Muslim Multi-Party System.* Princeton: Princeton University Press, 1959.

Keddie, Nikki R. *Sayyid Jamal ed-Din Afghani: A Political Biography.* Berke-ley: University of California Press, 1972.

Kedourie, Elie. *Afghani and Abduh: An Essay on Religious Unbelief and Political Activism in Modern Islam.* London: Frank Cass & Co. Ltd., 1966.

_____. *Nationalism in Asia and Africa.* London: Weidenfeld and Nicol-son, 1970.

Kepel, Gilles. *Le Prophete et Pharaon: Les Mouvements Islamistes dans l'Eg-ypte Contemporaine.* Paris: Editions La Decouverte, 1984.

_____. *La Revanche de Dieu, Chretiens, Juifs et Musulmans a la reconquete du monde.* Paris: Editions du Seuil, 1991.

Landau, Jacob M. *The Politics of Pan-Islam.* Oxford: Clarendon Press, 1994.

Lewis, Bernard. *The Middle East and the West.* Bloomington: Indiana Uni-versity Press, 1964.

_____. *Islam and the West.* New York: Oxford University Press, 1993.

Malik, Hafeez. *Sir Sayyid Ahmad Khan and Muslim Modernization in India and Pakistan.* New York: Columbia University Press, 1980.

_____, ed. *Iqbal: Poet-Philosopher of Pakistan.* New York: Columbia Uni-versity Press, 1971.

Malley, Robert. *The Call from Algeria: Third Worldism, Revolution, and the Turn to Islam.* Berkeley: University of California Press, 1996.

Martin, Vanessa. *Islam and Modernism: The Iranian Revolution of 1906.* London: Tauris, 1989.

Mazrui, Ali. *Africa's International Relations: The Diplomacy of Dependency and Change.* Boulder, Colo.: Westview, 1977.

Minovi, Mujtaba, ed. *Nameh-e-Tansar (Book of Tansar).* Teheran: Kharazmi, 1354 (1975).

Moadel, Mansoor. *Class, Politics and Ideology in the Iranian Revolution.* New York: Columbia University Press, 1993.

Morgenthau, Hans J. *Politics among Nations.* New York: Alfred A. Knopf, 1958.

Munson, Henry J. R. *Religion and Power in Morocco.* New Haven: Yale University Press, 1993.

Northedge, F. S. *The Foreign Policies of the Powers.* London: Faber & Faber, 1968.

Pipes, Daniel. *In the Path of God: Islam and Political Power.* New York: Basic Books, 1983.

Piscatori, James P. *Islam in a World of Nation States.* Cambridge: Cambridge University Press, 1986.

_____. *Islamic Fundamentalism and the Gulf Crisis.* Chicago: The American Academy of Arts and Sciences, 1991.

_____, ed. *Islam in the Political Process.* Cambridge: Cambridge University Press, 1983.

Quandt, William B. *Saudi Arabia in the 1980s: Foreign Policy, Security and Oil.* Washington, D.C.: The Brookings Institution, 1981.

Rahman, Fazlur. *Islam and Modernity.* Chicago: University of Chicago Press, 1982.

Rajaee, Farhang. *Islamic Values and World View: Khomeini on Man, the State and International Politics.* Lanham, Md.: University Press of America, 1983.

Ramazani, R. K. *The Foreign Policy of Iran: A Developing Nation in World Affairs 1500–1941.* Charlottesville, Va.: University Press of Virginia, 1966.

_____. *Iran's Foreign Policy 1941–1973: A Study of Foreign Policy in Modernizing Nations.* Charlottesville, Va.: University Press of Virginia, 1975.

Raoudja, Ahmed. *Les Freres et la Mosquee: Enquete sur le Mouvement Islamiste en Algerie.* Paris: Karthala, 1990.

Robins, Philip. *Turkey and the Middle East.* London: Pinter Publishers/Royal Institute of International Affairs, 1990.

Said, Edward. *Orientalism.* New York: Vintage Books, 1978.

Salem, Norma. *Habib Bourguiba, Islam and the Creation of Tunisia.* London: Croom Helm, 1984.

Schacht, Joseph and C. E. Bosworth, eds. *The Legacy of Islam.* Oxford: Oxford University Press, 1979.

Sivan, Emmanuel. *Radical Islam: Medieval Theology and Modern Politics*. New Haven: Yale University Press, 1985.

Smith, Donald E., ed. *Religion and Political Modernization*. New Haven: Yale University Press, 1974.

Toprak, Binnaz. *Islam and Political Development in Turkey*. Leiden: E. J. Brill, 1981.

Toynbee, Arnold. *The Study of History*. New York: Oxford University Press, 1963.

Von der Mehden, Fred R. *Religion and Nationalism in Southeast Asia*. Madison: University of Wisconsin Press, 1986.

Waardenburg, J. D. *L'Islam dans le Miroir de l'Occident*. Paris: Mouton, 1963.

Watt, Montgomery. *Islamic Political Thought: The Basic Concepts*. Edinburgh: Edinburgh University Press, 1968.

Articles

Abrahamian, Ervand. "The Guerrilla Movements in Iran, 1963–1977." *Middle East Research and Information Project (MERIP) Report* 86 (March–April 1980).

Amirahmadi, Hooshang. "Emerging Civil Society in Iran." *SAIS Review* (Summer–Fall 1986).

Batatu, Hanna. "Iraq's Underground Shi'a Movements: Characteristics, Causes and Prospects." *Middle East Journal* 35, no. 4 (Autumn 1981).

Bill, James. "Resurgent Islam in the Persian Gulf." *Foreign Affairs* 63, no. 1 (Fall 1984).

Bozeman, Adda. "Iran, U.S. Foreign Policy, and the Tradition of Persian Statecraft." *Orbis* (Summer 1979).

Dekmejian, R. Hrair. "The Arab Anatomy of Islamic Revival: Legitimacy Crisis, Ethnic Conflict, and the Search for Islamic Alternatives." *Middle East Journal* 34, no. 1 (Winter 1980).

_____. "The Rise of Political Islamism in Saudi Arabia." *Middle East Journal* 48, no. 4 (Autumn 1994).

Esposito, John L., and John D. Voll. "Islam's Democratic Essence." *Middle East Quarterly* (September 1994).

Esposito, John L., and James P. Piscatori. "Democratization and Islam." *Middle East Journal* 45, no. 3 (Summer 1991).

Fandy, Mamoun. "Tribe versus Islam: The Post-Colonial Arab State and the Democratic Imperative." *Middle East Policy* 48 (1994).

_____. "Egypt's Islamic Group: Regional Revenge?" *Middle East Journal* 48, no. 4 (Autumn 1994).

Feroz, Ahmad. "Islamic Reassertion in Turkey." *Third World Quarterly* 10, no. 2 (April 1988).

Fuller, Graham. "Islamic Fundamentalism: No Long-Term Threat." *Washington Post* (January 13, 1992).

_____. "The Clash of Ideas: The Next Ideology." *Foreign Policy* 98 (Spring 1995).

Gates, Henry Louis. "Blood and Irony." *Economist* (September 11–17, 1993).

Gelb, Leslie. "The Free Election Trap." *New York Times* (May 29, 1991).

Haddar, Leon T. "What Green Peril?" *Foreign Affairs* 72, no. 2 (Spring 1993).

Hanafi, Hassan. "Des Ideologies Modernistes a l'Islam Revolution-naire." *Peuples mediterraneens* 21 (October–December 1982).

Hunter, Shireen T. "Iran and the Spread of Revolutionary Islam." *Third World Quarterly* 10, no. 2 (1988).

_____. "Islamic Fundamentalism: What It Really Is and Why It Frightens the West." *SAIS Review* (Winter–Spring 1988).

_____. "Islam and the Future of Middle Eastern Societies." *Relazioni Internazionali* 56 (March 1992).

Huntington, Samuel P. "The Clash of Civilizations." *Foreign Affairs* 72, no. 3 (Summer 1993).

Ibrahim, Saad Eddin. "An Islamic Alternative in Egypt: The Muslim Brotherhood and Sadat." *Arab Studies Quarterly* 4, nos. 1–2, (Spring 1982).

_____. "Islamic Activism: A Rejoinder." *Security Dialogue* 25, no. 2 (1994).

Kramer, Martin. "Islam versus Democracy." *Commentary* (January 1993).

Kristol, Irving. "A Post-Wilsonian Foreign Policy." *Wall Street Journal Europe* (August 7, 1996).

Leach, Hugh. "Observing Islam from Within and Without." *Asian Affairs* 21, part 1 (February 1991).

Leffler, Melyn P. "Inside Enemy Archives: The Cold War Reopened." *Foreign Affairs* 75, no. 4 (Summer 1996).

Lewis, Bernard. "The Roots of Muslim Rage." *Atlantic Monthly* (September 1990).

_____. "Islam and Liberal Democracy." *Atlantic Monthly* (February 1993).

Maley, William. "Taliban Triumphant." *World Today* 52, no. 11 (November 1966).

Miller, Judith. "The Challenge of Radical Islam." *Foreign Affairs* 72, no. 2 (Spring 1993).

Mortimer, Edward. "On the Middle Path." *Financial Times* (July 10, 1996).

Noorbakhsh, Mehdi. "The Middle East, Islam and the United States: The Special Case of Iran." *Middle East Policy* 11, no. 3 (1993).

Pelletreau, Robert H., Daniel Pipes, and John L. Esposito. "Symposium: Resurgent Islam in the Middle East." *Middle East Policy* 3, no. 2 (1994).

Perlmutter, Amos. "Wishful Thinking about Islamic Fundamentalism." *Washington Post* (January 19, 1992).

Pipes, Daniel. "Fundamentalist Muslims between America and Russia." *Foreign Affairs* 64, no. 5 (Summer 1986).

_____. "The Muslims Are Coming! The Muslims Are Coming!" *National Review* (November 19, 1990).

Power, Carla. "Secularist Radicalism." *Newsweek* (July 16, 1997).

Rubenstein, Richard E., and Farle Crocker. "Challenging Huntington." *Foreign Policy* 96 (Fall 1994).

Sadowski, Yahya. "The New Orientalism and the Democracy Debate." *Middle East Research and Information Project (MERIP) Report* 183 (July–August 1993).

Said, Abdul Aziz. "Islamic Fundamentalism and the West." *Mediterranean Quarterly* 3, no. 4 (Fall 1992).

Salamé, Ghassan. "Islam and the West." *Foreign Policy* 90 (Spring 1993).

Surush, Abdul-Karim. "Shari'ati va Jameeh-e-Shenasi-e-Din" ("Shari'ati and the Sociology of Religion"). *Kian* 3 (third year), no. 13 (June–July 1994).

Turabi, Hassan. "Islam, Democracy, the State and the West." *Middle East Policy* 1, no. 3 (1992).

Vakili, Valla. *Debating Religion and Politics in Iran: The Political Thought of Abdol Karim Soroush.* Occasional Paper Series no. 2, Council on Foreign Relations, New York (1996).

Index

About the Author

Shireen Tahmasseb Hunter is director of Islamic Studies at the Center for Strategic and International Studies in Washington, D.C., where she has also served as deputy director of the CSIS Middle East Program. Previously she was visiting senior research fellow at the Center for European Policy Studies in Brussels, where she conducted the Mediterranean Program.

Dr. Hunter holds degrees from Tehran University, the London School of Economics, and the Institut Universitaire des Hautes Etudes Internationales in Geneva. Her publications include *The Algerian Crisis: Origins, Evolution and Lessons for the Maghreb and Europe* (1996), *Central Asia since Independence* (1996), *Turkey at the Crossroads: Islamic Past or European Future?* (1995), *The Transcaucasus in Transition: Nation-Building and Conflict* (1994), *Iran after Khomeini* (1992), *Iran and the World: Continuity in a Revolutionary Decade* (1990), *The Politics of Islamic Revivalism: Diversity and Unity* (1988), and *OPEC and the Third World: The Politics of Aid* (1984). She has contributed to numerous edited volumes, and her articles have appeared in such journals as *Foreign Affairs, Foreign Policy, The Washington Quarterly, SAIS Review, Current History, Third World Quarterly, Middle East Journal, Central Asia Monitor, International Spectator, Security Dialogue*, and *Relazione Internazionali*.

Dr. Hunter has lectured widely in the United States, Canada, Europe, the Middle East, Asia, and the former Soviet Union. She is fluent in English, French, Persian, and Azeri Turkish.